IMAGES
of America

HASKELL COUNTY

I0806177

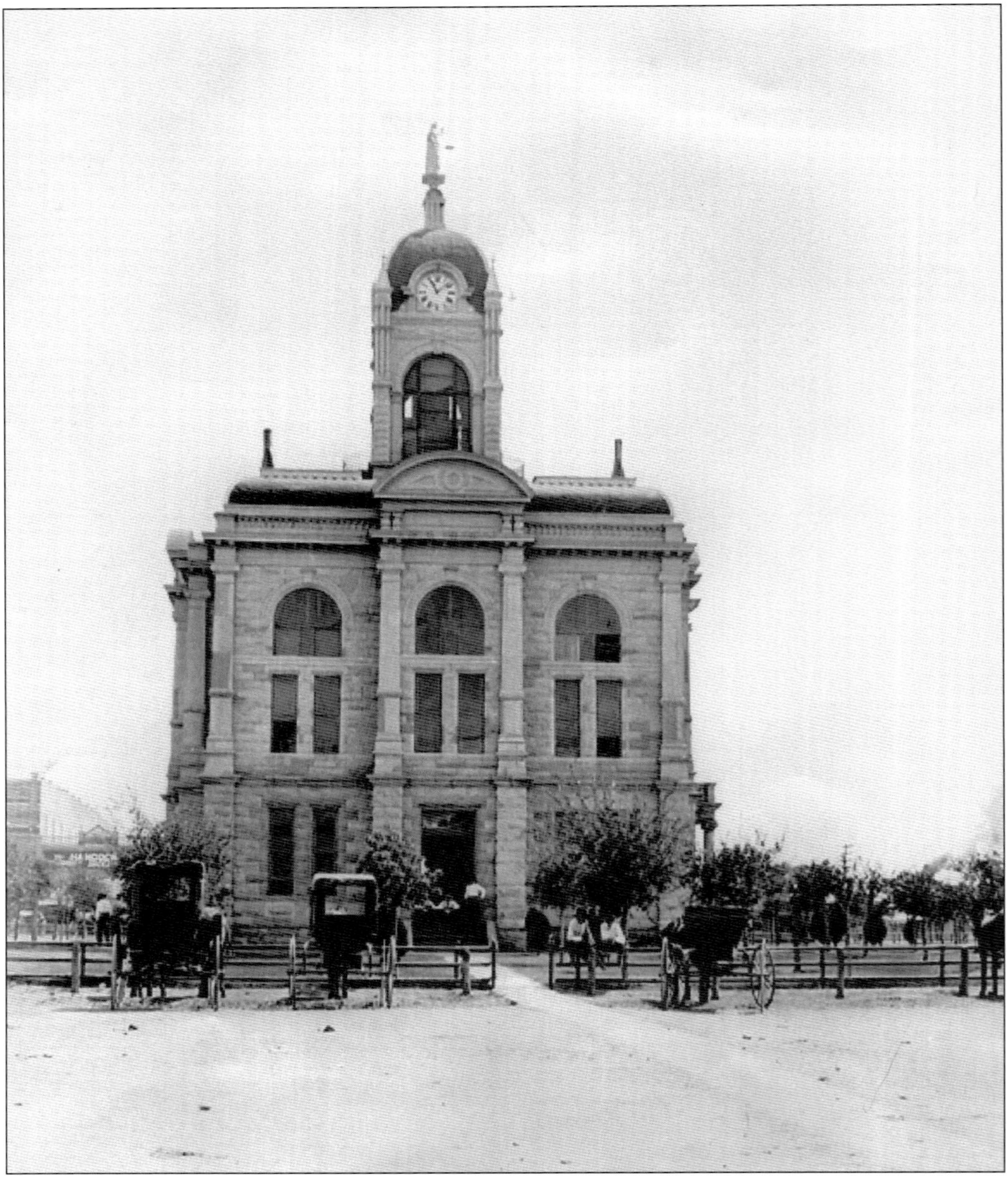

By 1891, Haskell County had become widely settled. Commissioners determined that the county's original two-story wood-frame courthouse was no longer adequate. A contract was awarded to Lamour and Watson to erect a native stone building, pictured here, one block south of the original courthouse site. Judge H. G. McConnell was presiding county judge. Including the tower, Seth Thomas clock, and furnishings, the final cost was $55,000. (Courtesy of Haskell County Historical and Genealogical Society.)

On the Cover: This striking native stone structure rises above 903 square miles of Texas prairie known as Haskell County. Completed in 1892, the courthouse and its citizens were captured here by a photographer by the name of McCall. He captioned this undated photograph, "A busy day in Haskell, Texas." The view looks north across the county seat. In the original photograph, an early-day gazebo is visible on the northwest corner of the square. (Courtesy of Hess Hartsfield.)

IMAGES
of America

HASKELL COUNTY

Haskell County Historical
and Genealogical Society

ARCADIA
PUBLISHING

ISBN 978-0-7385-7887-3

Published by Arcadia Publishing
Charleston SC, Chicago IL, Portsmouth NH, San Francisco CA

Printed in the United States of America

Library of Congress Control Number: 2009934029

For all general information contact Arcadia Publishing at:
Telephone 843-853-2070
Fax 843-853-0044
E-mail sales@arcadiapublishing.com
For customer service and orders:
Toll-Free 1-888-313-2665

Visit us on the Internet at www.arcadiapublishing.com

To the pioneers of Haskell County, whose character and spirit continue to inspire those who follow in their footsteps.

Contents

Acknowledgments

When the Haskell County Historical and Genealogical Society was formed, one of its primary purposes was the preservation of historical photographs. In keeping with that purpose, the society has sought in this publication to preserve chapters of county heritage through images and stories shared by its people. Through previous donations of photographs, the society had a sizeable collection from which to begin, but we are indebted to those who shared new images and new stories. We only regret that because of editorial constraints, all of them could not be included.

Without the work of groups and individuals who came before us in recording Haskell County history, this work would not be possible. We acknowledge the immeasurable contribution of all who spent untold hours compiling and publishing extensive works on Haskell County history. These include the following publications: *R. E. Sherrill's History of Haskell County, Haskell County and its Pioneers, Cowpokes and Sodbusters, Just Passing through Weinert, Putting Paint Creek on the Map, The Early History of Sagerton, the Story of Rule, Texas, A History of O'Brien, When the Rails Were Laid*, and *A Century in the Rochester Area.* We also benefited from the extensive county school history published by the Haskell Free Press and from family collections of county residents. *Pioneer Trails*, the newsletter of the historical society, was a rich resource. We have made every effort to ensure historical accuracy but realize that at times the record is difficult to establish and, despite best efforts, errors are made.

This project was born of the talents and resources of many people who donated time, photographs, and stories and who expressed enthusiasm for the work. We recognize all those who have a tie to Haskell County, for they, too, have had a hand in writing our story.

The Haskell County Historical and Genealogical Society has sought here to capture the image and the essence of a land beloved of its people. There is more to our story than any one book can hold, and it is our hope that more chapters of our heritage will find their way to the printed page.

INTRODUCTION

Though the story of the land runs far back in time, Haskell County was first platted on the map of Texas February 1, 1858. The name was chosen in honor of Charles Ready Haskell, martyred at Goliad in the struggle for Texas independence on Palm Sunday 1836. Within the county's 903 square miles lay abundant resources, but to coax these from the prairie would require another kind of resource, that of the dreamer, the visionary—the pioneer. Our greatest resource has always been in the dreams, the vision, and the will of our people.

Haskell County was carved from the Fannin and Milam Land Districts. It is bordered on the north by Knox, the east by Throckmorton, the south by Jones, and the west by Stonewall Counties. When originally surveyed, the western boundary was 10 miles west of the present line. This was adjusted in 1876, making the county 30 miles square. There were a significant number of land surveys in the area of what would become Haskell County as early as 1855.

The Rio de los Brazos de Dios, the "River of the Arms of God," cradles the land on two sides, the Double Mountain Fork on the west and the Clear Fork to the southeast. The Double Mountain Fork of the Brazos flows north along the western border where it joins the Salt Fork west of Rochester. It is at this point that the Brazos River proper has its beginning. From here the river runs west of and parallel to the Haskell-Stonewall County line before bending to the northeast into Knox County, eventually turning south toward the Gulf of Mexico. Clear springs occasionally may be found in the Brazos River breaks. Several creeks run through the eastern portion of Haskell County, draining into the Clear Fork, which joins the main Brazos channel near Graham, Texas. These creeks were known and well defined by the earliest mapmakers of the day. The Salt Fork and Double Mountain Fork seem to have presented more of a cartographical challenge.

Miller's Creek in the northeast quadrant drains that section of the county. Though located in Baylor and Throckmorton Counties, Miller's Creek Reservoir is a popular recreational destination and a water source for communities in Haskell County. Lake Stamford, built southeast of Haskell in the early 1950s, is also a popular recreation area and water source.

Native Americans traversed the prairies of Haskell County for centuries, hunting the buffalo, antelope, and deer that grazed the treeless grassland. The Comanche and Kiowa were the principal tribes. When Anglo settlers sought to claim the same ground, several battles were fought within the county.

A cast of historically significant travelers left footprints in Haskell County. Sixteenth-century explorers bearing the flag of the Spanish Crown are said to have crossed portions of the county in their search for fabled treasure. Capt. Randolph B. Marcy led an expeditionary force across Texas in 1849. His favorable report of the country was widely published. The trail marked by Captain Marcy became a well-traveled thoroughfare for immigrants headed to the western gold fields. One of the first of those groups camped on a creek they called California. Their legacy remains to this day, as the creek still bears the name.

Following the Civil War, Col. Ranald S. Mackenzie established a strategic supply route along the southern border of Haskell County. Known as the Mackenzie Trail, it was heavily relied upon by 4th U.S. Cavalry engaged in the Red River War against Native Americans.

Following Mackenzie's defeat of the native tribes, buffalo hunters moved out onto the Texas plains to take part in the booming enterprise of supplying buffalo hides to eastern tanners. The great hunts in Texas had their beginning near the town of Weinert when a party including famed hunter J. Wright Mooar took 2,000 hides in the winter of 1875–1876. The Mackenzie Trail then became a thoroughfare for wagons piled high with hides and, later, bones gathered by settlers.

The demise of the buffalo opened the range for a new enterprise: cattle ranching. A herd was located in the southwest corner of the county near Flat Top Mountain in 1874, but the first permanent ranching enterprise was established by George T. Reynolds and J. A. Matthews on Paint Creek in 1876. By 1880, more cattlemen came. They shared the prairie with wild game and large herds of horses in the area of Wild Horse Prairie. Ranching became a cornerstone of the Haskell County economy.

In 1884, a petition was circulated to have the county organized. According to R. E. Sherrill's *History of Haskell County*, anyone passing through the county was asked to sign. The document may also have contained the signatures of a few dogs and saddle horses. Organization was achieved, however, with the town of Haskell, formerly known as Rice Springs, designated as the county seat.

As news of this promising country made its way east, settlers came ready to establish farms and all the trappings of community—homes, churches, schools, and civic organizations. In 1886, the *Haskell Free Press* printed its first edition. On horseback, by wagon, or on foot, settlers found their way to Haskell County. Their optimistic reports to friends and family drew even more. The census of 1900 recorded only 2,300 county residents. Ten years later, the population had grown to over 16,000.

Railroads were a crucial ingredient to ensure the county's growth and were heavily courted. The towns of O'Brien, Rochester, Rule, and Sagerton were serviced by the Kansas City, Mexico, and Orient. Sagerton boasted a second line in the Stamford and Northwestern (later leased to the Wichita Valley Railway). The Wichita Valley Railroad ran through Weinert and Haskell. Communities bypassed by the railroads, such as Marcy, did not survive for long.

Oil was discovered in the county in 1929 and continues to have a significant impact on the area economy.

Education has always received priority in Haskell County. The foundation of commitment laid by over 60 country schools set the standard from which our modern campuses have received the state's highest rankings for achievement.

Today Haskell County is one of the most diverse and most productive agricultural regions in Texas. Within the 30 square miles comprising Haskell County lie 576,000 acres of land. Rangeland comprises some 200,000 of these acres. The balance consists of deep soils favorable to crop production. The first significant farming venture was that of George Cook in the western portion of the county. Fertile soils produce peanuts, wheat, grain sorghum, and other crops, but cotton has traditionally been king. Shallow water began to provide irrigation to a large section of the county in the 1950s. The Seymour Aquifer spans 430 square miles beneath Haskell and Knox Counties. Good water may generally be found at a depth of 40 to 60 feet. This made possible Haskell County becoming one of the most productive peanut-producing counties in Texas in the 1980s. Modern irrigation methods have had a significant impact on the county economy.

Fabled treasure drew the first nonnative peoples to this land between the forks of the Brazos. Searching for gold, they missed the real treasure in this land beloved of its people. Today Haskell County residents share this treasure with visitors who come to enjoy recreation on area waterways; hunt wild hogs, geese, deer, quail, and dove; or enjoy the quiet, starlit nights and spectacular sunsets.

One

To the Place of Beginning

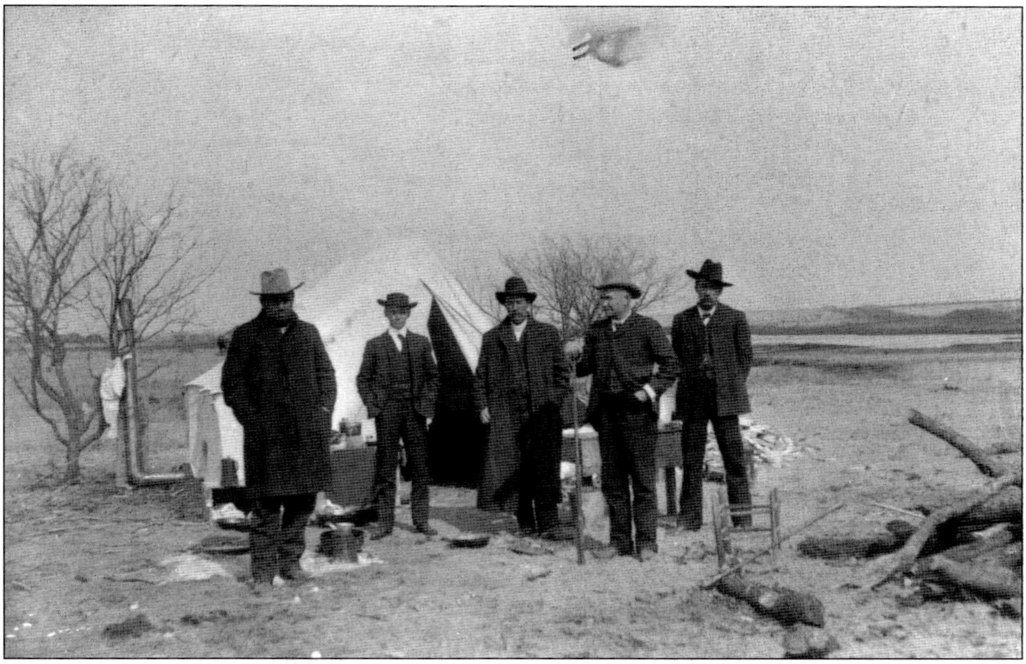

Surveyors played a crucial role in the development of Haskell County. Their work laid the legal foundation for land ownership and town building upon which other trappings of community would rest. Surveyors of the town of Weinert are shown here at their camp on Lake Creek. From left to right are Herman Weinert, Ed Fuller, ? Sowell, L. E. Buie, and B. E. Sparks. (Courtesy of Harlan Weinert.)

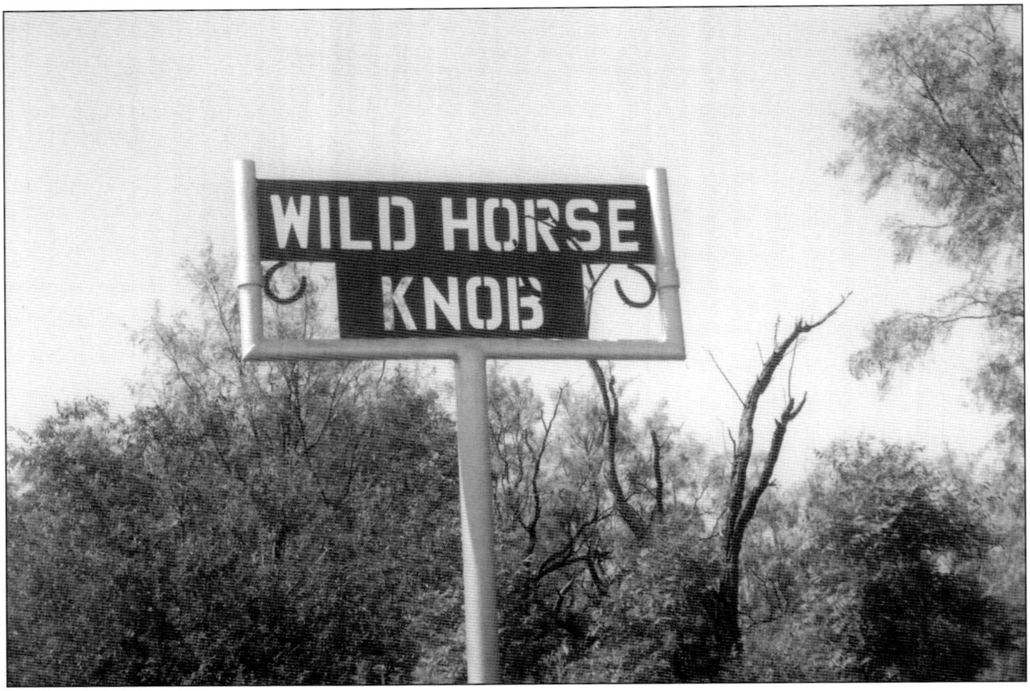

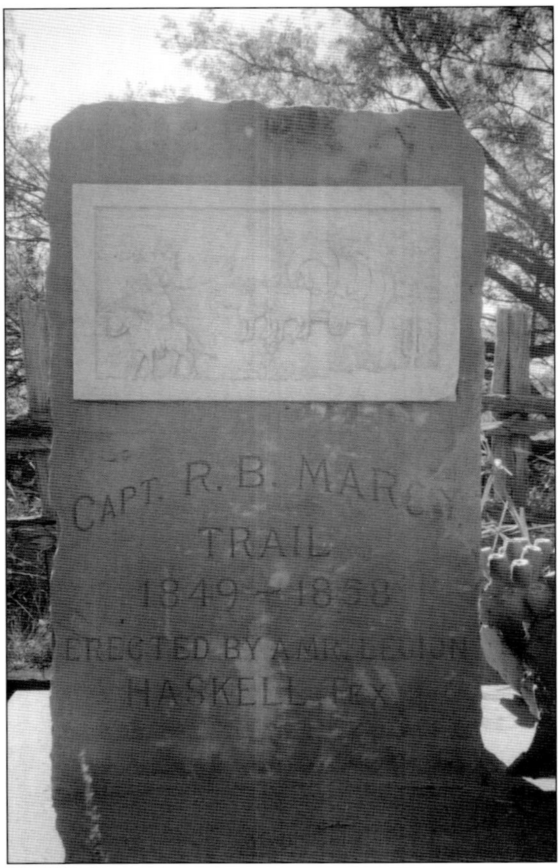

Wild horses roaming the central prairies gave name to this geographic landmark, one of the highest points in Haskell County. The wild horses often led astray gentle horses and so were sometimes hunted. The horses were, at other times, captured and sold for working stock. Once known for its abundance of wildflowers, the view from Wild Horse Knob gradually came to be primarily of cotton fields. (Courtesy of Susan Turner.)

In 1849, Capt. Randolph Barnes Marcy escorted a wagon train westward across the Texas panhandle, scouting military and commercial roads across Texas. On his more southern return, he reached Haskell County about October 20 and camped on Paint Creek. His favorable description of the country was widely published. The Marcy Trail became a prominent immigrant thoroughfare to California gold fields and is commemorated in this monument south of Haskell, Texas. (Courtesy of Susan Turner.)

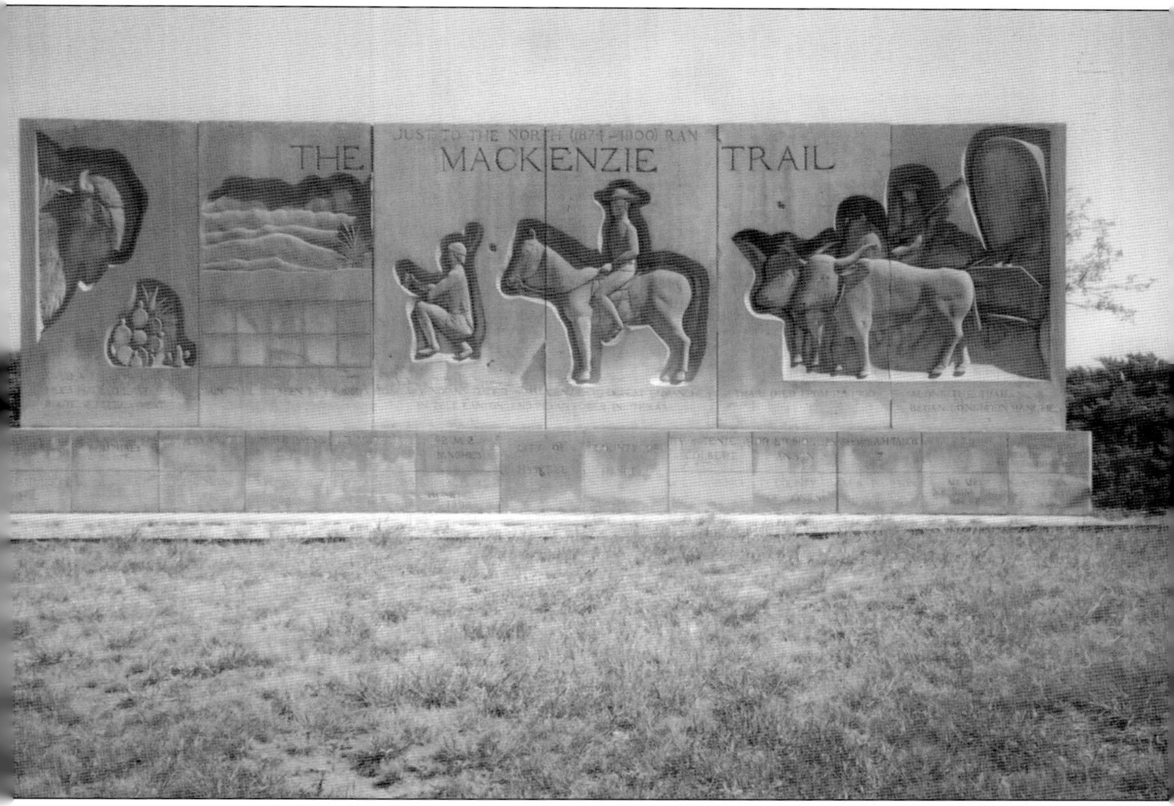

During its engagement in the 1874–1875 Red River War of the Texas panhandle, the 4th U.S. Cavalry, under the command of Col. Ranald Slidell Mackenzie, established a supply route from Fort Griffin in Shackleford County northwesterly across Haskell County up the Llano Estacado. It was Quartermaster Henry Lawton who actually laid out the road. Troops and supply wagons followed this route during a series of campaigns in the Texas panhandle against Comanche, Kiowa, and Cheyenne Indians. With a reliable supply line, troops were able to stay in the field during fall and winter when forage for cavalry horses was short. Known as the Mackenzie Trail, the road later transported thousands of buffalo hides to market and was well traveled by cattlemen and settlers. This hand-carved monument sits in southern Haskell County at the intersection of State Highways 6 and 277 near the town of Stamford. (Courtesy of Susan Turner.)

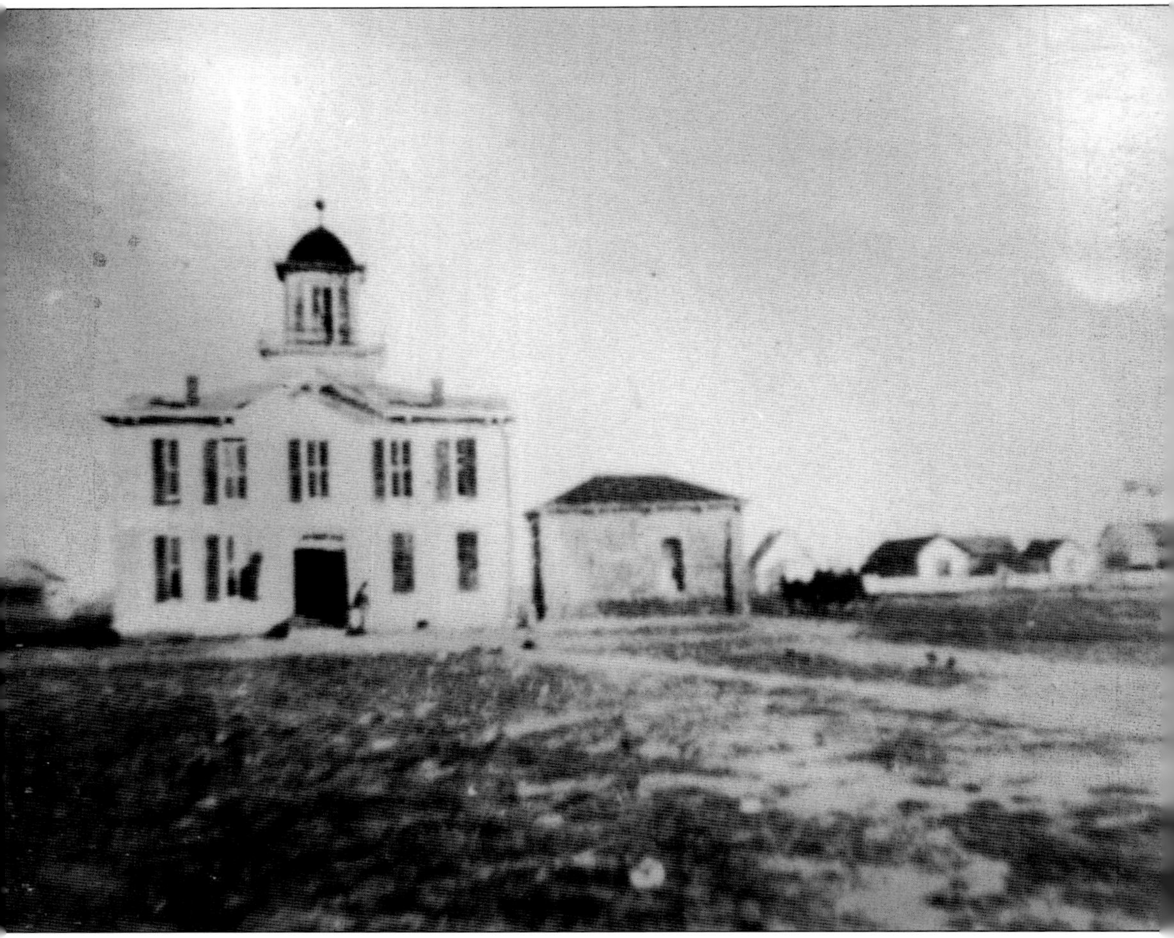

The Texas legislature created Haskell County February 1, 1858, naming it in honor of Charles Ready Haskell, killed in the Goliad massacre on Palm Sunday 1836. The county was not organized at the time, however, nor surveyed. In 1884, a petition requesting organization was delivered to Throckmorton County to which Haskell County was attached for judicial purposes. Throckmorton commissioners called an election for January 13, 1885. Thomas F. Tucker was elected the first county judge, with Haskell designated as the county seat. Commissioners met February 9, 1885, and voted "to order court record blanks, books, seals, etc, for the sum of $700.00." On February 10, the court approved a 25¢ poll tax and designated a building owned by William Harvey to serve as a courtroom until a courthouse could be built. The first trial took place in the building belonging to Harvey. In the summer of 1885, a two-story frame wooden courthouse was erected at 201 North Avenue E, a block north of the present courthouse. A building adjacent to the courthouse served as the clerk's office. (Courtesy of Haskell County Historical and Genealogical Society.)

Two

LEVEL FLATS COVERING THOUSANDS OF ACRES

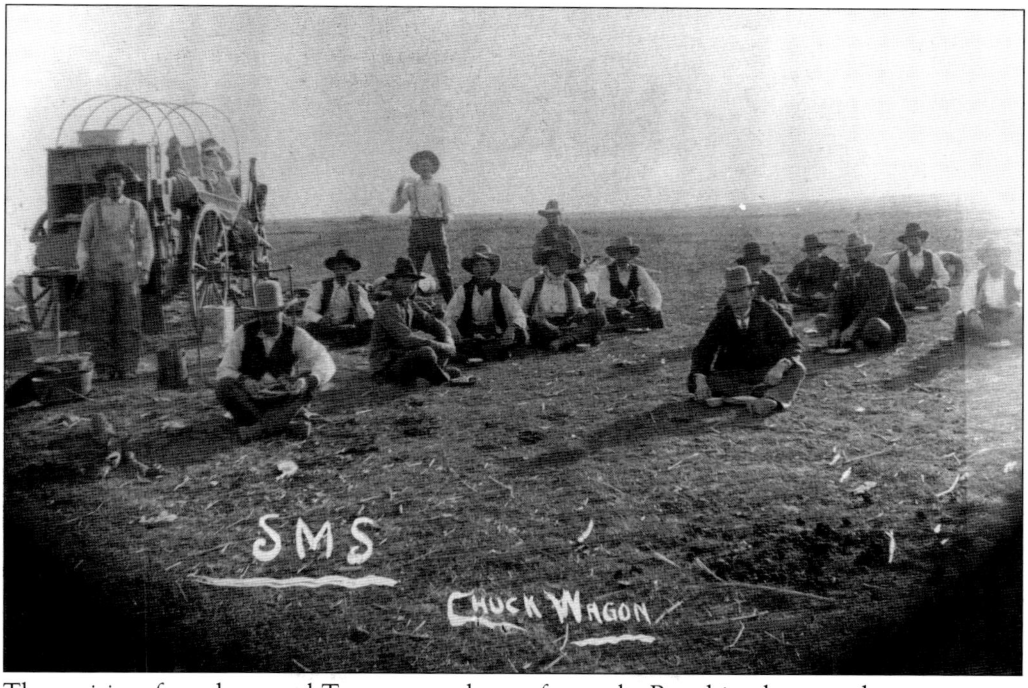

The prairies of north central Texas were a haven for cattle. Ranching became the cornerstone of the Haskell County economy when John A. Matthews and George T. Reynolds established a headquarters on Paint Creek in 1876. The SMS Flat Top Ranch, established in the early 1880s, is located partially in southwestern Haskell County. Named for Flat Top Mountain near Sagerton, it was one of the first ranches in this part of Texas to be fenced. (Courtesy of Gary Mathis.)

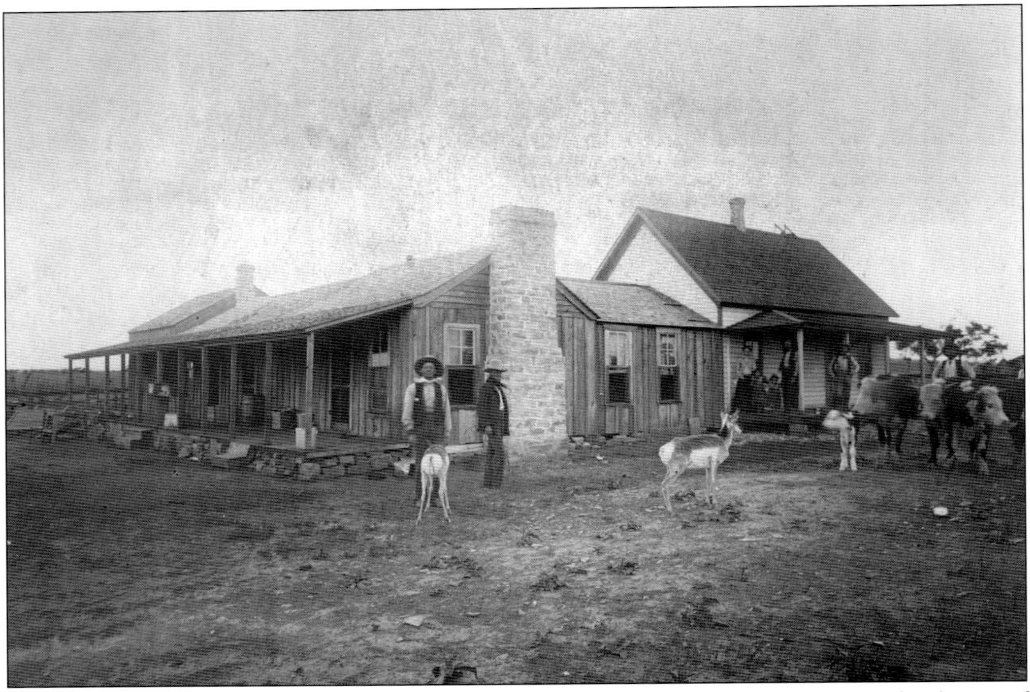

Svante Magnus Swenson, friend and associate of Sam Houston, purchased thousands of acres of grass in north central Texas, stocking it with cattle wearing the SMS brand. This ranch house was located on the SMS Throckmorton Ranch, which originally included part of eastern Haskell County. Cattle from this ranch were driven to Wichita Valley Railroad pens at Haskell for shipment to stockyards in Fort Worth, Kansas City, and Denver. (Courtesy of Gary Mathis.)

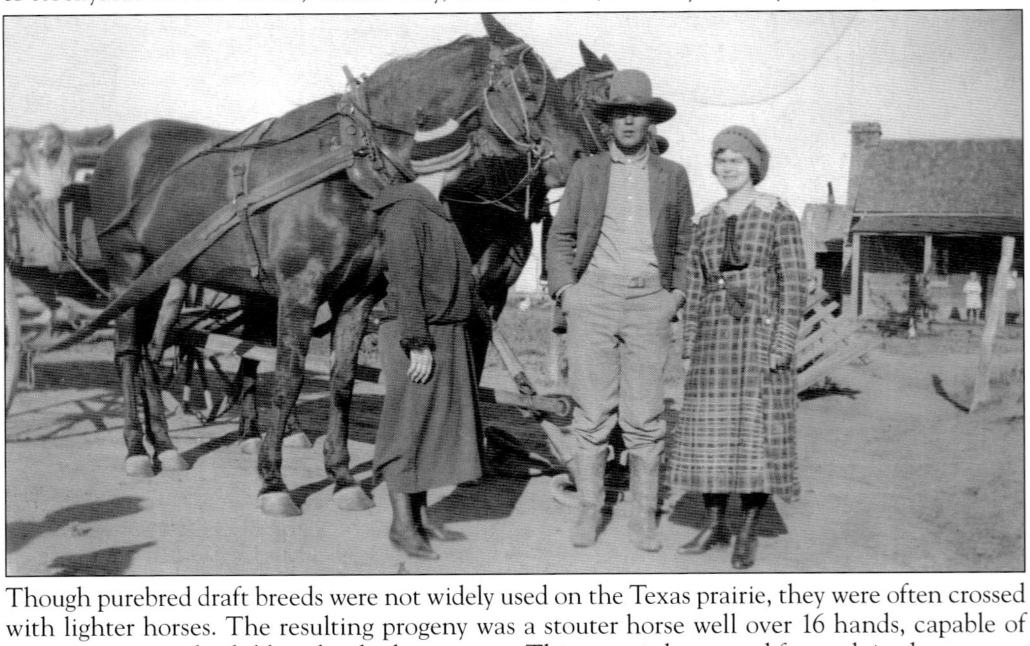

Though purebred draft breeds were not widely used on the Texas prairie, they were often crossed with lighter horses. The resulting progeny was a stouter horse well over 16 hands, capable of greater power in the fields or hitched to wagons. This team is harnessed for work in the western sandhills of Haskell County. Ann Roberson stands at left. The others are unidentified. (Courtesy of Billi Jo Roberson.)

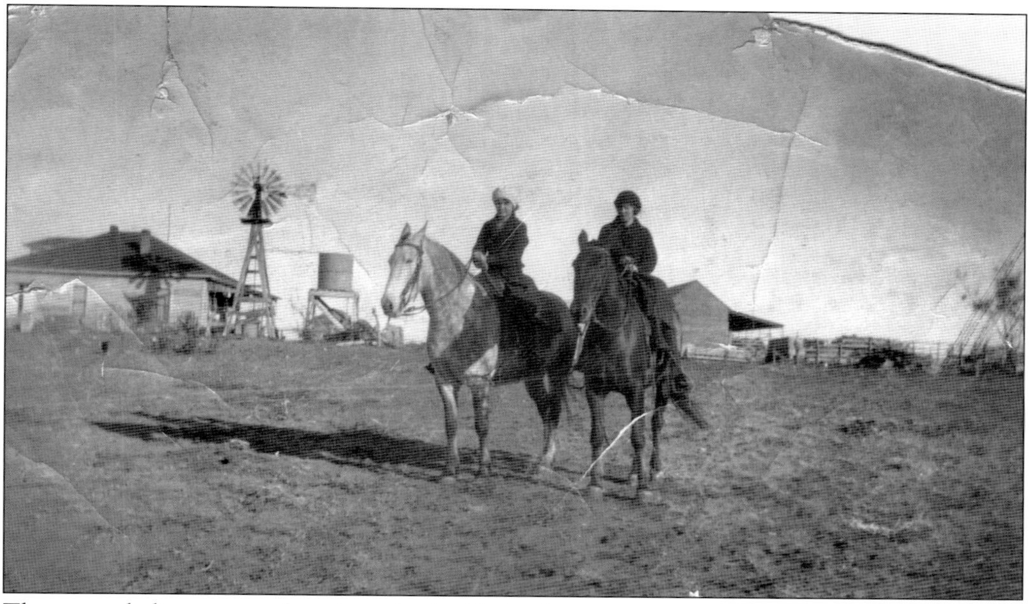

These two ladies are out for a horseback ride in the country near the Salt Fork of the Brazos River. The lady on the dark horse is Mrs. Terry (Gertrude) Karr Roberson, mother of one-time Haskell County judge B. O. Roberson. The community of Jud, Texas, was named for her father-in-law, Jud Roberson, who came to Haskell County in 1895. Roberson is riding sidesaddle. The windmill near the barn was a common sight on farms throughout the county. (Courtesy of Billi Jo Roberson.)

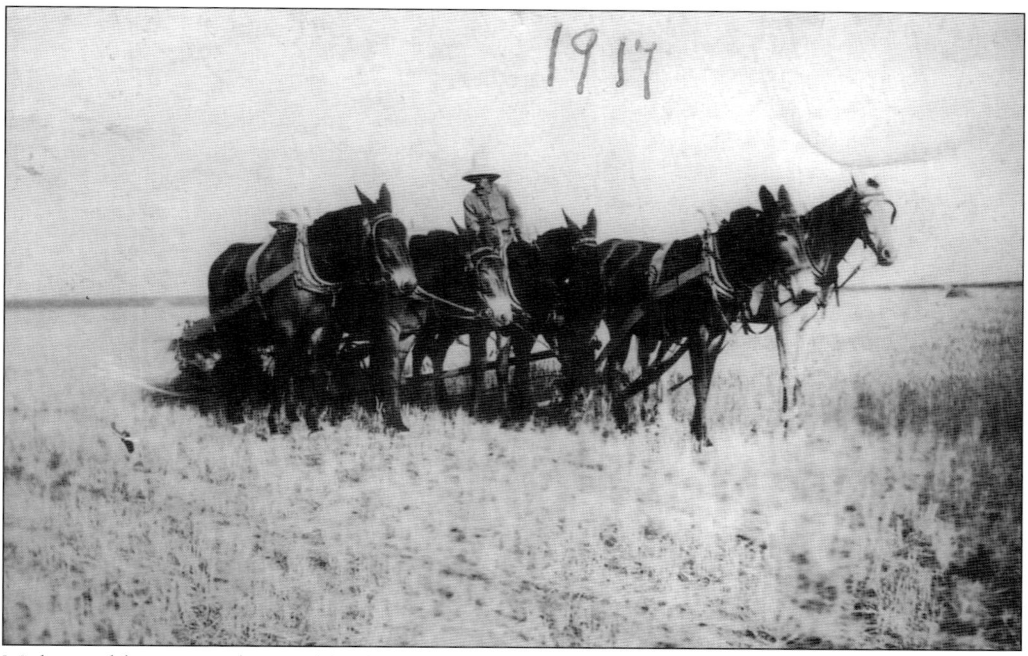

Mules and horses made possible the development of the agricultural economy of early Haskell County. A large farm might have 20 or 30 mules working hundreds of acres, but most farmers had from 6 to 12. They were depended on to plow, plant, cultivate, deliver a harvest to market, and bring supplies to the farm. (Courtesy of Haskell County Historical and Genealogical Society.)

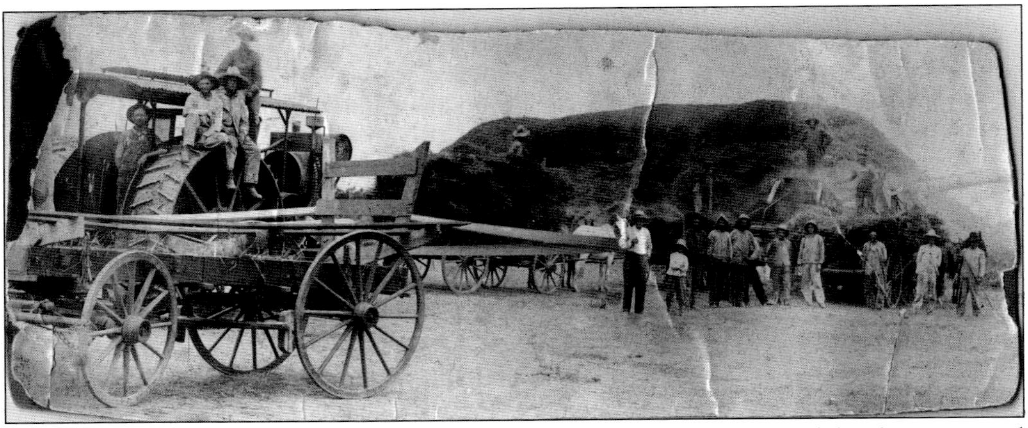

Grain production in Haskell County was second only to cotton. Steam-powered threshers separated the grain from the straw. Neighbors joined together, hauling their crop to a central location. This thresher, owned by George A. Turnbow, is threshing wheat near Josselet Switch north of Haskell. Turnbow stands at far right. (Courtesy of Doris Reeves.)

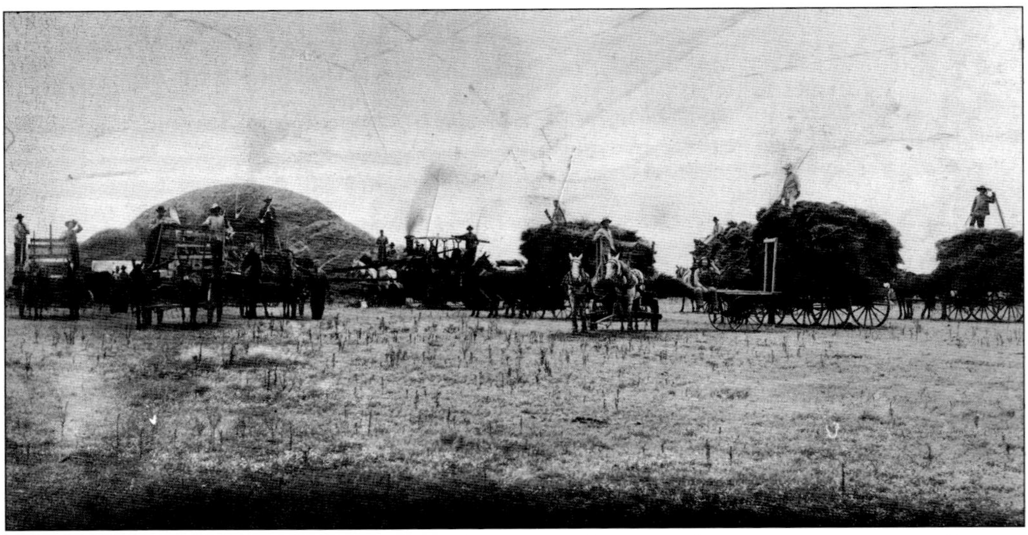

This 1913 photograph of R. P. Glenn's threshing crew illustrates the enormous amount of horse-, mule-, and manpower required for cultivating crops. Entire neighboring families joined together at harvest. Women had the task of feeding large crews of laborers, and young children carried food and water to the fields. One combine operator now does the work of dozens of laborers. (Courtesy of Tommy Matthews.)

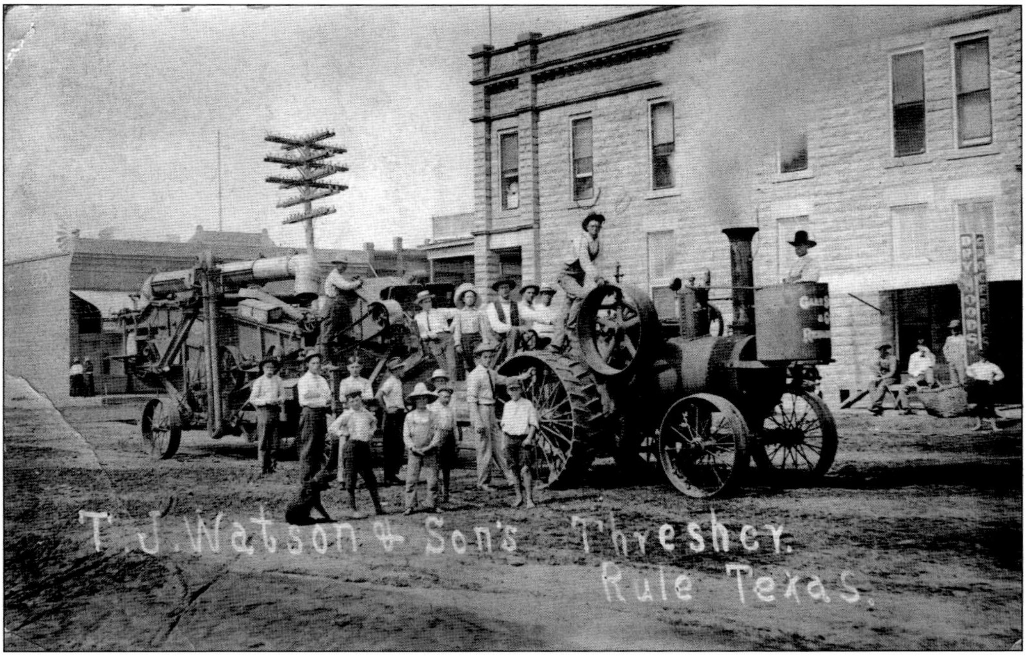

Thomas Jefferson Watson and Sons' thresher pauses on a street in Rule, Texas. Water hauled to the field provided the steam power for these machines. On threshing day, the owner of the thresher had to arrive early to build up steam for the day's threshing. Mr. Watson and his sons are among the group in this photograph. (Courtesy of Linda Lane-Bloise.)

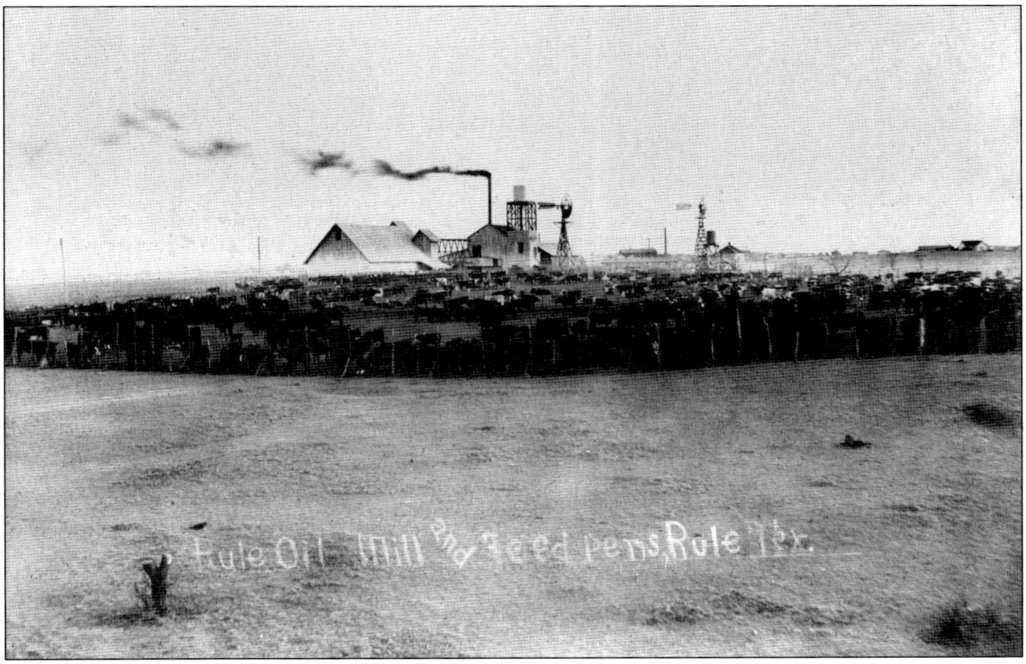

Around 1908, with increased cotton production in the county, A. C. Foster, W. A. Earnest, and J. L. Jones built the Rule Cotton Oil Mill north of Rule. The name was changed to Rule Jayton Cotton Oil Mill in 1917. The mill processed cottonseed into oil. The byproducts, cottonseed hulls and meal, were sold as feed or fed to cattle in pens adjacent to the mill. (Courtesy of Bill Jones.)

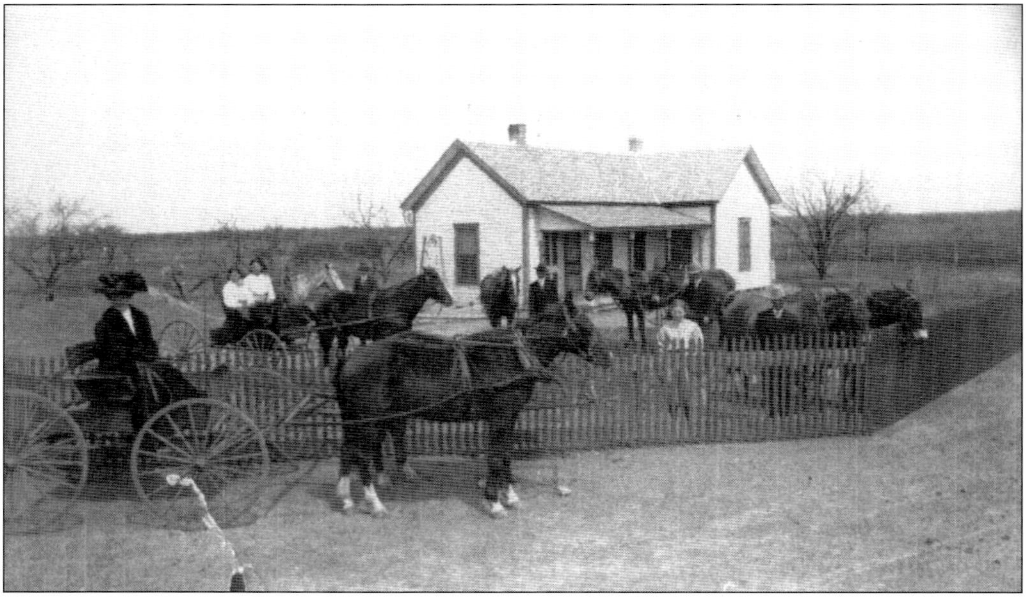

This photograph of the Fred Monke farm near the Myers community was made in March 1911. Mrs. Fred (Emma) Monke is seated in the buggy in the foreground. Fred Monke stands near the fence, with Mrs. Ed (Doris) Monke on his right. Ed Monke holds the team of mules, and the Patterson sisters are seated in the second buggy. The gentlemen holding the saddle horses are unidentified. (Courtesy of Haskell County Historical and Genealogical Society.)

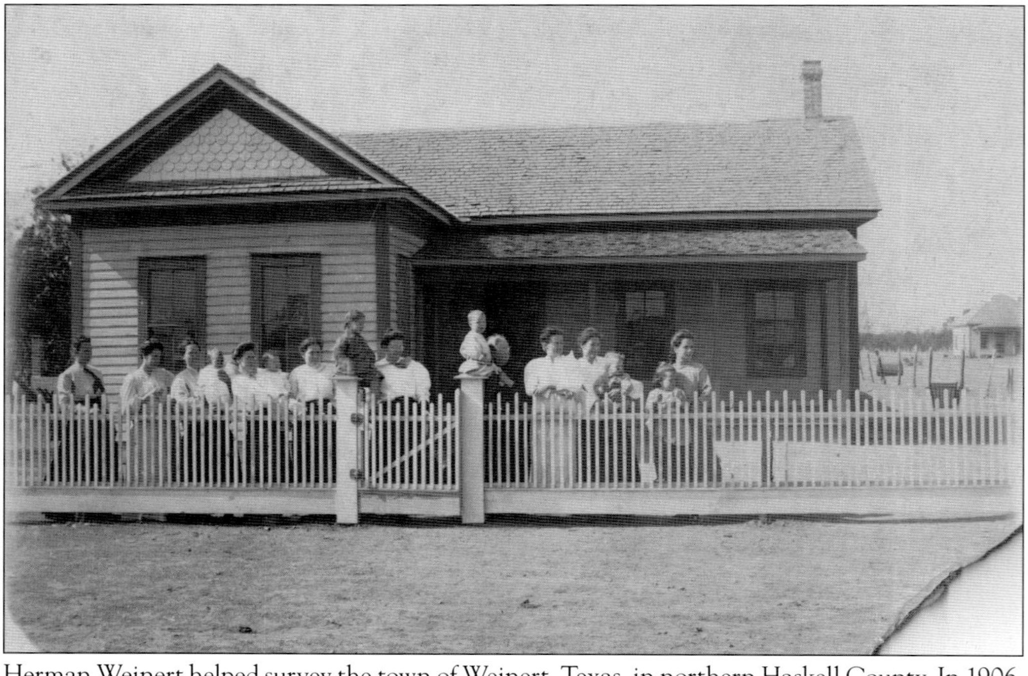

Herman Weinert helped survey the town of Weinert, Texas, in northern Haskell County. In 1906, he built one of the first homes in that community. When his wife, Annie, and children came to Haskell County from their former home in Seguin, they rode the train as far as Stamford and traveled by buggy the remaining 30 miles. Herman Weinert constructed the first church building, Weinert Presbyterian Church, in the town. (Courtesy of Harlan Weinert.)

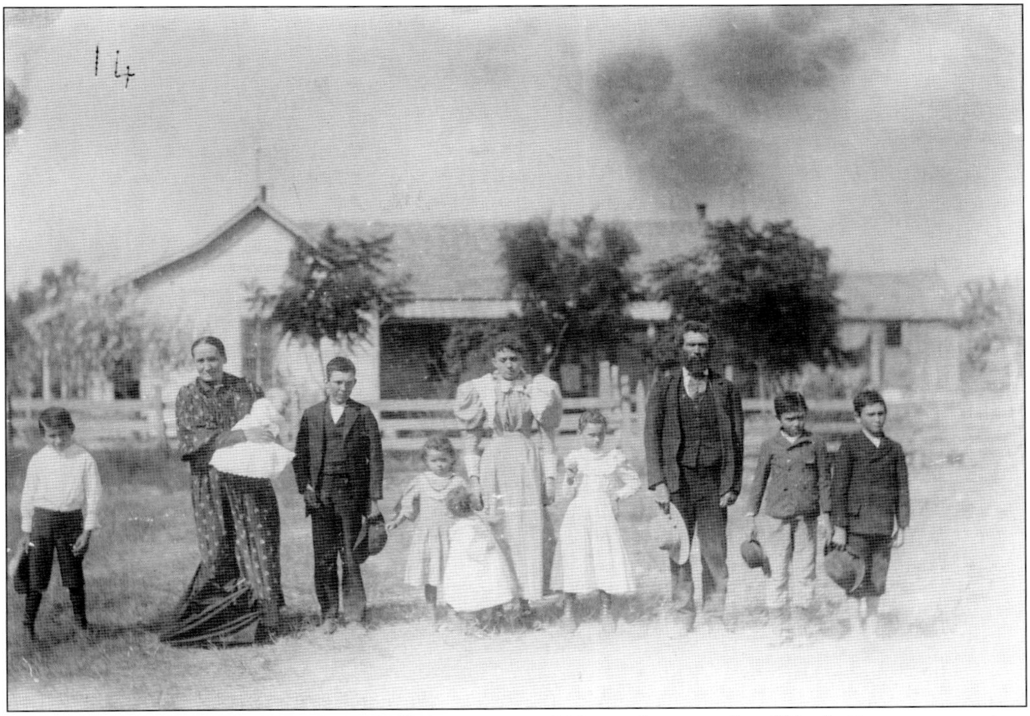

Victor Joseph Josselet came to Haskell County in 1908, settling north of Haskell in an area that came to be called Josselet Switch. His family is shown in front of their home. From left to right are Andrew, Catherina (holding Jessie), Felix, Annie, Esther, Lydia, Ardonia, Victor Joseph, Paul, and Dave Josselet. (Courtesy of Nancy Toliver.)

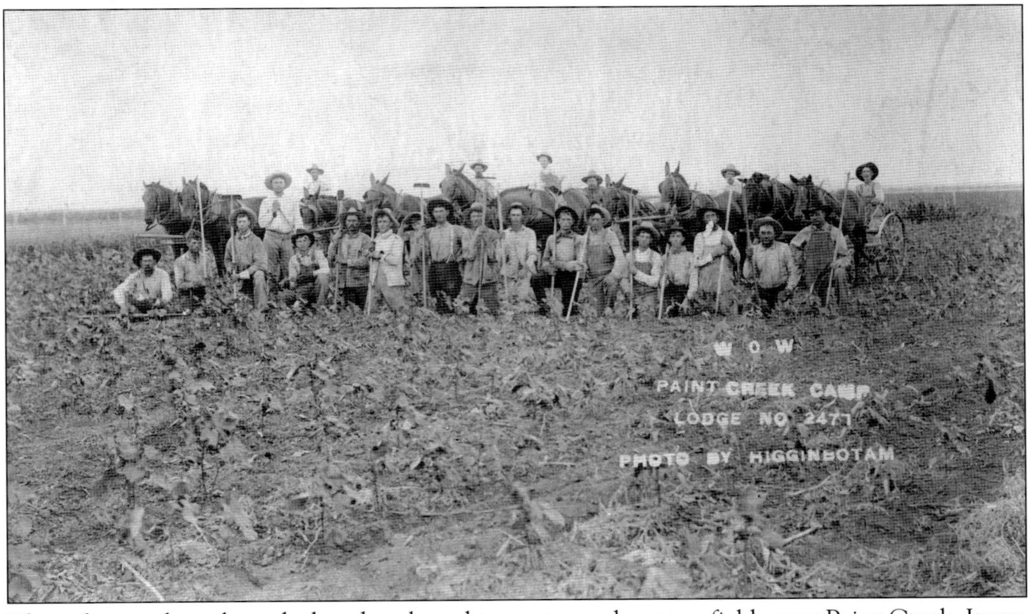

These farmers have brought hand tools and teams to work cotton fields near Paint Creek. It was common for neighbors to join together to help with field work. This photograph includes a caption, which reads, "WOW Paint Creek Camp Lodge #2477. Photo by Higginbotam." Third from right is Wayne Perry, great-grandfather of Texas governor Rick Perry. (Courtesy of J. R. Perry.)

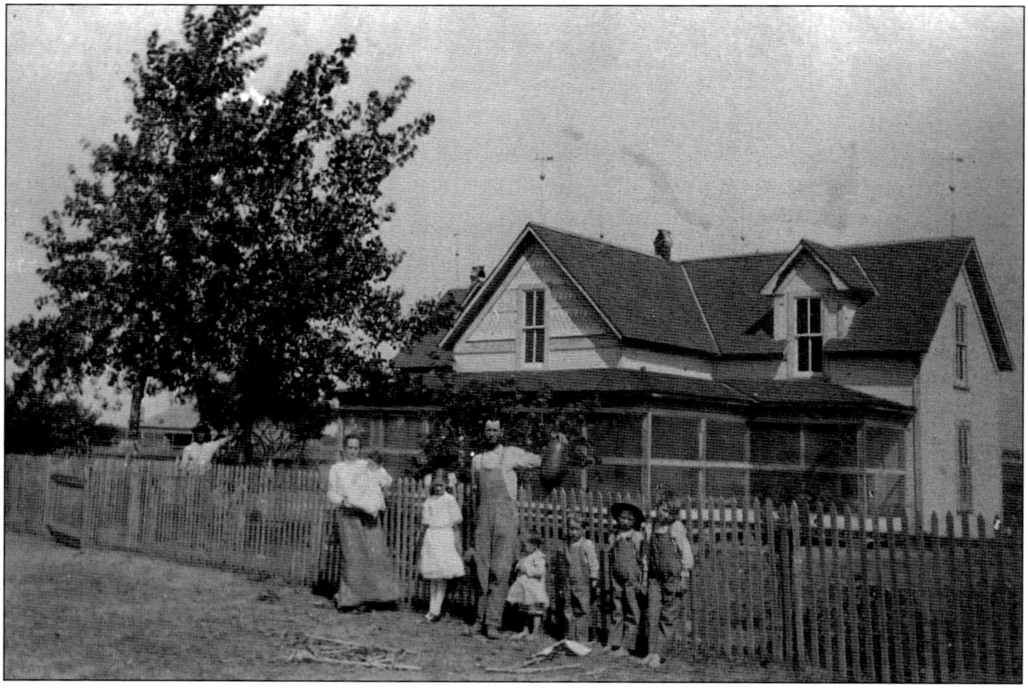

This 1911 photograph, taken in the area of the Brushy community of Haskell County, is of the James Riley Griffith family. Pictured in front of the picket fence surrounding their home are, from left to right, Mollie (holding Bill), Fay, James Riley, Sammie, Elmer, Allen, and Roy Griffith. James Riley Griffith holds a watermelon. The man leaning against the tree is unidentified. (Courtesy of Marilyn Griffith.)

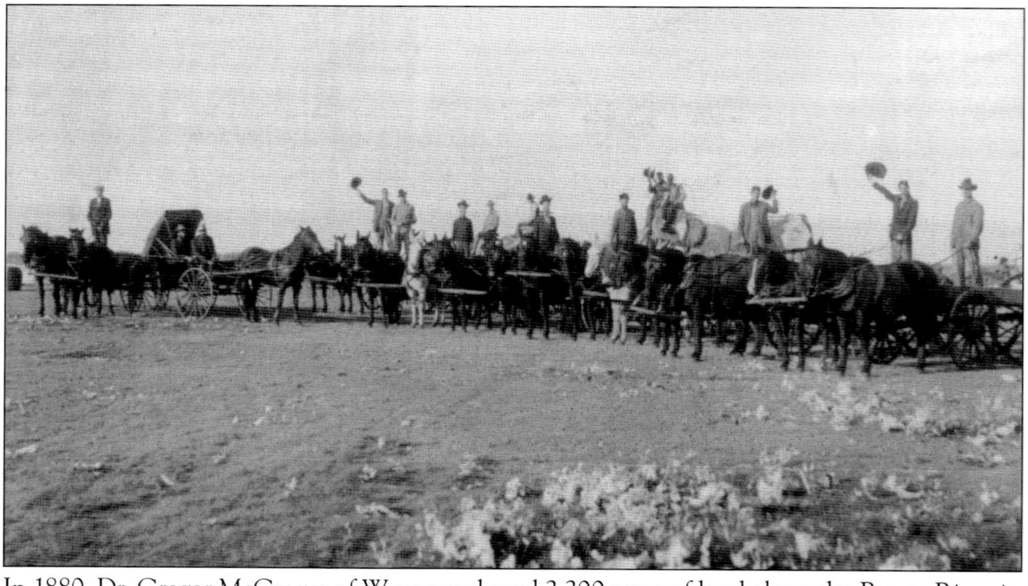

In 1880, Dr. Gregor McGregor of Waco purchased 2,200 acres of land along the Brazos River in western Haskell County. His son, Charles, married Juliana Huber in Germany, and they sailed to America about 1903 to make their home in West Texas. On this large acreage lived several tenant families. This photograph shows a group of them lined up in a cotton field on the McGregor Farm west of O'Brien. (Courtesy of Sharon Mullino.)

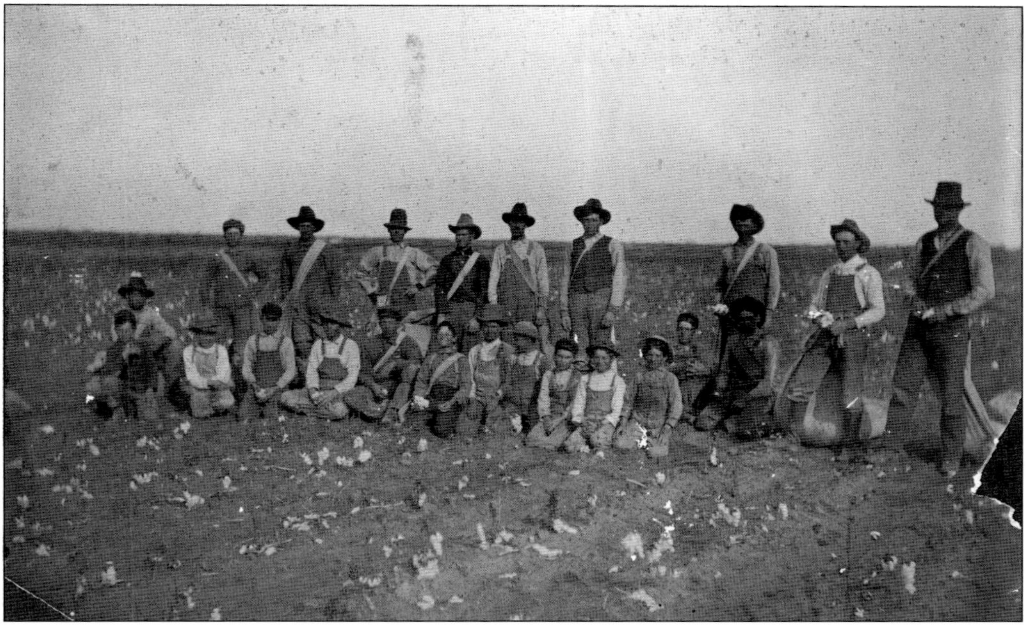

By 1900, cattle and sheep grazing were giving way to the cultivation of crops. Prior to mechanized agriculture, neighbors joined together to work the fields. In this photograph, members of the Josselet and Toliver families pick cotton near Josselet Switch north of Haskell. George A. Turnbow is on the far right, third from right is Felix Josselet, fourth from right is Andrew Josselet, and sixth from right is Owen Toliver. (Courtesy of Nancy Toliver.)

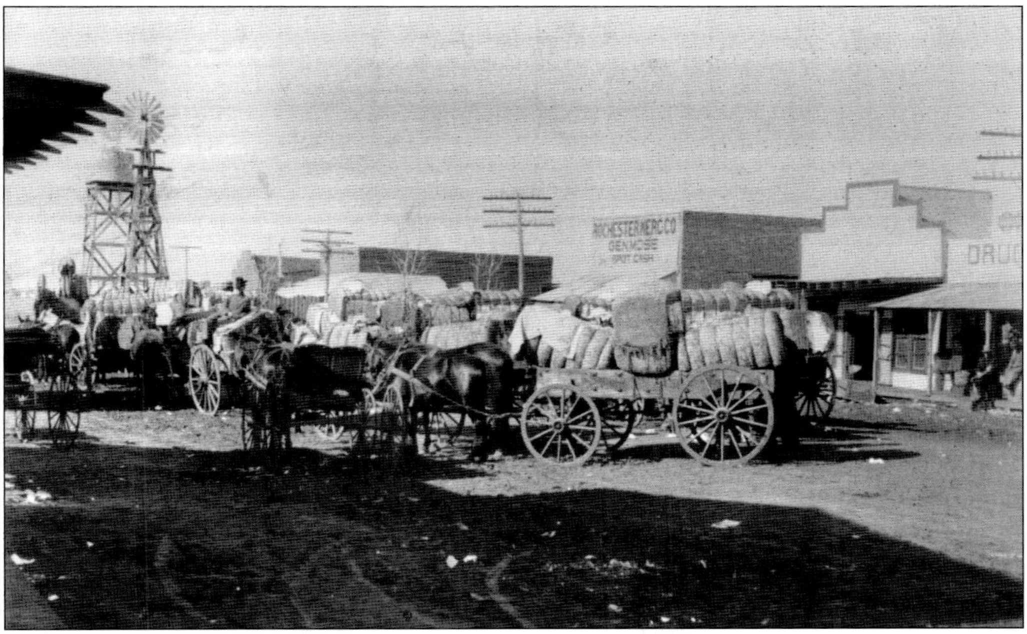

Rochester Mercantile is visible in the background of this photograph depicting wagons on Carothers Avenue. In the rush of cotton harvest, this was a common sight. After ginning, growers carried bales to a public weigher and received a receipt honored by cotton buyers in purchasing the crop. Before the railroads came through, bales were freighted to Abilene and later Stamford for shipment. (Courtesy of Sharon Mullino.)

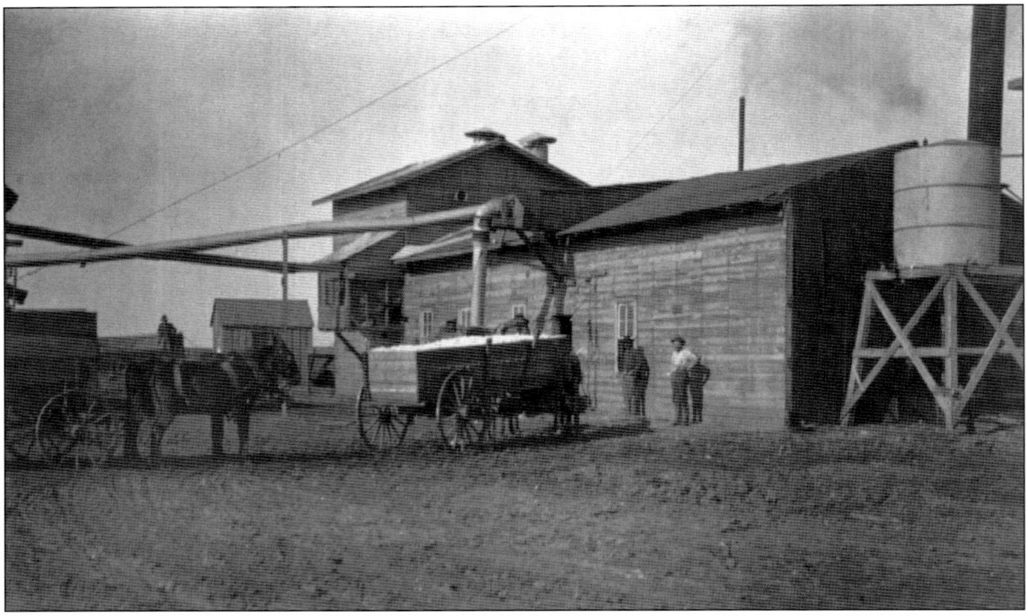

This scene shows a wagonload of cotton under the suction at Carney (later O'Brien) gin. Though the entire county produced less than 1,000 bales in 1899, today Haskell County is a major Rolling Plains cotton producer. Gins were built in every area of the county where cotton was grown. Causey and Causey built a gin near Jud in 1885 before there was anything else there. The Rule Co-op gin, established in 1913, is the oldest continuously operating co-op gin in the world. (Courtesy of C. H. Underwood.)

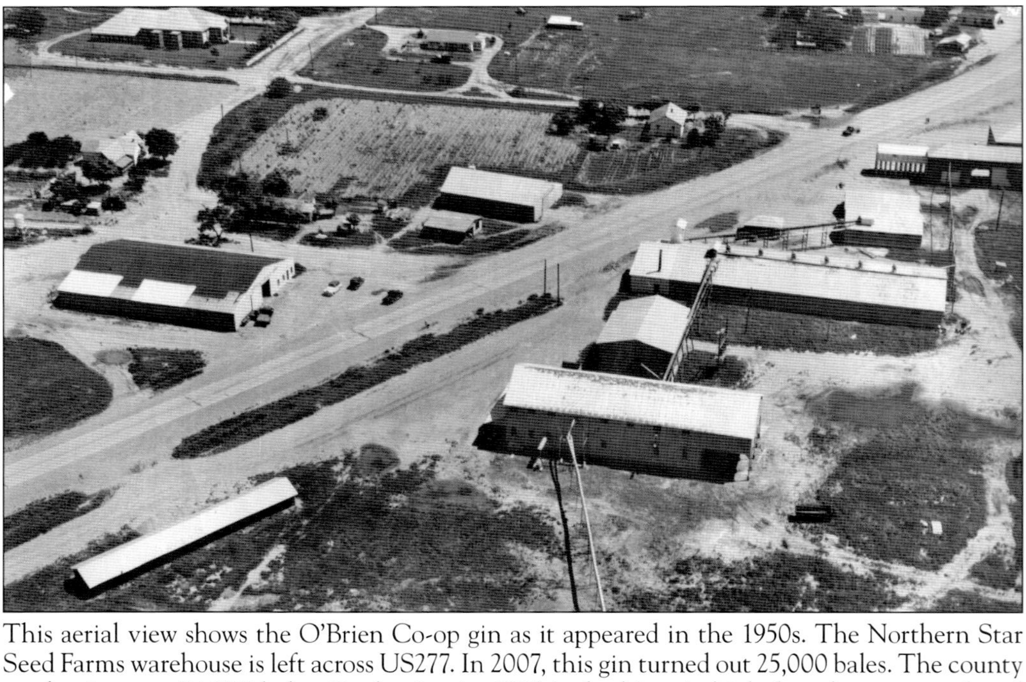

This aerial view shows the O'Brien Co-op gin as it appeared in the 1950s. The Northern Star Seed Farms warehouse is left across US277. In 2007, this gin turned out 25,000 bales. The county production was 94,000 bales. Production in 1979 is the historic high, but that was produced from more acres. O'Brien First Baptist Church is seen in the upper left corner. (Courtesy of C. H. Underwood.)

Bumper Cotton Crop on Behringer Farm Near Rule

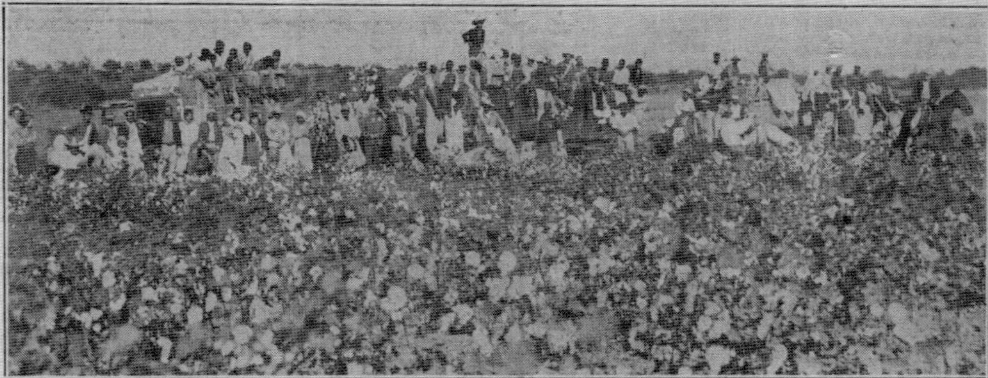

Pictured above are one hundred and sixty cotton pickers, Mexicans and Negroes, gathering a bumper crop from the river bottom lands in the western part of Haskell county. This particular tract of two hundred and fifty acres owned by John Behringer, on the forks of the Brazos and "Salty" River will yield a bale to the acre or more. Pickers are pulling more than twenty bales daily. With 985 acres planted in cotton Mr. Behringer expects to make at least 650 bales. Many of the stalks in the bottom land are higher than a man's head and have fallen to the ground. Planted later than last season, production on the same land is greatly increased this year with improved method of planting. All of the cotton is being placed in the government loan bringing eight to eight and a half cents for 13-16 and 7-8 staple.

Adjoining the farm is a six section ranch leased from J. E. Grissom, stocked with a fine herd of thoroughbred Hereford cattle. The herd of three hundred with six registered bulls is one of the finest in West Texas and plenty of winter forage is assured them on six hundred acres of wheat already up.

A typical West Texas ranchman, Mr. Behringer is proving what a successful farmer can accomplish with the right management. Of course, it isn't every year that such a tremendous crop is harvested but this exemplifies what West Texas really is in a good year.

A "bumper" cotton crop produced on the 250-acre John Behringer farm west of Rule is the subject of this photograph. According to the caption, 160 cotton pickers were harvesting the crop produced in the bottom lands near the "Salty River," a nickname for the Salt Fork of the Brazos River. Many of the stalks were higher than a man's head. The cotton was to be placed in the government loan at about 8¢ a pound. (Courtesy of Village Primitive Antique Store.)

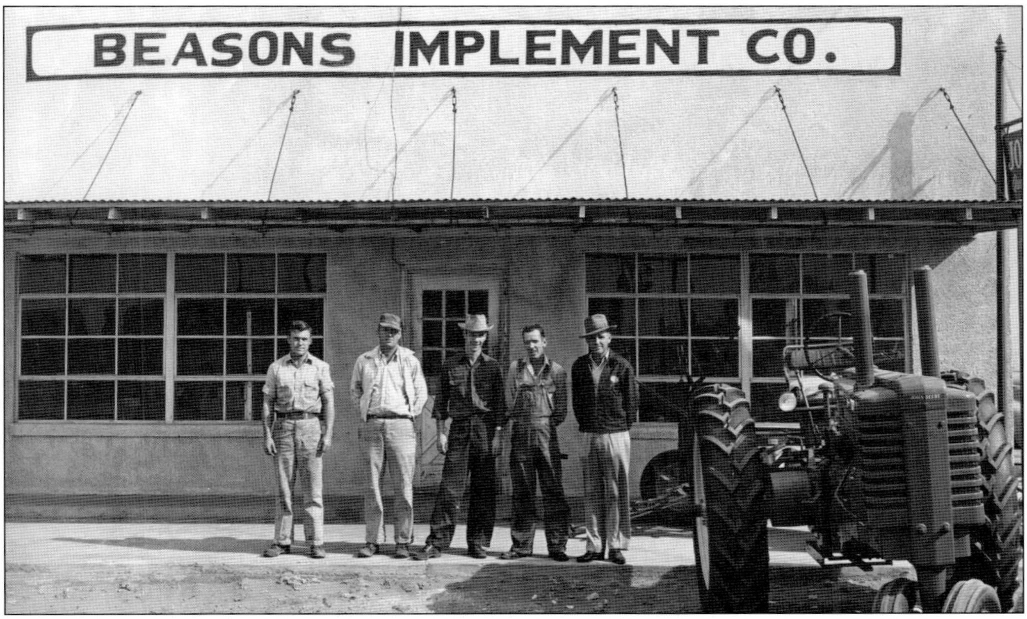

Beason Implement Company in Rochester was a John Deere dealership operated from about 1949 until 1963. The company was located at Farm Road 617 and Highway 6. Tractors and farm implements were shipped in by train on flatcars and in boxcars. From left to right are Robert P. Cypert, Harvey Byrd, Kenneth Newberry, Elvin Watkins, and Tolbert Beason. The tractor is an early 1950s model G John Deere. (Courtesy of Lorene Ardell Beason.)

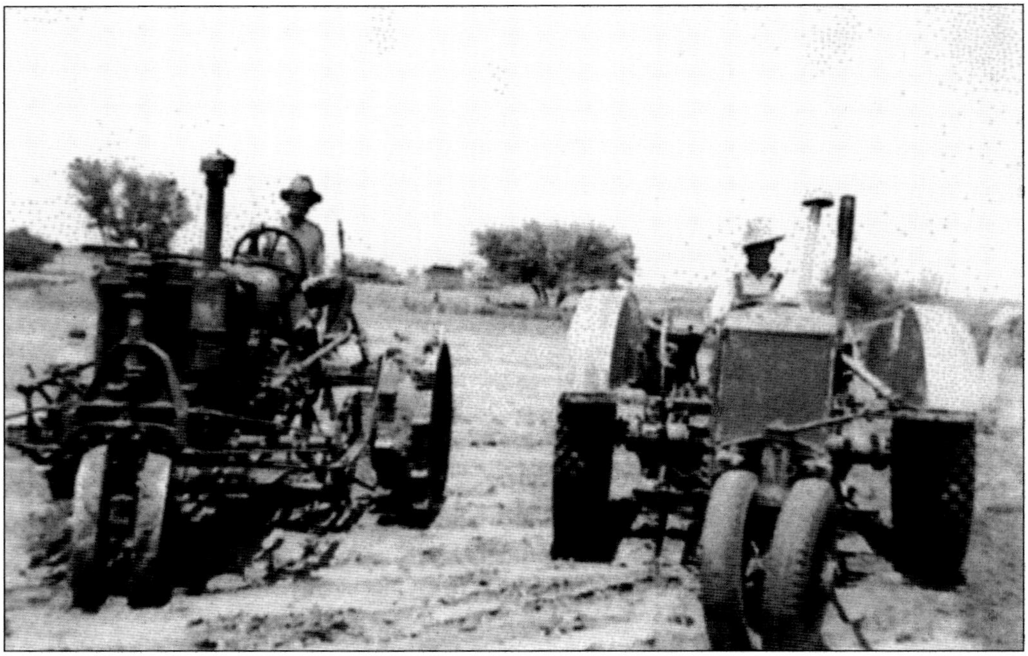

Luther Toliver (left), driving his 1946 International Harvester Farmall tractor, and Johnny Perrin, with a new Case Tractor, illustrate a revolution in American agriculture. Horses and mules continued to reign after World War I, but in the 1930s, tractors began to replace them on the farm. In addition to saving labor, acres once planted to feed crops for horses and mules could now be planted to cotton. (Courtesy of Nancy Toliver.)

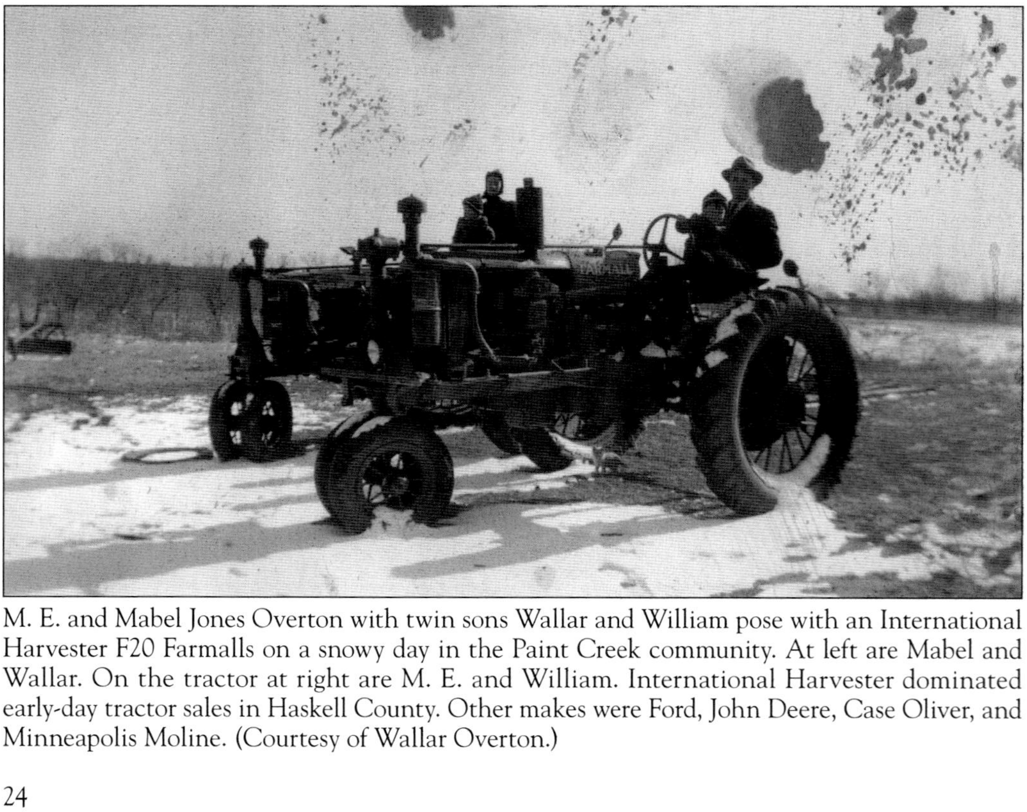

M. E. and Mabel Jones Overton with twin sons Wallar and William pose with an International Harvester F20 Farmalls on a snowy day in the Paint Creek community. At left are Mabel and Wallar. On the tractor at right are M. E. and William. International Harvester dominated early-day tractor sales in Haskell County. Other makes were Ford, John Deere, Case Oliver, and Minneapolis Moline. (Courtesy of Wallar Overton.)

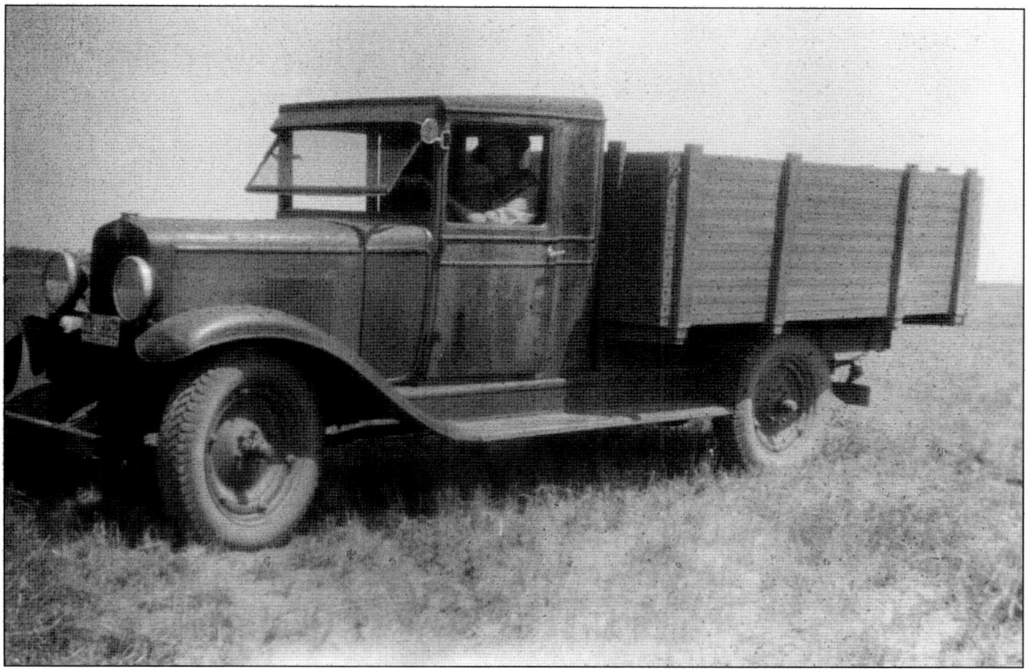

Along with tractors and mechanized harvesting equipment came heavy-duty trucks. Though small by today's standards, they were a significant change over mule-drawn wagons. This 1942 model with an unidentified driver is helping with the wheat harvest on the Luther Toliver farm north of Haskell. (Courtesy of Nancy Toliver.)

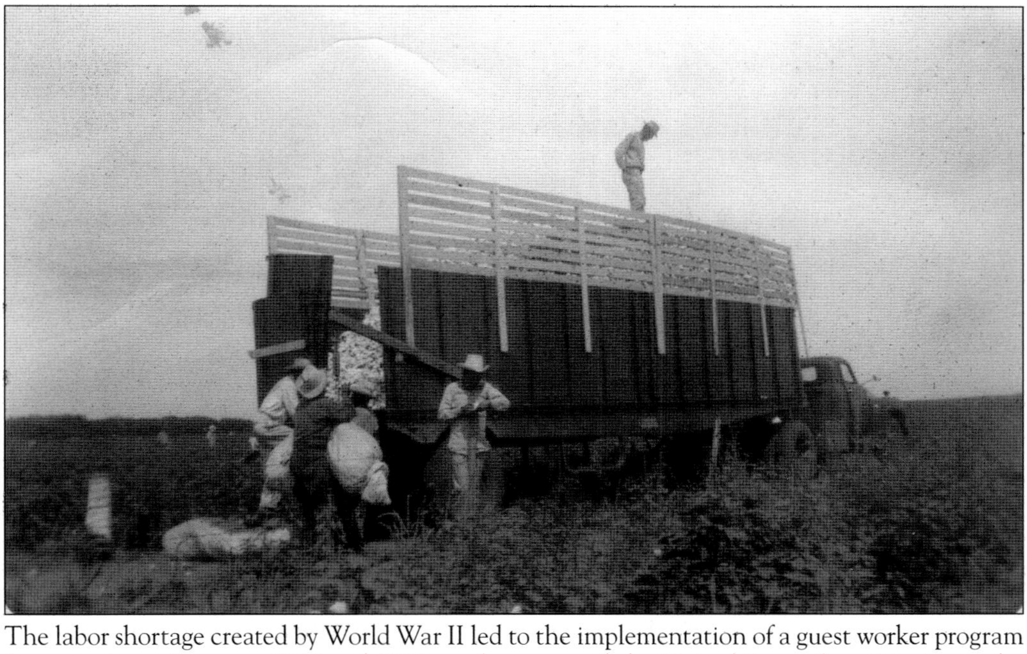

The labor shortage created by World War II led to the implementation of a guest worker program for agriculture. Between 1942 and 1964, workers entered the United States from Mexico under what was known as the Bracero Program. This photograph depicts a cotton harvest near O'Brien. Cotton sacks were weighed on scales at the back of the trailer. The International truck could haul several thousand pounds of lint cotton. (Courtesy of C. H. Underwood.)

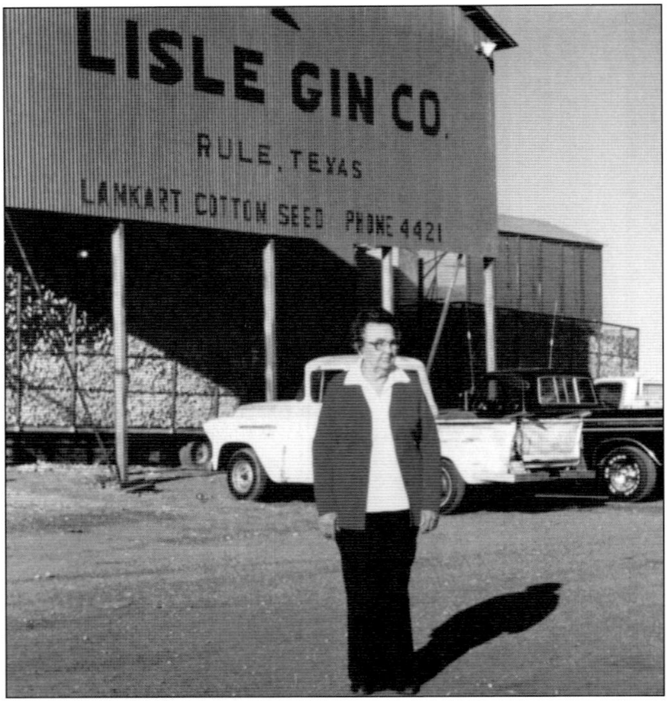

A true pioneer, Ola Mae Pike Lisle was born in Indian Territory in 1901. Her family later farmed in the interior of Mexico, returning to Texas when the Mexican revolution began. When her husband, James A. Lisle Sr., died in 1927, she assumed management of Lisle Gin Company in Rule to support her family. A devoted community leader, among her many honors was being commissioned a Yellow Rose of Texas by Gov. Ann Richards. (Courtesy of Jo Ruth Lisle.)

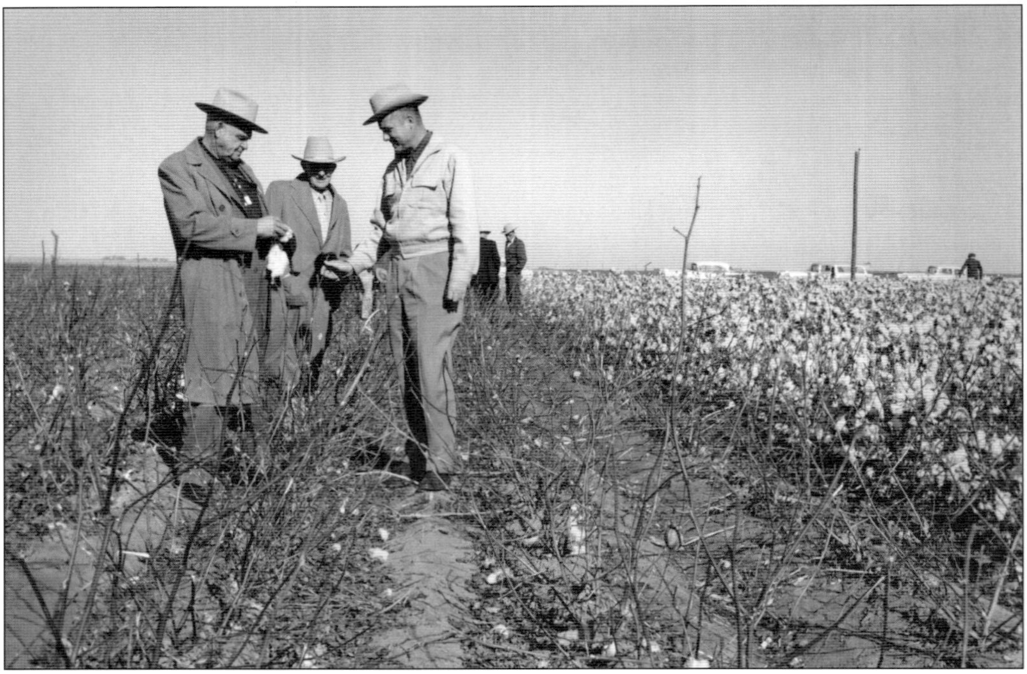

Northern Star Seed Farms was a cottonseed-producing company in O'Brien. Beginning in the 1950s, the company crossbred established cotton varieties to develop improved varieties that performed ideally in the Rolling Plains region of Texas. Working with O'Brien Co-op Gin and area cotton growers, Northern Star came to be known among cotton producers throughout the United States. Its varieties were top performers for that era in yield and quality. From left to right are ? Woodward, J. S. Mogford, and unidentified. (Courtesy of C. H. Underwood.)

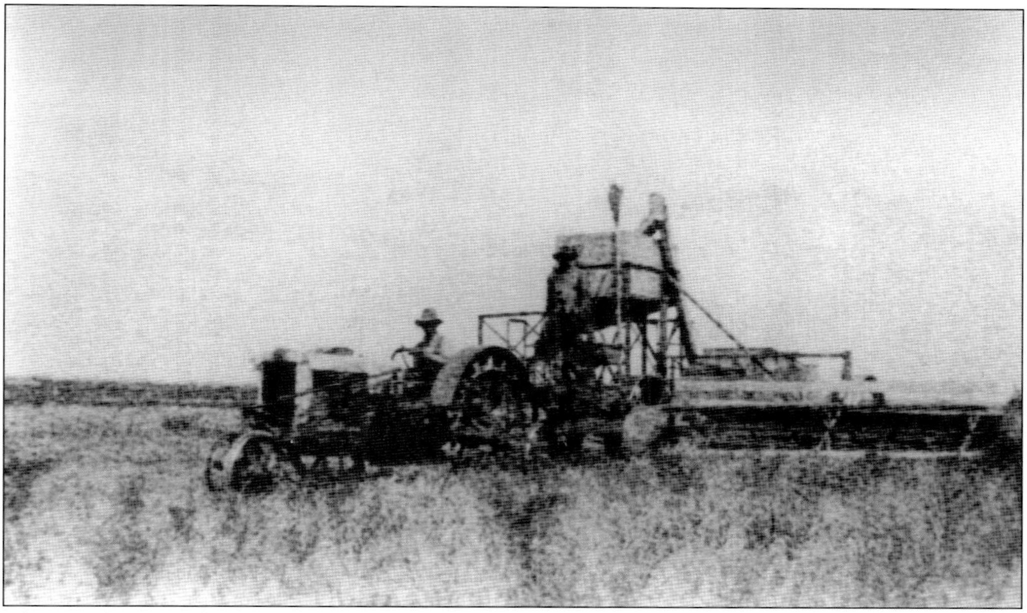

The combine in the undated photograph above is operated by Gus Rueffer in the Mattson community. Wheat harvest once took the labor of many men over long days, first binding the wheat into bundles, stacking it in the fields to dry, and then hauling it to a thresher. In the 1930s, all the elements of harvesting wheat were combined into one machine. One unintentional result of this mechanization was loss of the social aspect surrounding large threshing crews. Gleaner Baldwin and International Harvester were two of the earliest manufacturers of drag-type combines. Later self-propelled models were developed. The combines below belong to the J. D. and Walter Davis crew harvesting fields near Weinert in the 1980s. Modern-day computerized combines with 30-foot headers harvest grain in a fraction of the time it once took. (Both courtesy of Mary Murphy.)

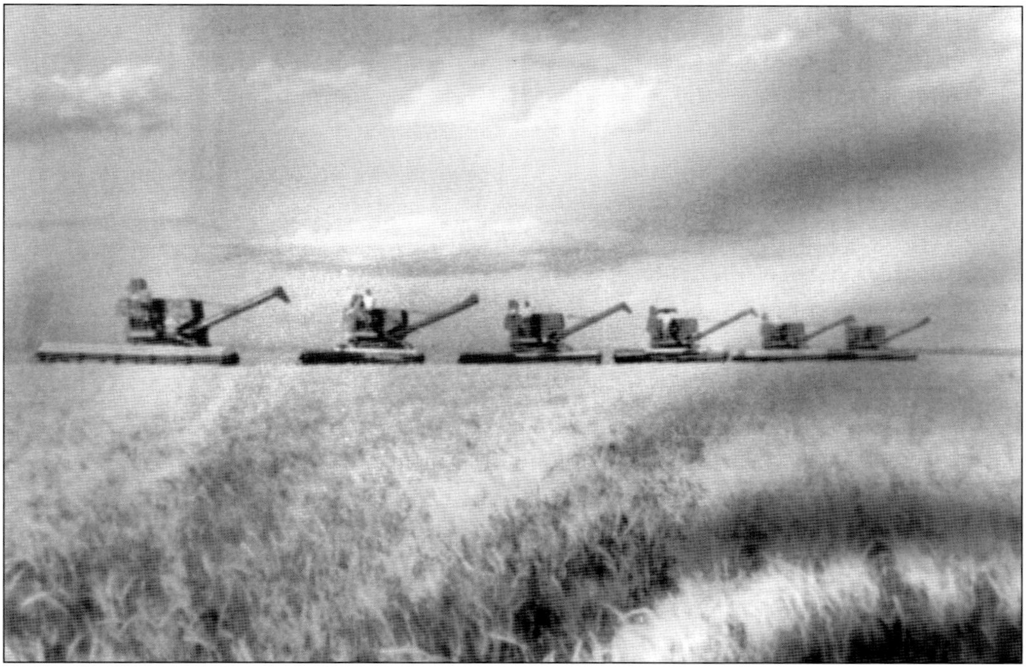

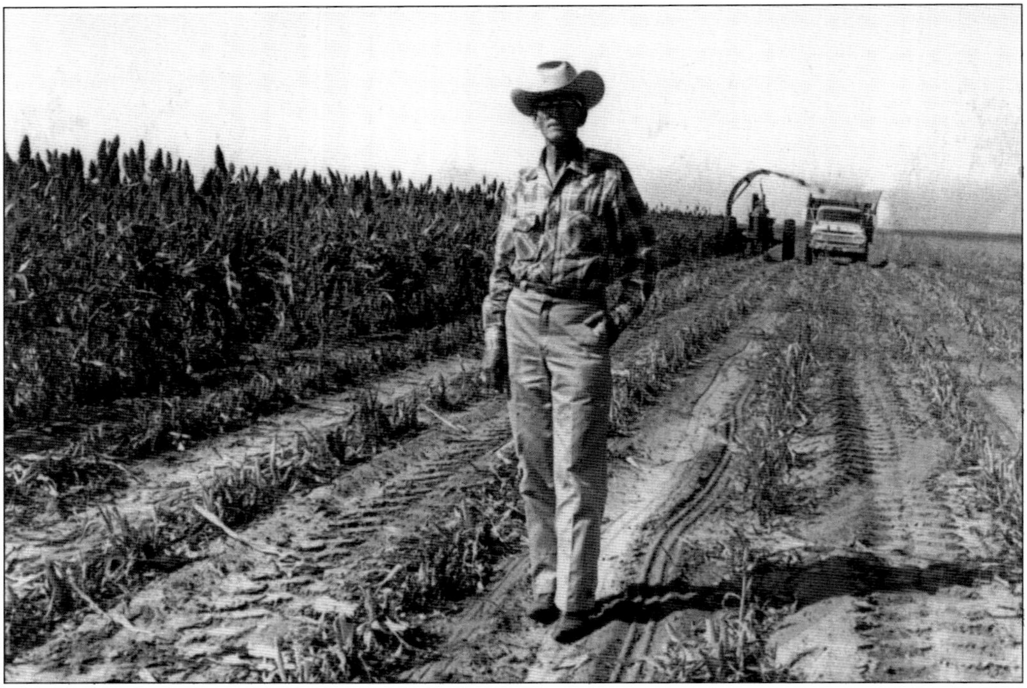

This field of red top cane is being chopped into silage on Ira Grinstead's farm near Rochester. Silage production provided winter feed for cattle, but in spite of mechanization, it was labor intensive. In this early-1960s photograph, a John Deere tractor pulls the silage cutter through the field as chopped cane is fed into a truck. The cane was then packed in ground silos for fermentation. (Courtesy of Sandra Fry.)

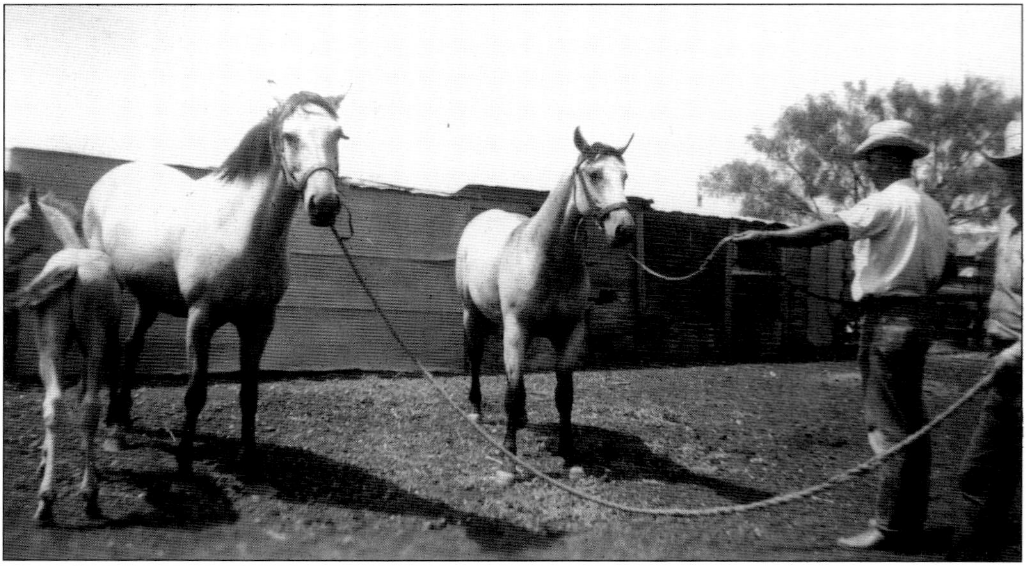

These horses are corralled near Bitter Lake. At the halter is Lynn Pace. At right is Scotty Green. Horses made possible a grazing economy from the county's natural resources of grass and water. Though wild horses were plentiful, early-day ranchers more often relied on gentle stock of improved bloodlines. Even as mechanized agriculture developed, horses were essential to the cattleman. A good cow pony was the subject of much admiration. (Courtesy of Lynn Pace.)

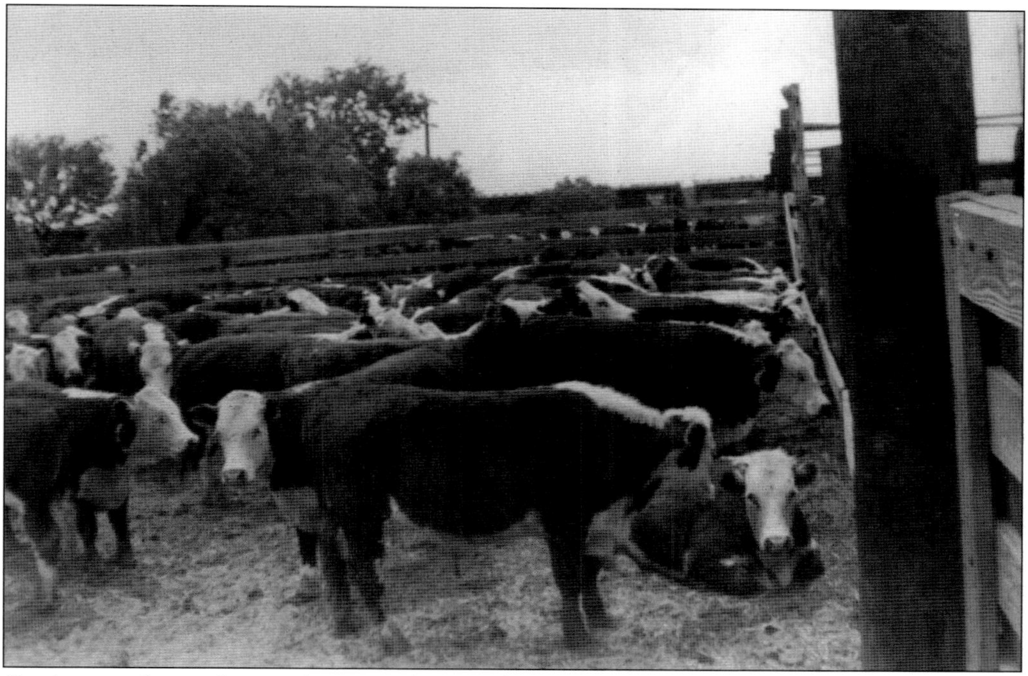

Cattle were driven from miles around to Wichita Valley Railroad pens in Haskell. Generally loaded 40 head per car, several hundred yearlings required many cars and two locomotives to pull them. Regulations required cattle to be unloaded and watered after a set number of hours. The owner or his representative could ride in the caboose and was given a return ride home. Here cattle belonging to Lynn Pace await shipment. (Courtesy of Lynn Pace.)

Rick Perry, 47th governor of the state of Texas and 1968 graduate of Paint Creek High School, served two terms as Texas commissioner of agriculture. Governor Perry's great-grandfather Wayne Perry was a pioneer settler of Haskell County. Pictured at pens on the Perry farm in 1986 are four generations of the Perry family. From left to right are Hoyt Perry, J. R. ("Ray") Perry, Gov. Rick Perry, and (center front) Rick's son Griffin. (Courtesy of J. R. Perry.)

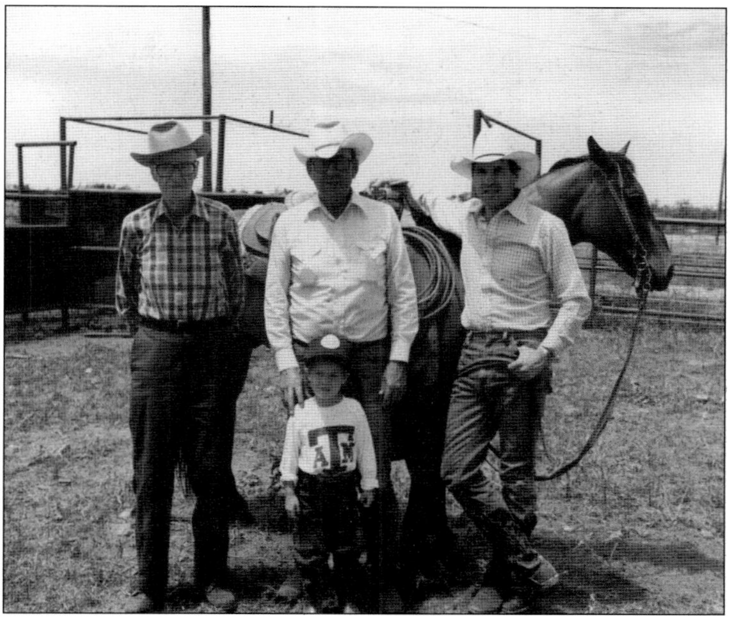

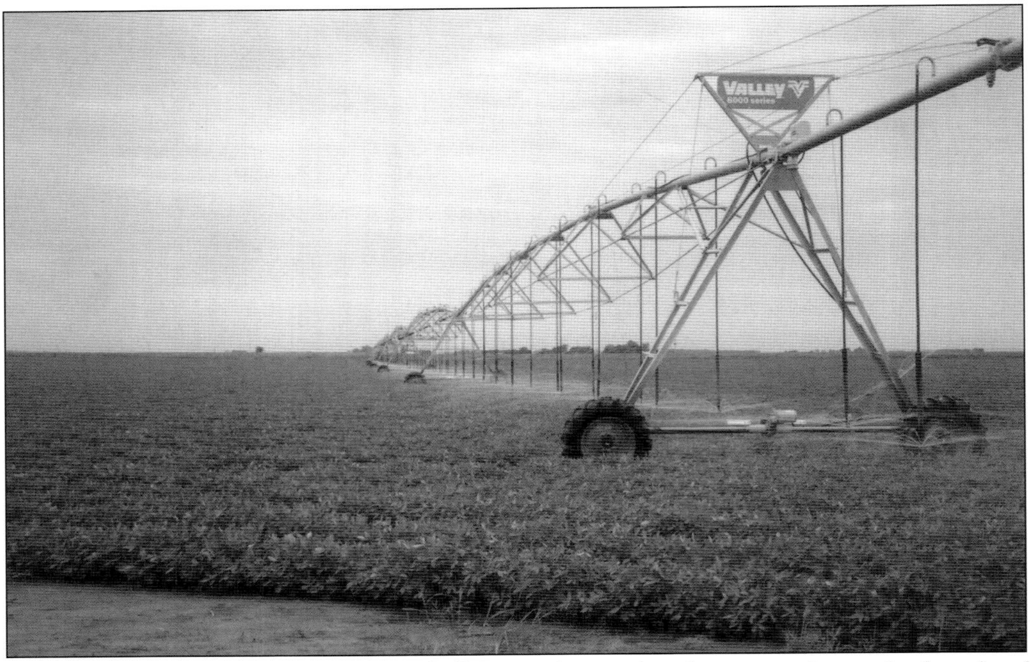

Irrigation began to play a key role in Haskell County's agricultural economy during the drought of the 1950s. While irrigation water is not found throughout the county, where present, it is drawn from a relatively shallow depth. Its source is the Seymour Aquifer. Modern irrigation systems distribute water efficiently over thousands of acres. This center pivot system waters a peanut field west of Rochester. (Courtesy of Susan Turner.)

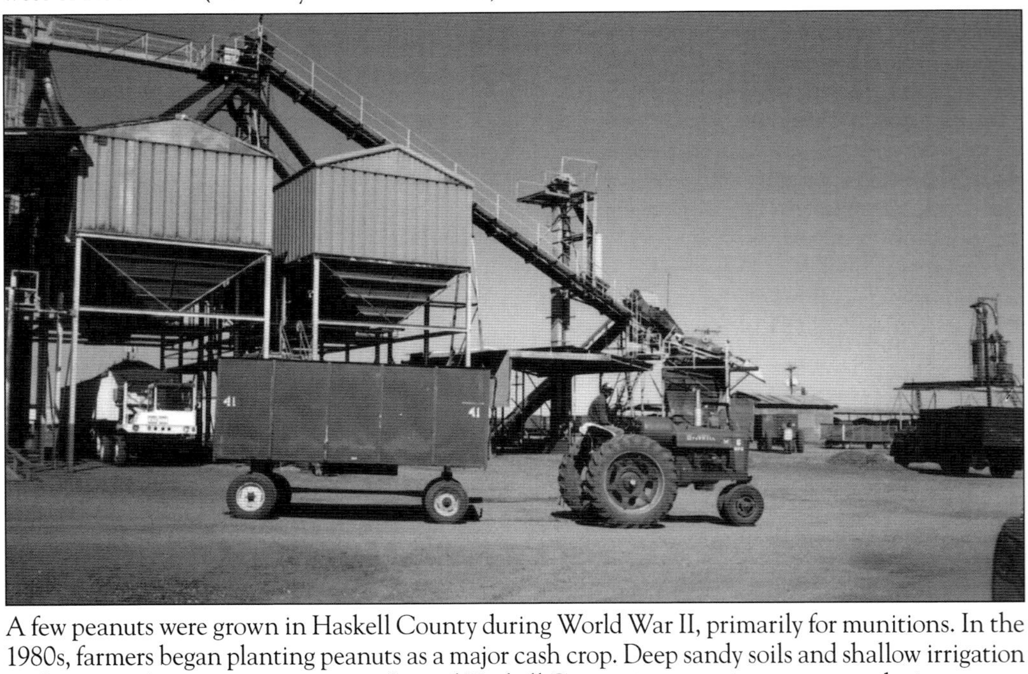

A few peanuts were grown in Haskell County during World War II, primarily for munitions. In the 1980s, farmers began planting peanuts as a major cash crop. Deep sandy soils and shallow irrigation in the county's western portion transformed Haskell County into a major peanut-producing county in Texas. A dryer was built at Rochester, which annually handles 10,000 tons. Vintage tractors work alongside modern equipment on this former gin yard. (Courtesy of Modelle Barton.)

Three

Places I Remember

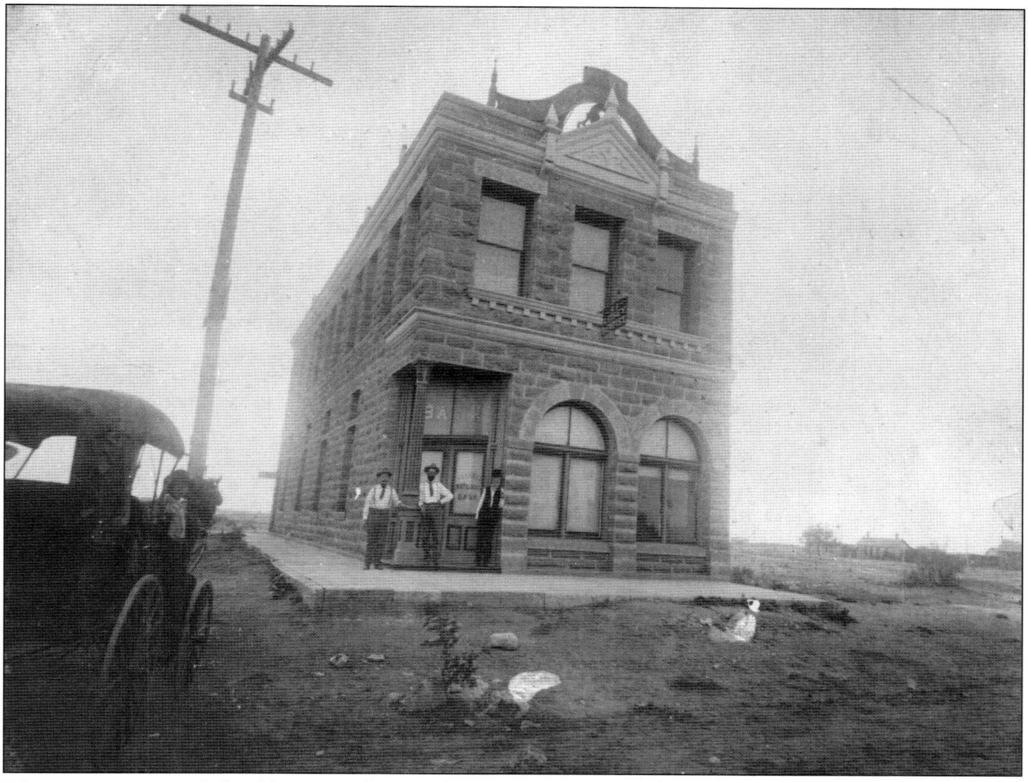

This two-story rock building on the northwest corner of the Haskell square was built to house the First National Bank, organized in 1890. Haskell National Bank was also organized that year by M. S. Pierson, Arthur C. Foster, H. G. McConnell, W. E. Johnson, J. L. Jones, J. G. Lowden, E. W. Taylor, and S. H. Johnson. M. S. Pierson was elected the first president. In 1895, First National sold the building to Haskell National Bank, which remained at this location until 1959. Here in front of the bank building are G. R. Crouch (left), Lee Pierson (center), and M. S. Pierson. Emmett Couch is pictured on the buggy. (Courtesy of Haskell County Historical and Genealogical Society.)

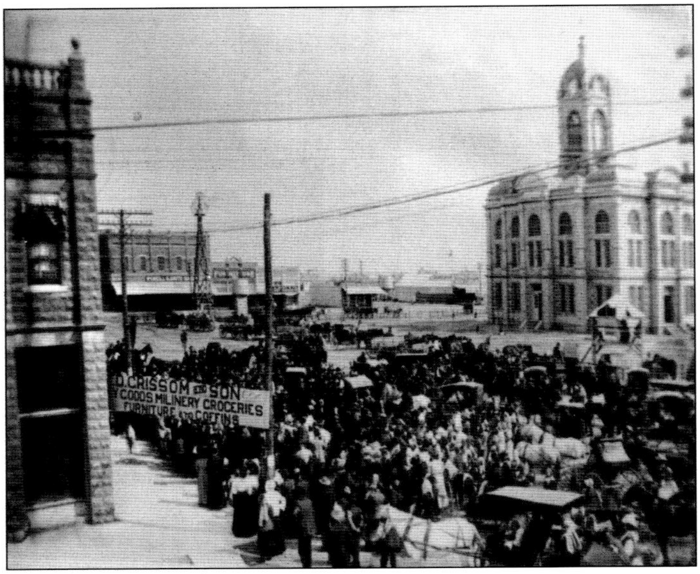

The Grissom's Department Store dynasty in Texas had its beginning in Haskell County. In 1906, C. D. Grissom opened his first store in the McConnell Building on the northwest corner of the square in Haskell. This photograph is perhaps of a sale or drawing considering the large crowd. A town windmill and water storage tank are visible, as well as the early-day gazebo on the northwest courthouse lawn. (Courtesy of Haskell County Historical and Genealogical Society.)

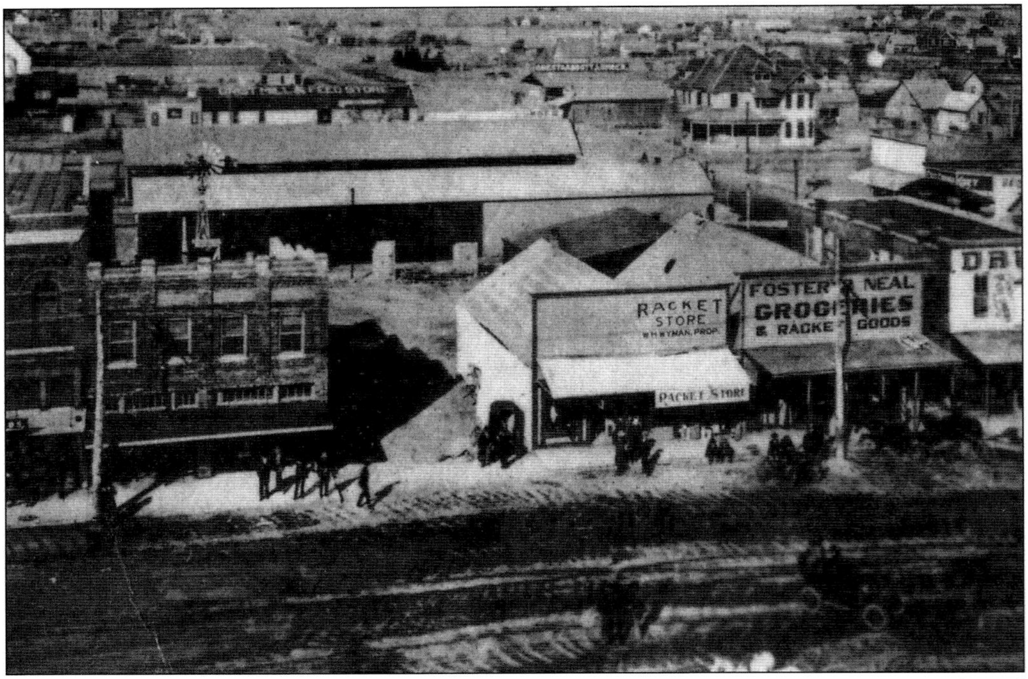

The three-story rooming house known as the Norton House is seen above the Foster and Neal Grocery sign in this view from the courthouse. A Racket Store was a general merchandise store. Foster and Neal Grocery and Collier Drug, forerunner of Oates Drug Store, shared the northside of Walton (North First) Street. Windmills, the town's water source in that day, and privies are located behind the stores' buildings. (Courtesy of Hess Hartsfield.)

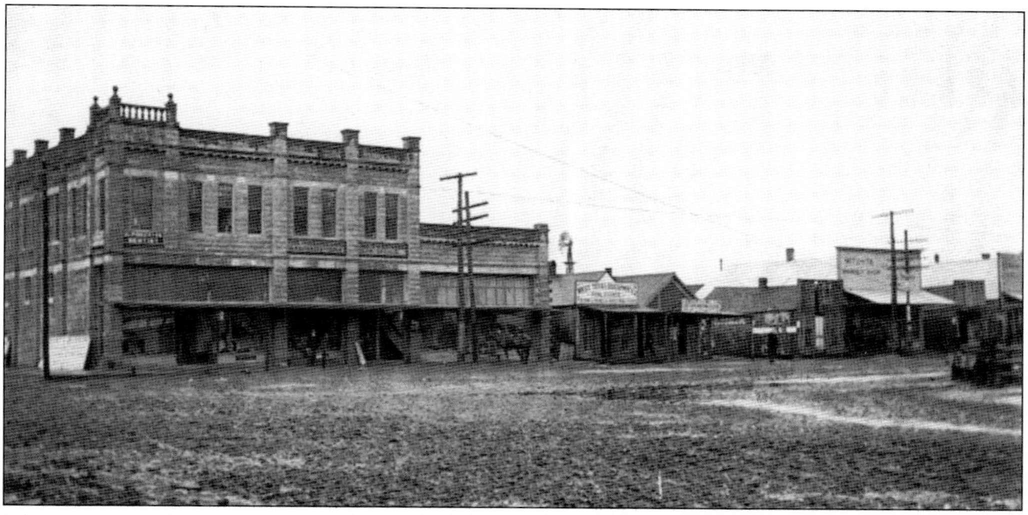

This photograph made about 1906 or 1907 shows the McConnell Building on the left. A dentist office is on the second floor, and a horse is tied to a utility pole outside. Many of the buildings around the square were originally three stories. H. G. McConnell was county judge when the second courthouse was built. The West Texas Development Company selling real estate occupied the north side of the square in this era of unpaved streets. (Courtesy of Haskell County Historical and Genealogical Society.)

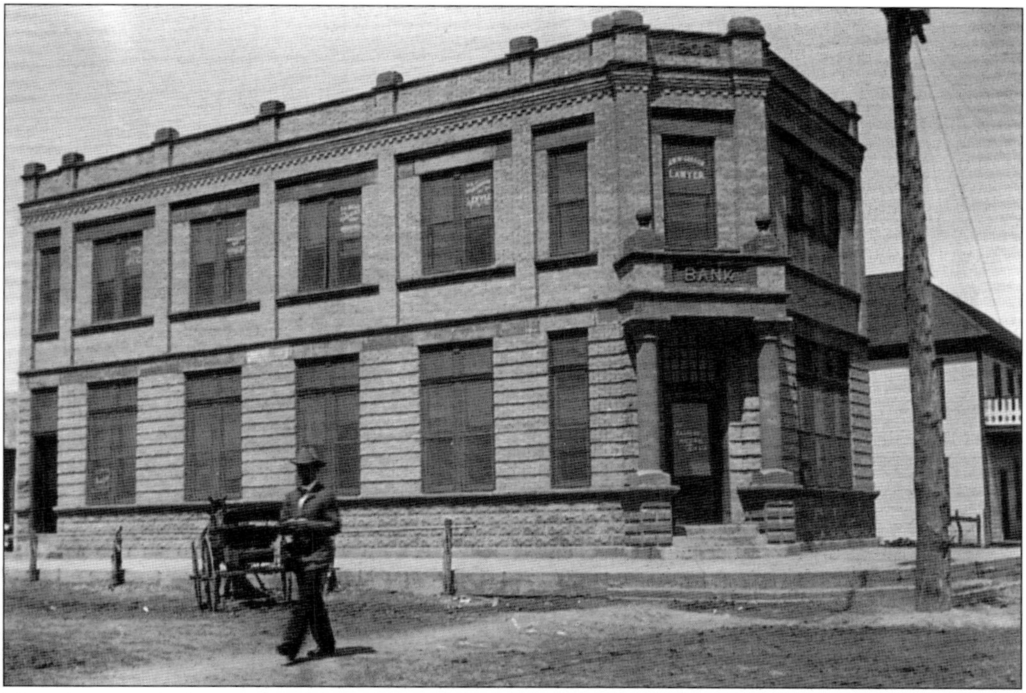

The Farmers Exchange Bank operating in 1904 on the southwest corner of the square merged with the Farmers National Bank in 1905. The charter was changed in 1913 to a state charter under Farmers State Bank. During the Depression of the 1930s, it reorganized as Farmers and Merchants State Bank. It occupied this building on the northeast corner of the square in Haskell. In 1947, it merged with Haskell National Bank. (Courtesy of Haskell County Historical and Genealogical Society.)

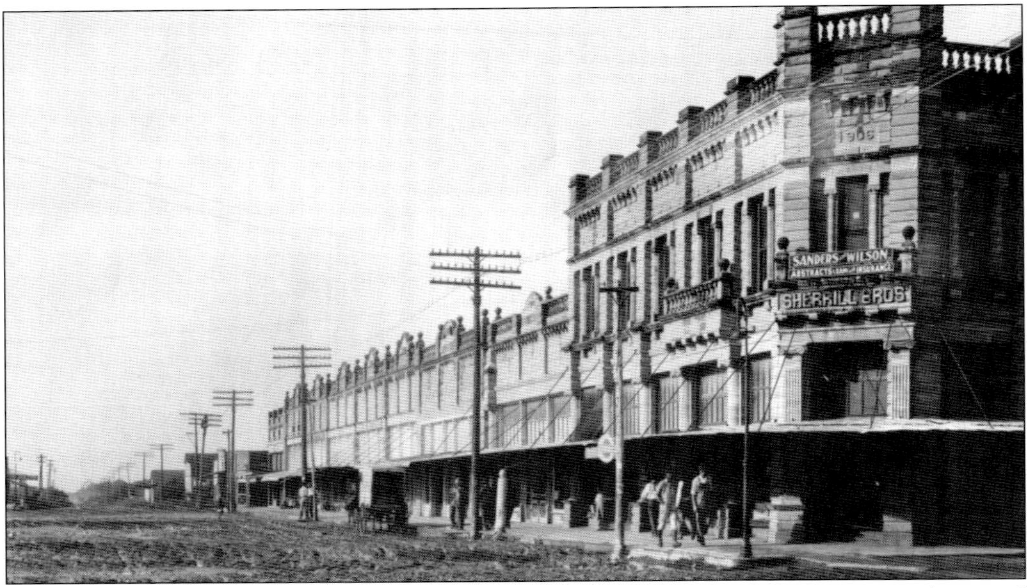

R. E. Sherrill, prominent historian and civic leader, came to Haskell County in 1890 and engaged in the hardware business. This ornate building on the west side of the square was one of the most recognizable buildings in the county. This view looks south down the muddy street. The men on the corner are wearing high-topped boots. Sherrill's thorough history of the county continues to be referenced by researchers. (Courtesy of Hess Hartsfield.)

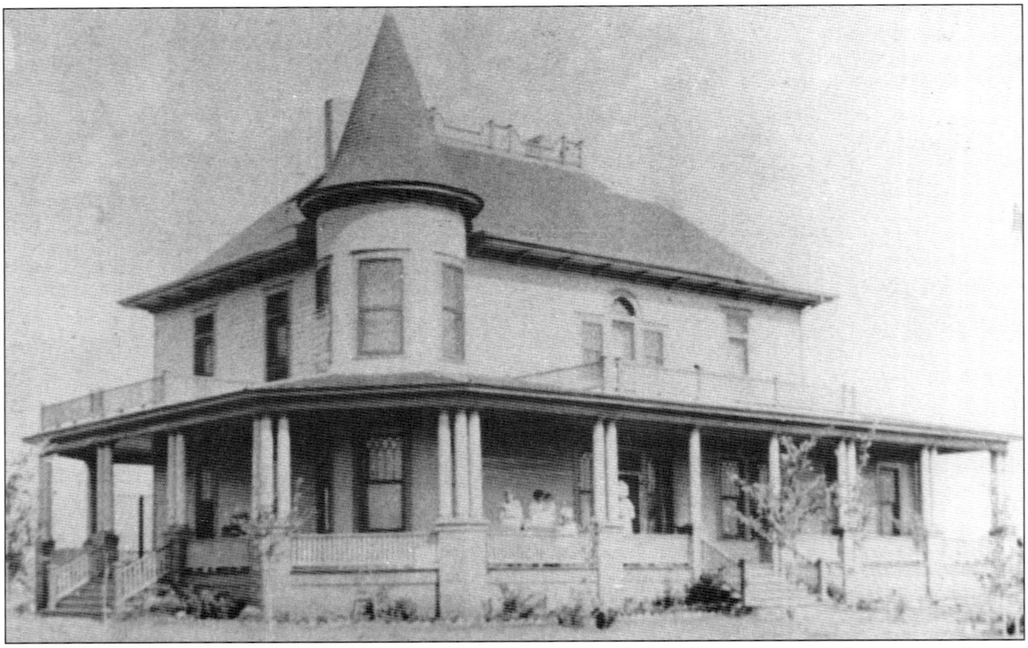
In 1906, Marion Stephens Shook and his wife, Jennie, built this two-story home at what is now North Sixteenth Street and Highway 277 in Haskell. They had come from Palo Pinto in 1879 to western Haskell County. From native prairie, they established a substantial ranching enterprise. When their children reached school age, the family moved to Haskell. The six-bedroom house had the first indoor bathrooms in Haskell. (Courtesy of Haskell County Historical and Genealogical Society.)

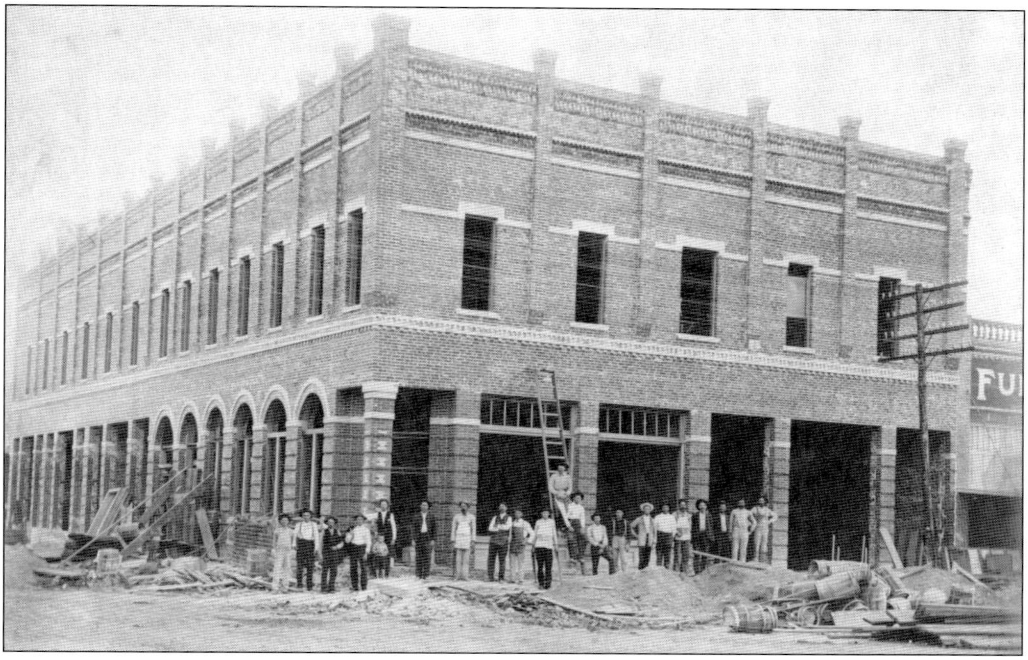

Once a railroad was secured, more substantial brick buildings began to rise around the Haskell square. This October 24, 1907, photograph is of a building on the northeast corner of the square. Its corner offices housed the Haskell State Bank, organized in 1907, until 1912. The Haskell Post Office occupied these offices at one time. McNeill and Smith Hardware occupied the remainder of the building. A furniture store is next door. (Courtesy of Texas Tech Southwest Collection.)

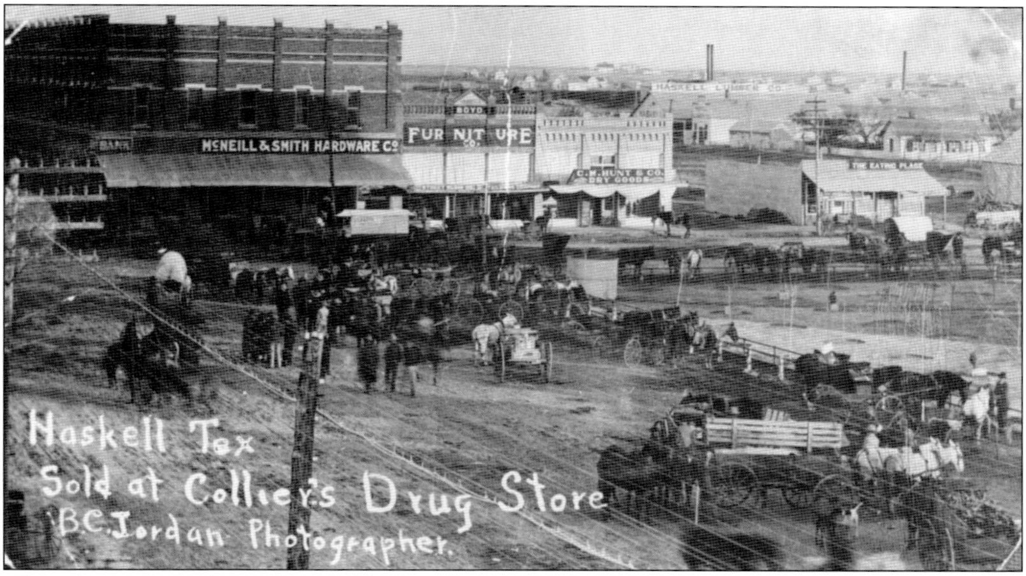

This photograph shows the building above at a later date, along with a flourishing Haskell business district. In the Boyd Furniture Company building are Street Music Company and Haskell Tailoring Company. Next door is C. M. Hunt and Company Dry Goods. In the next building are Haskell Plumbing and the Eating Place. Looking east, Haskell Lumber Company may be seen behind Campbell Street, now called Avenue D. (Courtesy of Haskell County Historical and Genealogical Society.)

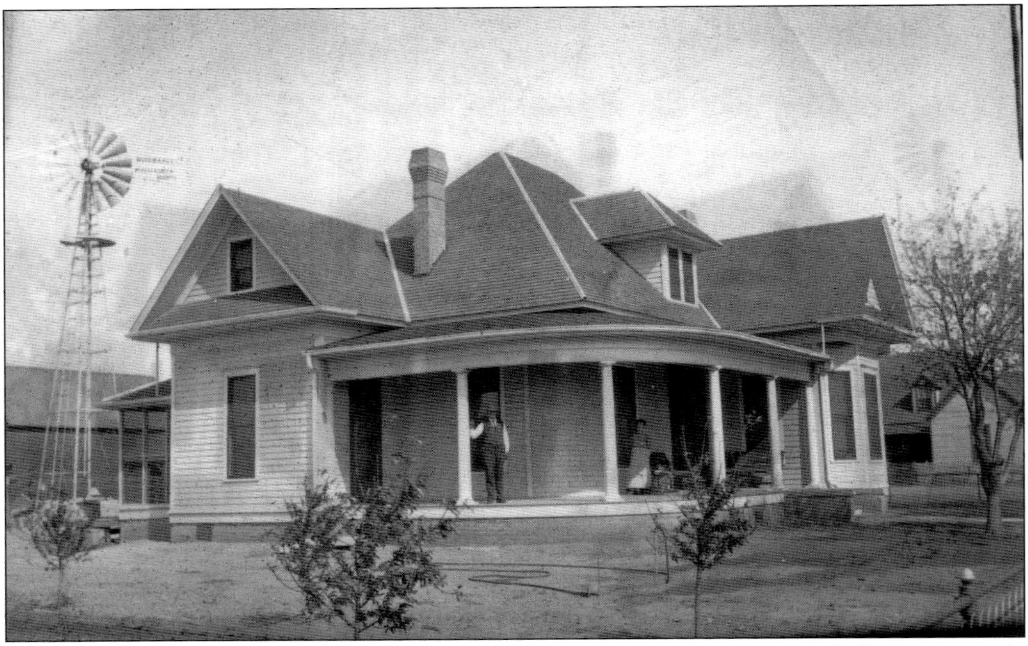

This home at 311 North Avenue F in Haskell was built by Spence Bevers, a Haskell County cattle rancher who arrived from Young and Palo Pinto Counties in 1887. The windmill in the backyard was one of many throughout the town. On the porch are Spence Bevers (left), Ola Bevers Frazier, and Byron Frazier (beside his mother, propped against the bench). The historical home is today known as the Bevers House Bed and Breakfast. (Courtesy of Woody Frazier.)

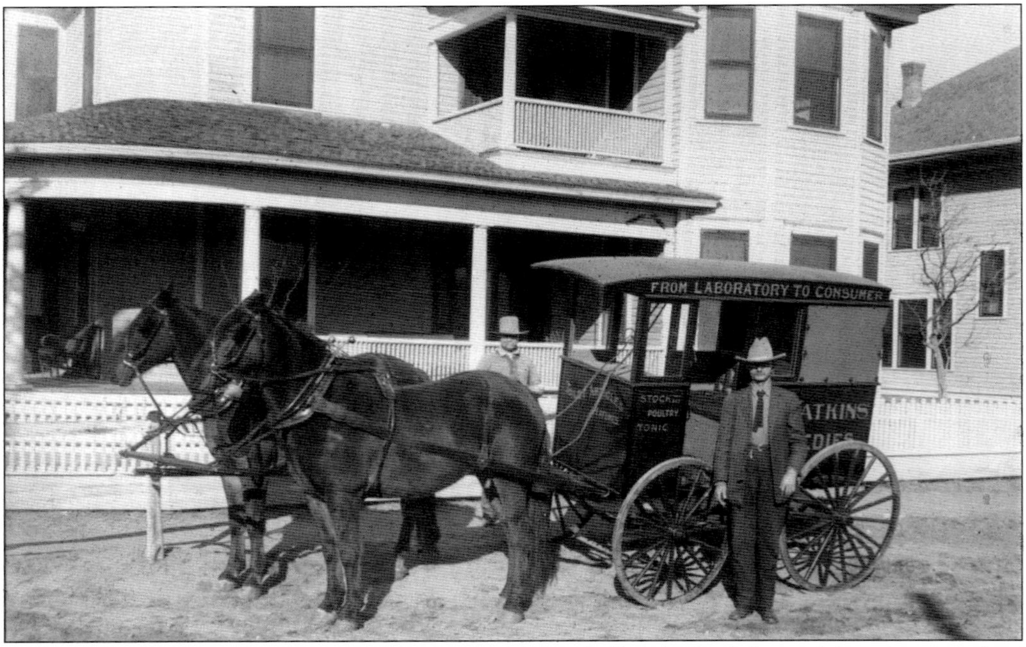

The Norton House at 301 North Second Street in Haskell is the backdrop of this photograph of a Watkins Products salesman with his wagon and team. Mrs. J. T. (Emily) Hunt once operated a boardinghouse here. The house is still standing at the present time. The two gentlemen are unidentified. (Courtesy of Haskell County Historical and Genealogical Society.)

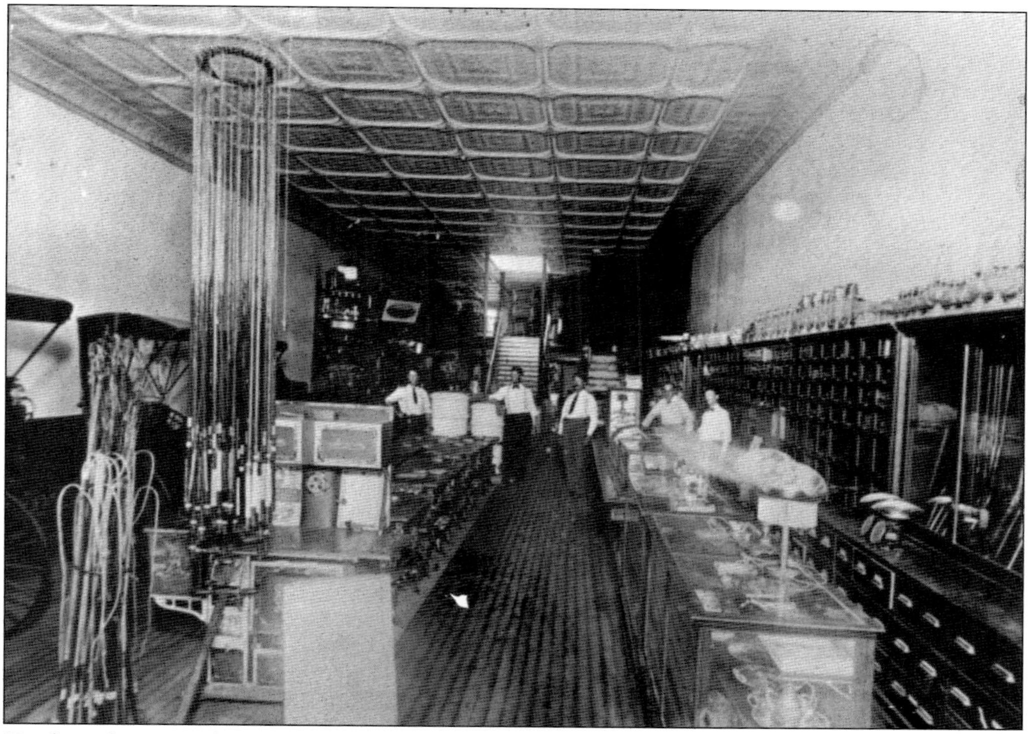

Herding sheep on the open range was the occupation of Burwell Cox when he came to Texas in 1888. He later formed a partnership with W. L. Cason. Cason and Cox Hardware Store dealt in farm equipment, furniture, and the undertaking business. Cason sold his interest to J. F. Jones in 1911, forming Jones, Cox, and Company. From left to right are Jim Killingsworth, Tom Russell, Burwell Cox, and Travis Arbuckle. The man on the far right is unidentified. (Courtesy of Wallace Cox.)

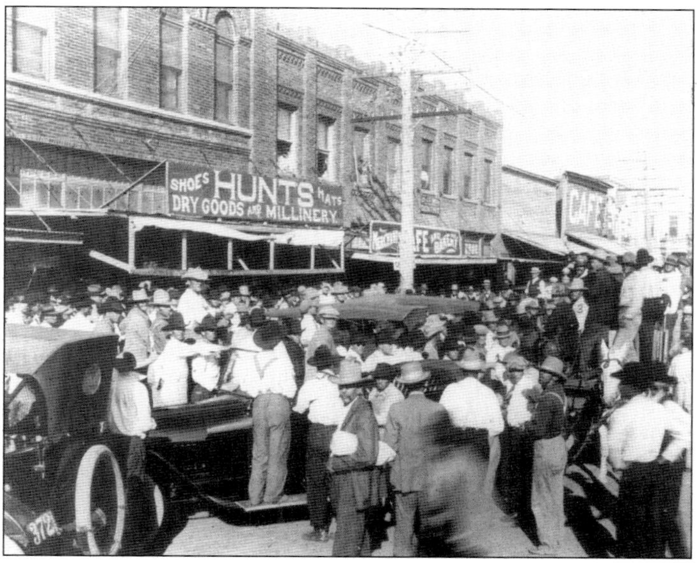

A large crowd has gathered on the north side of the Haskell square in 1916 for the drawing for a piano. The photograph identification states, "Six year old Floyd (Satch) Lusk drew the name of Alma Barton." Businesses looking east along what was once Walton Street (now North First Street) include Hunt's Dry Goods Company, Merchants Café and Bakery, and a café on the future site of Oates Drug Store. (Courtesy of Hess Hartsfield.)

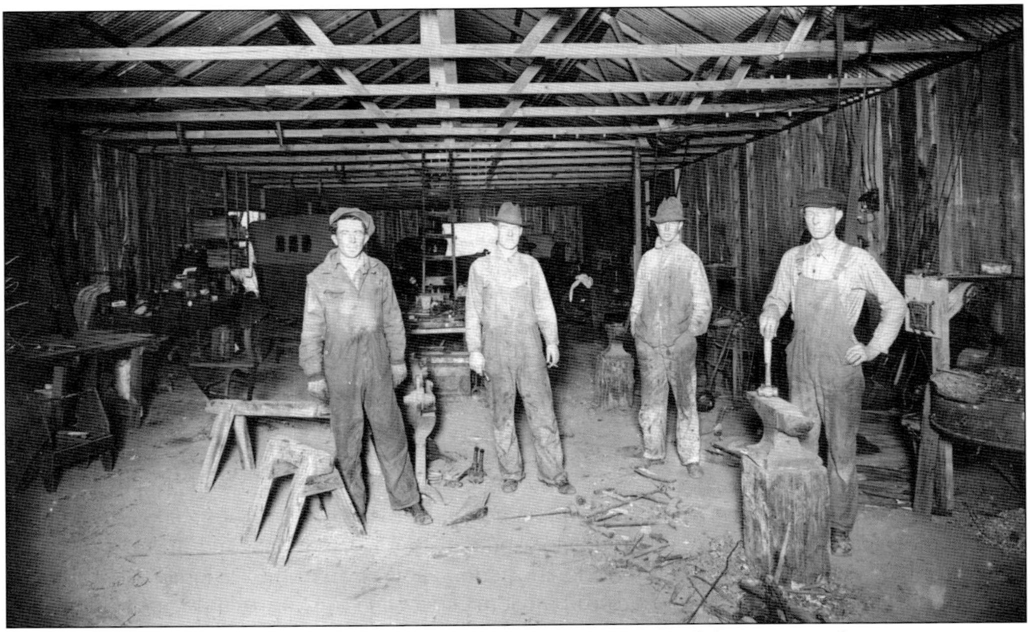

In the early days of Haskell County, blacksmith shops were essential for repairing buggies, carriages, wagons, plows, or anything powered by horses. Horses' shoes and feet received attention here from a farrier. Providing repairs to horseless carriages was a natural progression as seen by the automobile in the back of this photograph. E. E. McElroy stands near the anvil. (Courtesy of Haskell County Historical and Genealogical Society.)

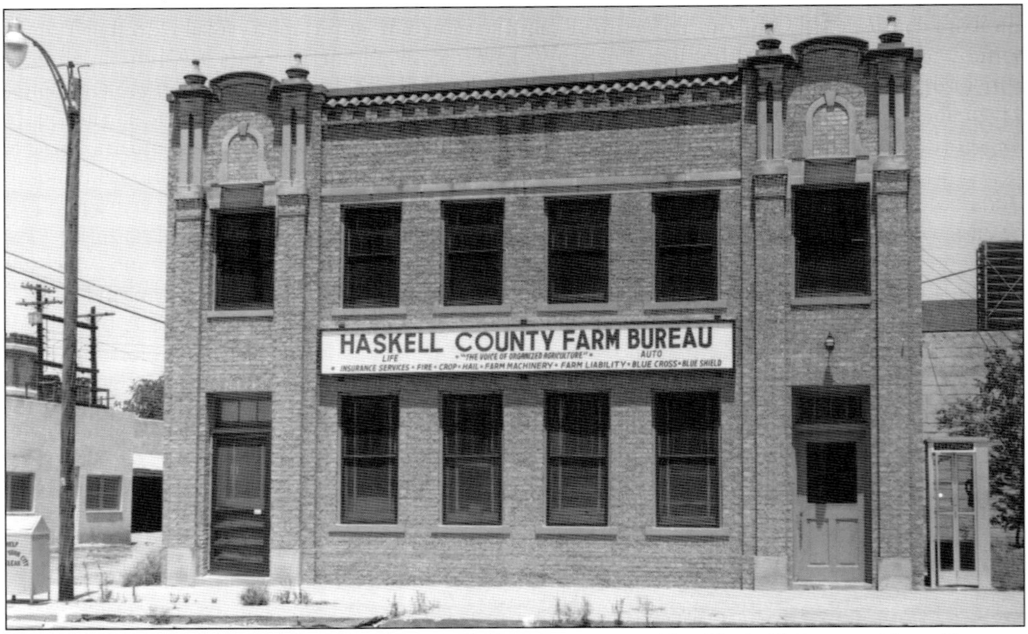

This building on North First Street in Haskell, now occupied by Haskell County Farm Bureau, once housed the Haskell Telephone, later General Telephone, office. Initially, customers were greeted with, "Number, please?" The service went to dial up in 1958. Note the bells at either end of the top of the building and the telephone booth outside. Haskell County Farm Bureau moved into the building in 1959. (Courtesy of Haskell County Farm Bureau.)

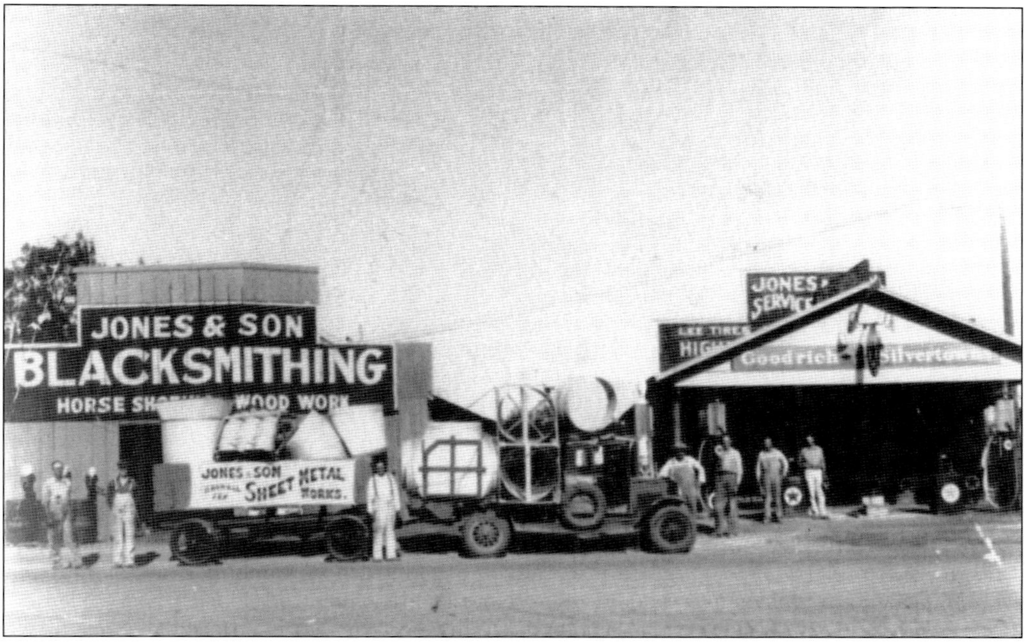

Jones and Son Sheet Metal was a partnership of Jesse Jones and his father, C. Jones. It was located just off the southwest corner of the square, west of the present-day Wild Horse Trading Post. There were three separate businesses: Jones and Son Sheet Metal works, a blacksmith shop, and a service station. C. Jones came to Haskell County in 1910 and served as a Baptist minister and missionary. (Courtesy of Hess Hartsfield.)

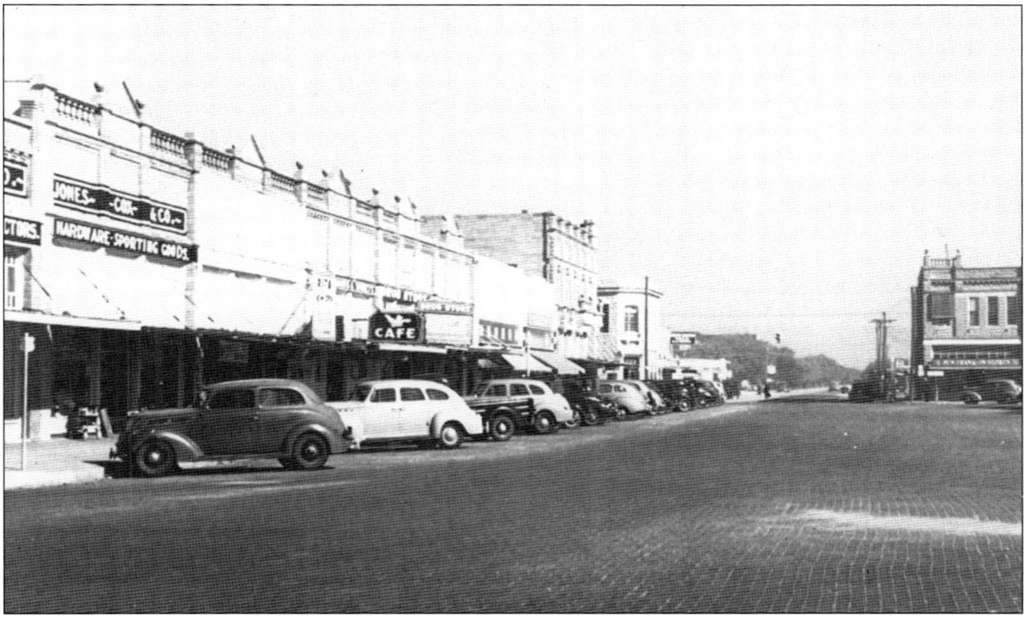

Wooden buildings on the west side of the square in Haskell were replaced by stone in 1906, when residents were assured that Haskell had indeed secured a railroad. The first occupants of the buildings included Samuel Luther Robertson's Dry Goods Store, the Oates store, and W. W. Fields Grocery. This photograph shows occupants in the 1930s. The McConnell Building, the first masonry building on the square, is visible on the right. (Courtesy of Hess Hartsfield.)

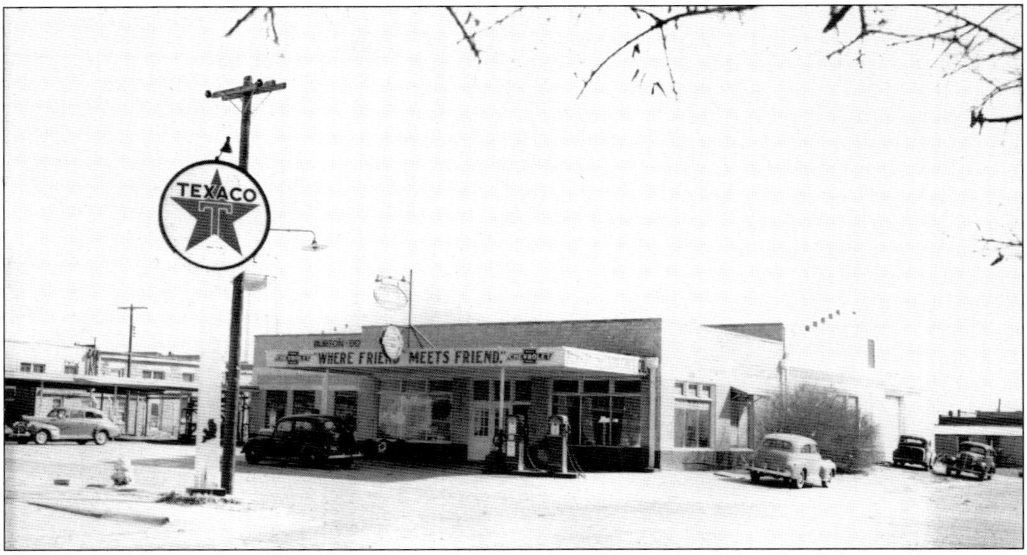

This undated photograph is of Burton Dodge, operated by R. L. Burton. The location was Avenue E and North First Street in Haskell. Bailey Toliver Chevrolet was later located on this site before moving to U.S. Highway 277 South. A 1937 advertisement from Reeves Burton Motor Company, then located on South First Street, lists a 1935 Tudor Ford for $450. (Courtesy of Woody Frazier.)

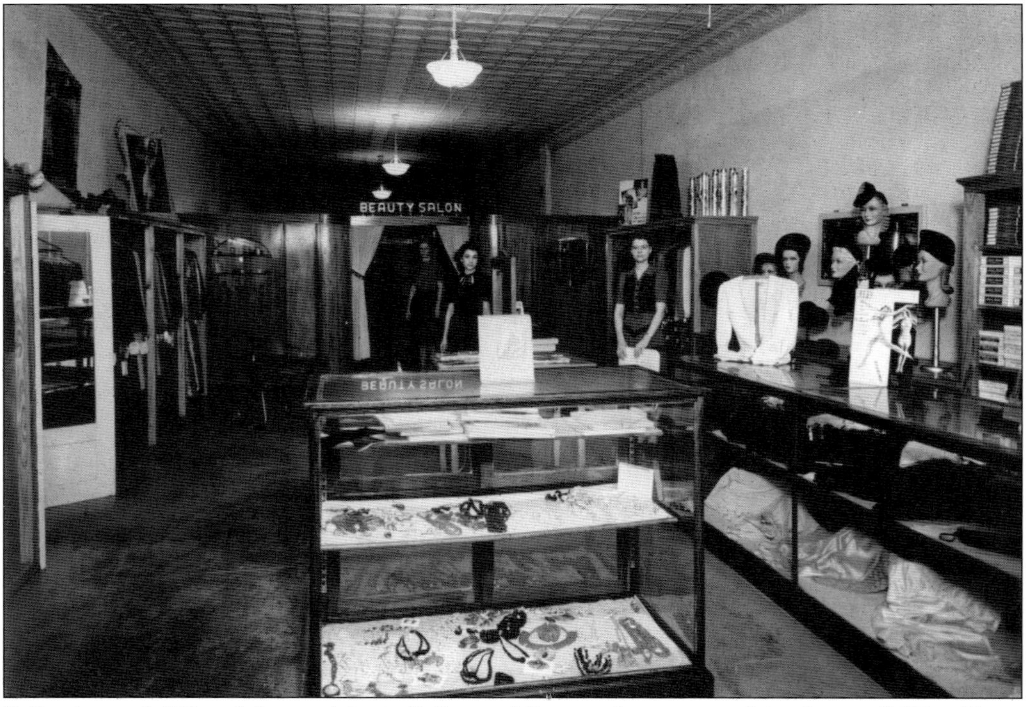

Following a childhood dream, Mattie Felker and Frances Lane created, in the small West Texas town of Haskell, an enterprise focused on ladies' fashion. Operated between 1940 and 1995, Lane-Felker attracted clientele from throughout the nation. Stanley Marcus, of Nieman Marcus in Dallas, once stated that Lane-Felker was his only competition in Texas. (Courtesy of Linda Lane-Bloise.)

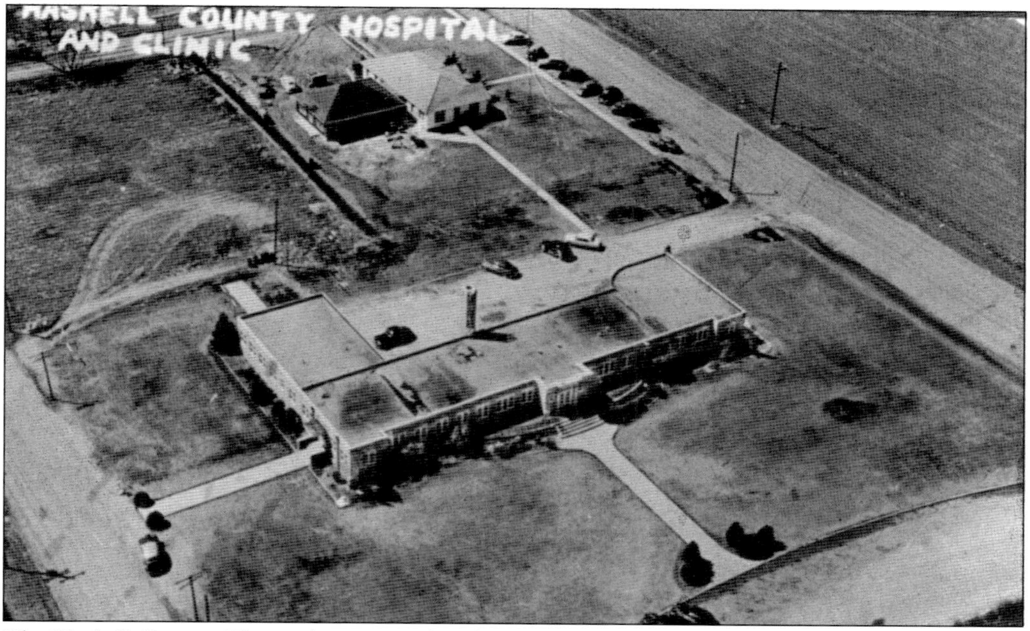

The Haskell County Hospital was completed at a cost of approximately $100,000. It was formally opened October 23, 1939. Verna Harwell was superintendent and business manager. Some of the doctors on the medical staff were J. F. Cadenhead of Weinert; ? Rogers, ? Davis, and ? Moch of Rule; ? Emory of Rochester; D. L. Cummins; L. F. Taylor; T. W. Williams; Gordon Phillips; Ernest M. Kimbrough; Frank C. Scott; J. D. Smith; and J. G. Vaughter. (Courtesy of Hess Hartsfield.)

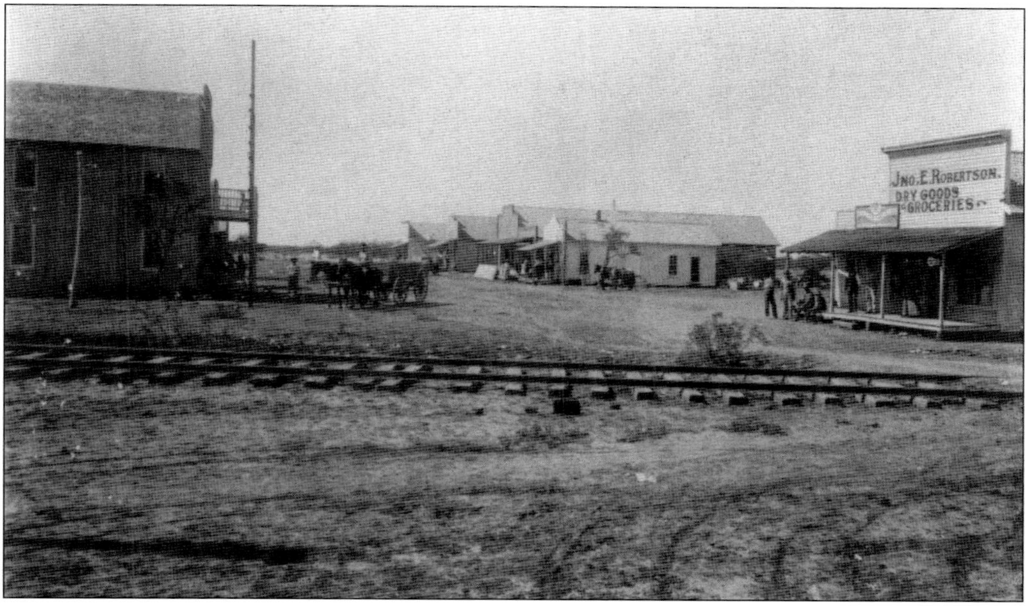

The Wichita Valley Railroad was chartered in 1905 to build from Seymour to Stamford, Texas. In the days of steam, the need for a strategically placed water source helped lead to the establishment of Weinert 11 miles north of Haskell. The business at right was owned by John E. Robertson. His son, French Robertson, onetime Haskell County attorney, later served as chairman of the Texas Prison Board. The French Robertson Unit near Abilene, Texas, is named for him. (Courtesy of Harlan Weinert.)

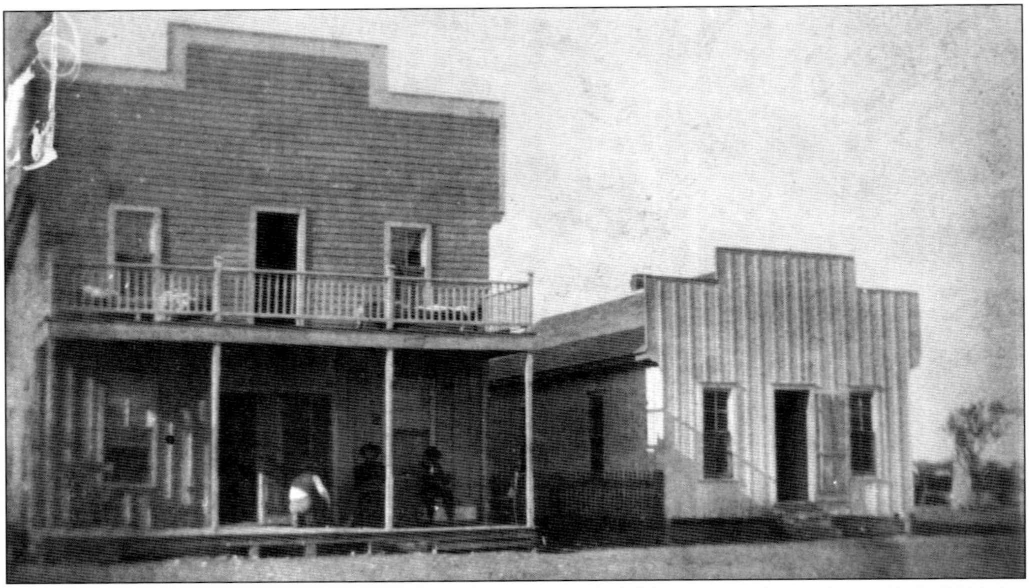

A cast of West Texans passed through the Weinert Hotel (left), pictured here about 1907. Wichita Valley Railroad employees, new settlers, and business entrepreneurs were among its guests. Local musicians performed in the evenings. The hotel, owned by Alexander Mayfield, was located on the south side of Main Street in Weinert. At right is the Red Cross Drug Store. Several doctors practiced here. (Courtesy of Mary Murphy.)

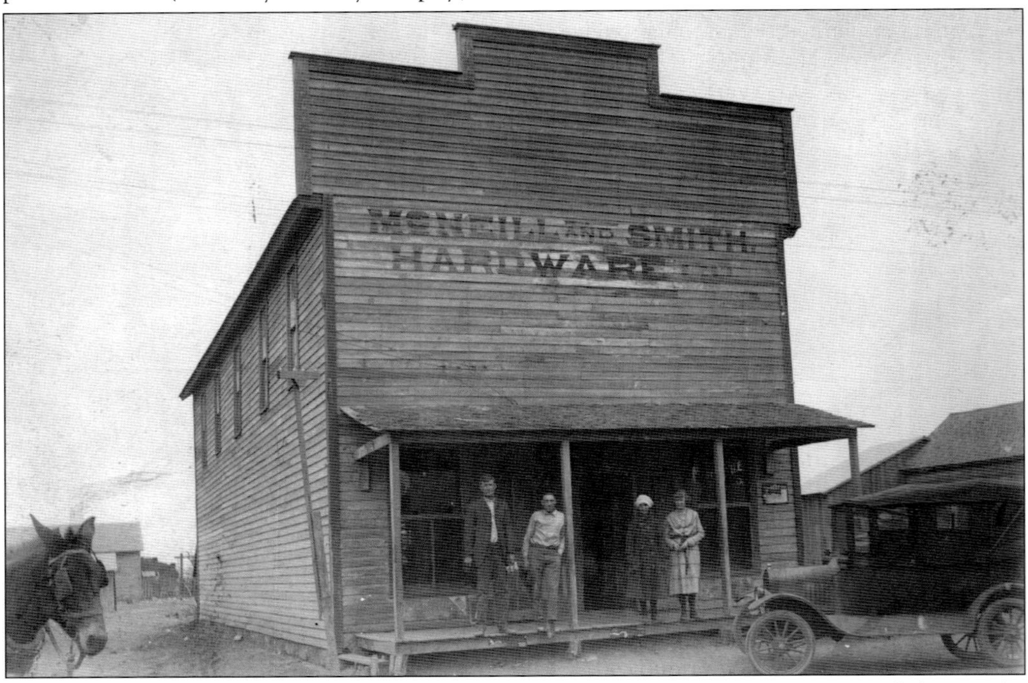

This building housed McNeill and Smith Hardware in Weinert in 1910. From left to right are Ed Howard, Al Marr, Willie Marr Runnels, and Margaret Marr Weinert. Margaret Marr Weinert operated a grocery store in the building with Al and Willie Marr. This building was destroyed by fire in 1923 and later rebuilt as Therwhanger Furniture and Hardware. (Courtesy of Harlan Weinert.)

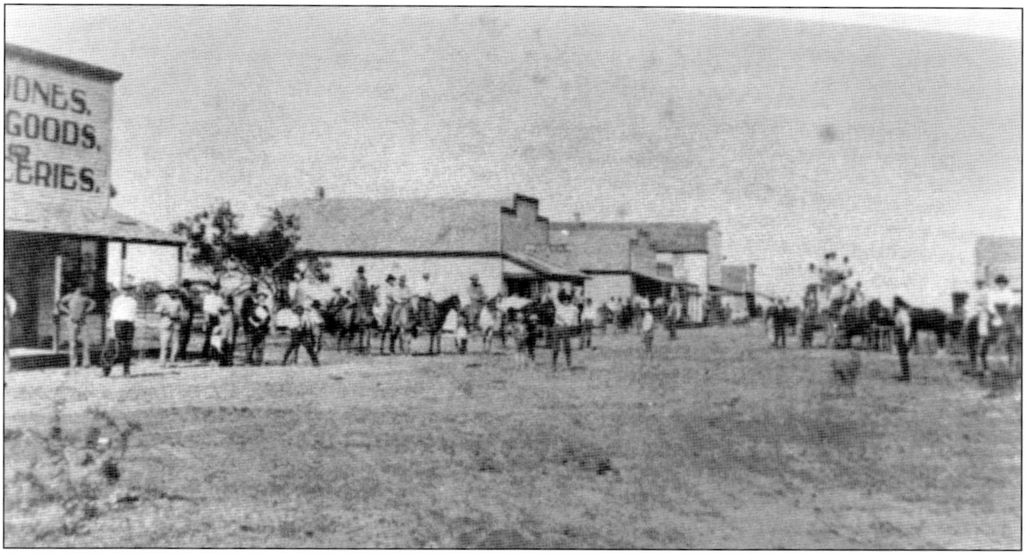

From its establishment in 1906 by the Wichita Valley Townsite Company, Weinert flourished for a time on the West Texas prairie. It has a deep and colorful ranching heritage, as shown in this 1907 photograph of cowboys on Main Street. It is said that this was sometimes the scene of bronc riding exhibitions. Several businesses may be seen looking east down Main Street. (Courtesy of Harlan Weinert.)

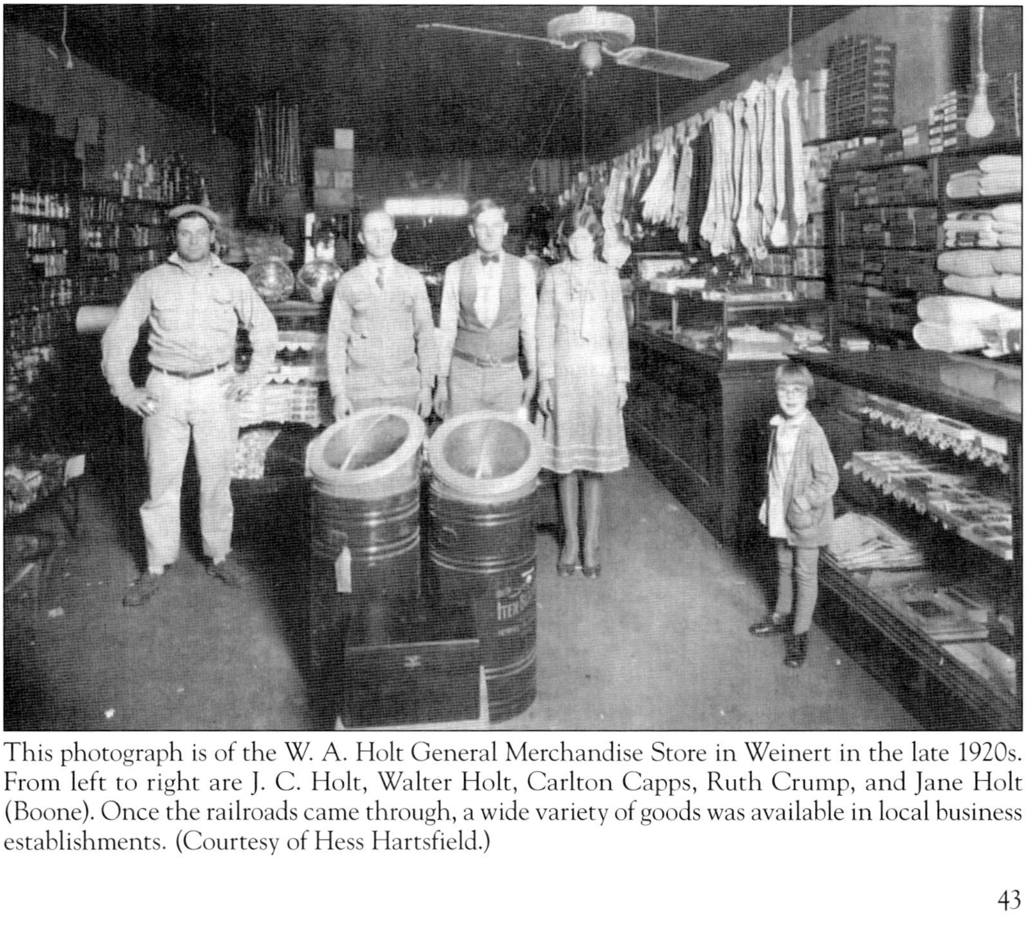

This photograph is of the W. A. Holt General Merchandise Store in Weinert in the late 1920s. From left to right are J. C. Holt, Walter Holt, Carlton Capps, Ruth Crump, and Jane Holt (Boone). Once the railroads came through, a wide variety of goods was available in local business establishments. (Courtesy of Hess Hartsfield.)

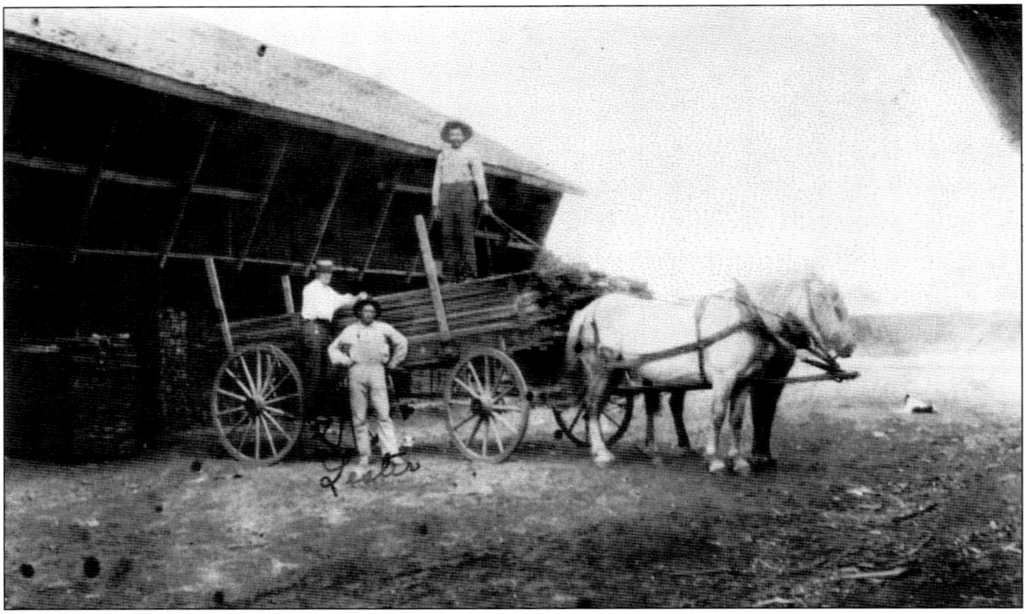

Before the railroads came, lumber had to be freighted by wagon from Abilene, Stamford, or Albany. When tracks were finally laid through Haskell County, it was possible for large supplies of building material, demanded by booming development, to be sold by local businesses such as Spencer Lumber Company in Weinert, pictured here. (Courtesy of Mary Murphy.)

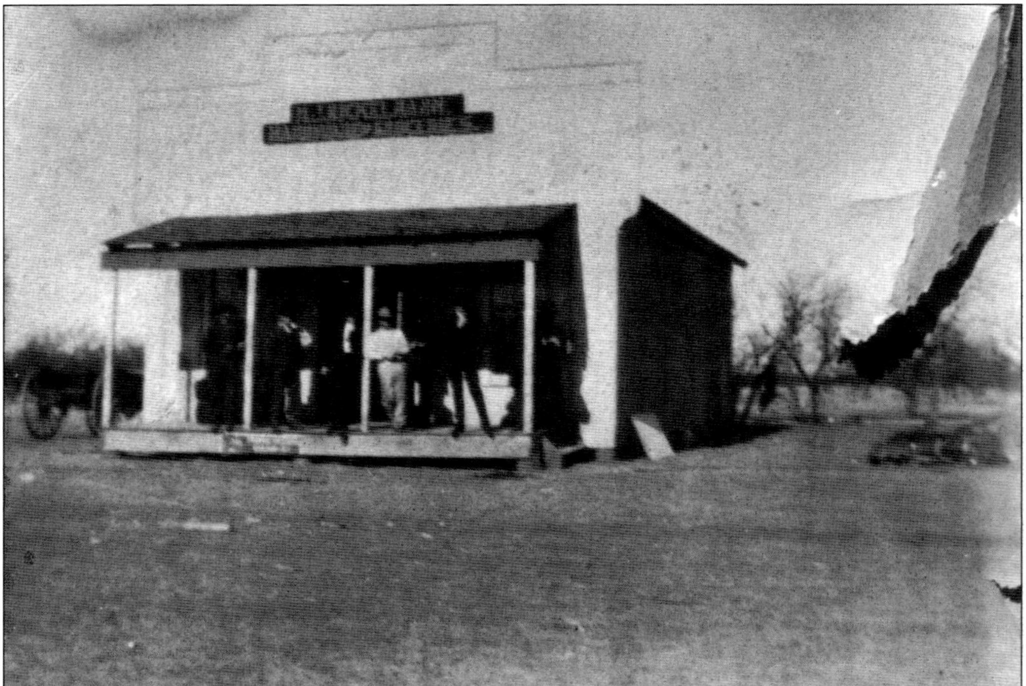

Rickelmann's Grocery, the first business to open in the new town of Weinert, was established in 1906. Joseph Rickelmann, proprietor, was appointed postmaster of Weinert in 1907, and the post office was operated out of his grocery store. (Courtesy of Haskell County Historical and Genealogical Society.)

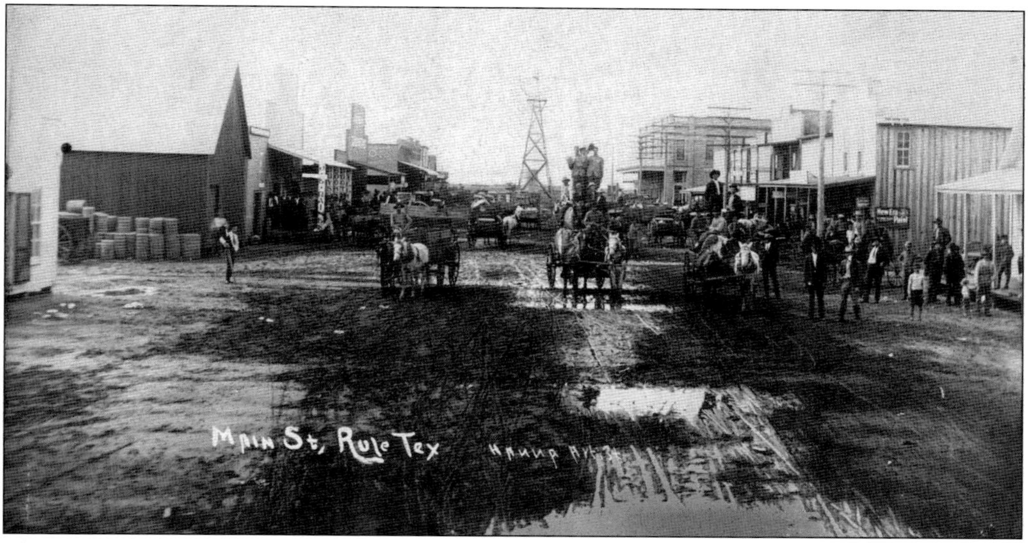

The Kansas City, Mexico, and Orient Railroad laid track through the western portion of Haskell County in the early 1900s. The town of Rule, pictured here about 1907, was established in 1906 on land purchased by the Orient Land Company. The name was chosen to honor W. A. Rule of the National Bank of Commerce in Kansas City, financial backers of the railroad. (Courtesy of Bill Jones.)

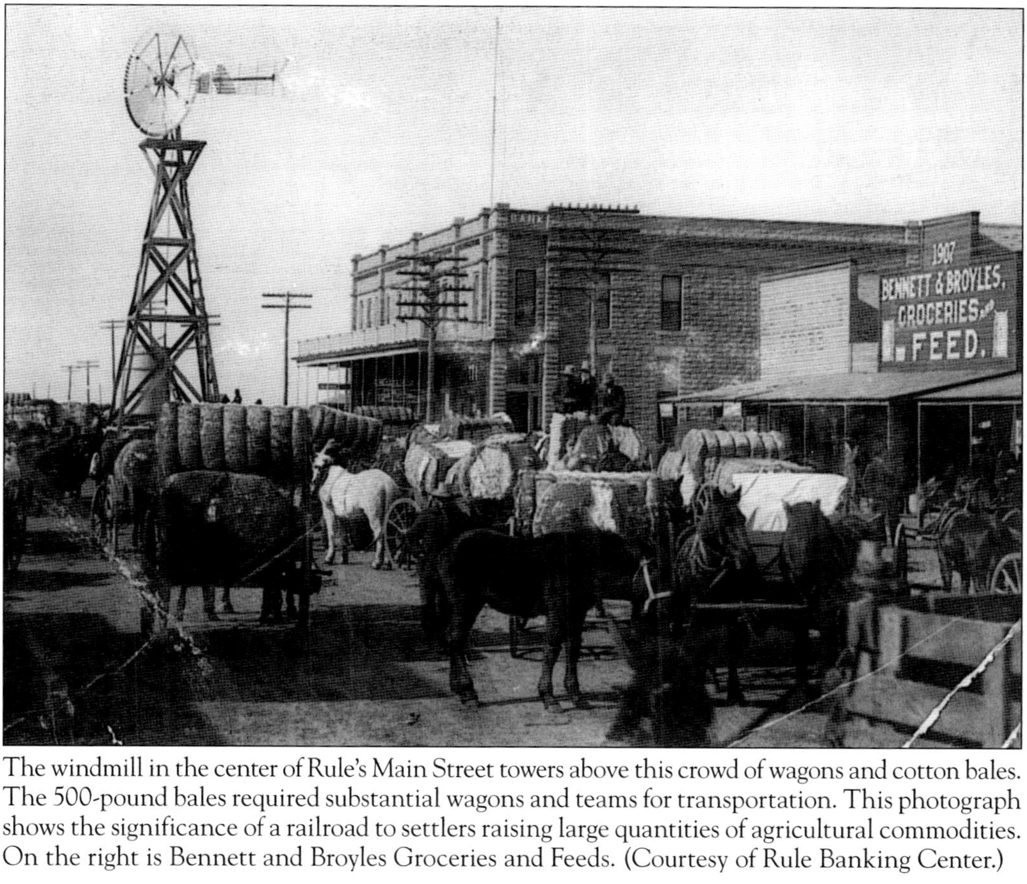

The windmill in the center of Rule's Main Street towers above this crowd of wagons and cotton bales. The 500-pound bales required substantial wagons and teams for transportation. This photograph shows the significance of a railroad to settlers raising large quantities of agricultural commodities. On the right is Bennett and Broyles Groceries and Feeds. (Courtesy of Rule Banking Center.)

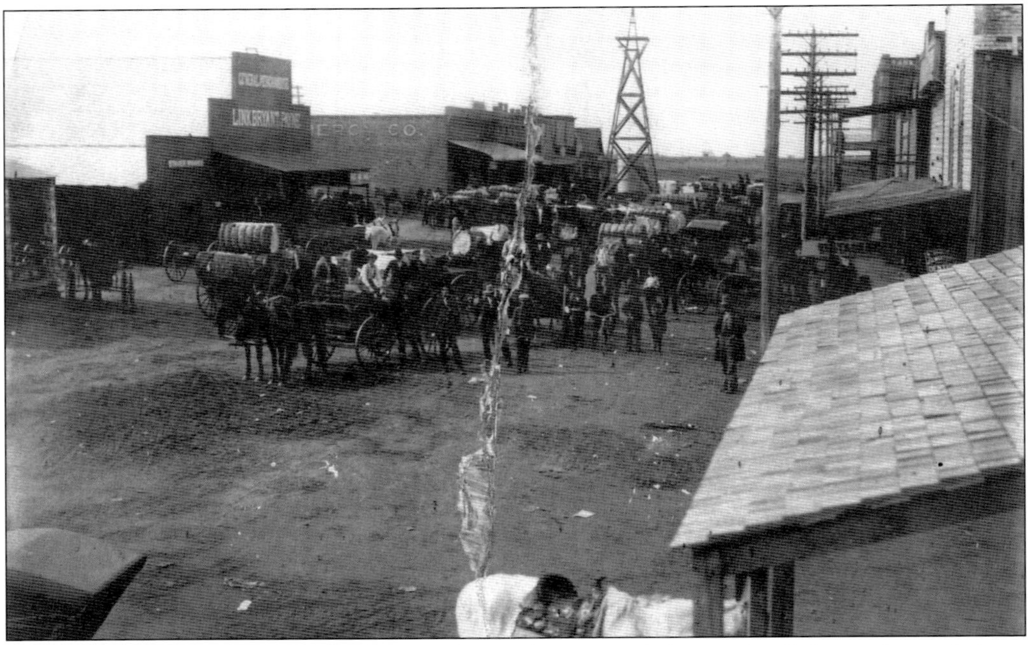

In this undated photograph of Rule, travelers gather around the windmill. It was located about where the traffic light is today. Link, Bryant, and Payne General Merchandise (left) had business establishments in several West Texas towns. The open prairie is evident in the distance. (Courtesy of Haskell County Historical and Genealogical Society.)

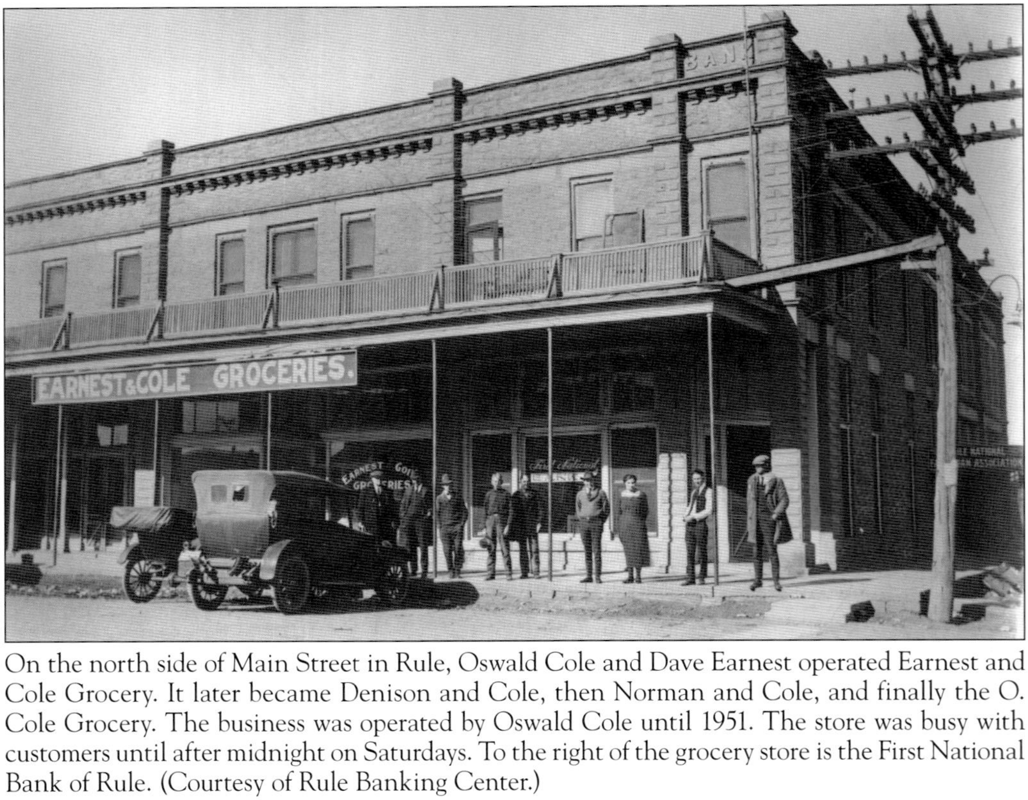

On the north side of Main Street in Rule, Oswald Cole and Dave Earnest operated Earnest and Cole Grocery. It later became Denison and Cole, then Norman and Cole, and finally the O. Cole Grocery. The business was operated by Oswald Cole until 1951. The store was busy with customers until after midnight on Saturdays. To the right of the grocery store is the First National Bank of Rule. (Courtesy of Rule Banking Center.)

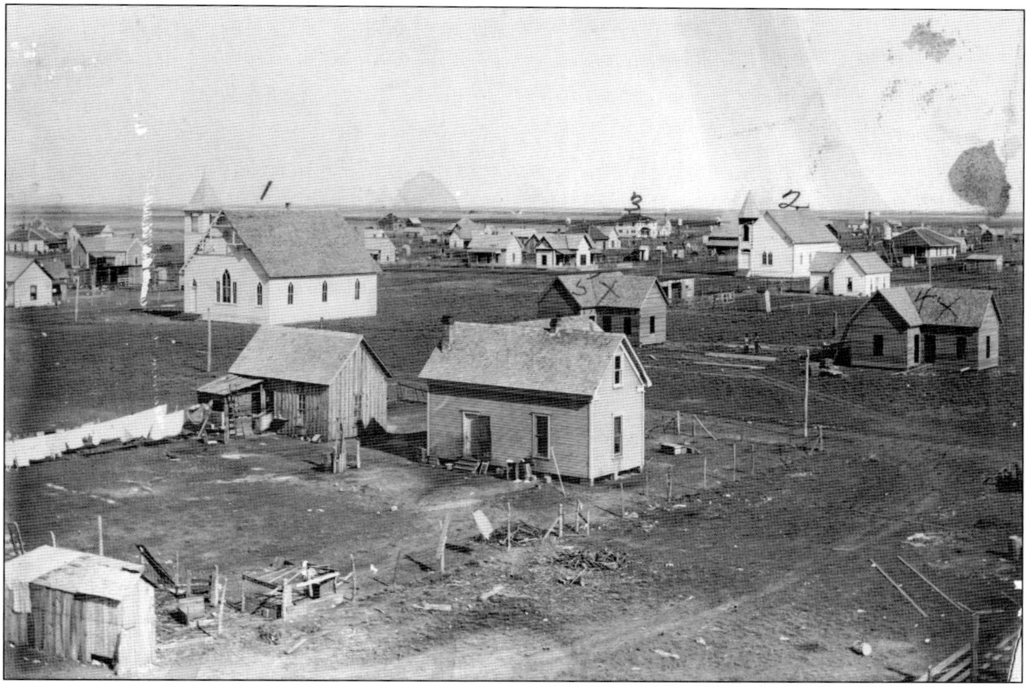

This view of Rule shows the marked absence of trees in the early days of Haskell County. In the photograph are 1) the First Baptist Church, 2) the First Christian Church, 3) identified as the Foster Home, 4) the Rhinehart Place, and 5) the nursery for the First Baptist Church. (Courtesy of Bill Jones.)

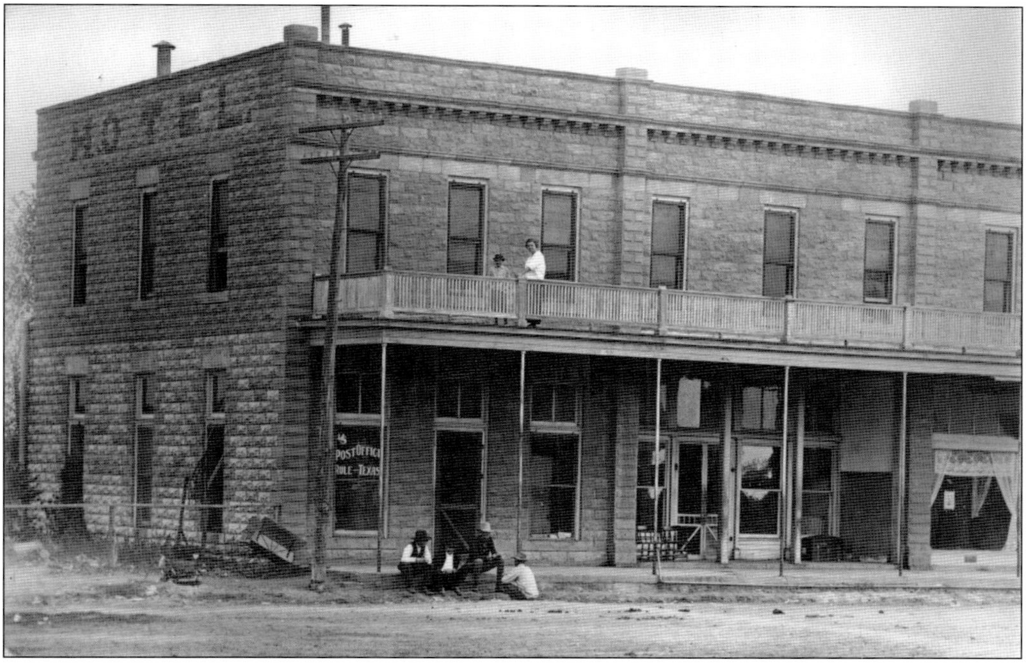

J. L. Jones and A. C. Foster built a two-story stone building in Rule known as the Foster and Jones Hotel. The post office shared the building for a time with several other businesses. This photograph was made in 1915. (Courtesy of Rule Banking Center.)

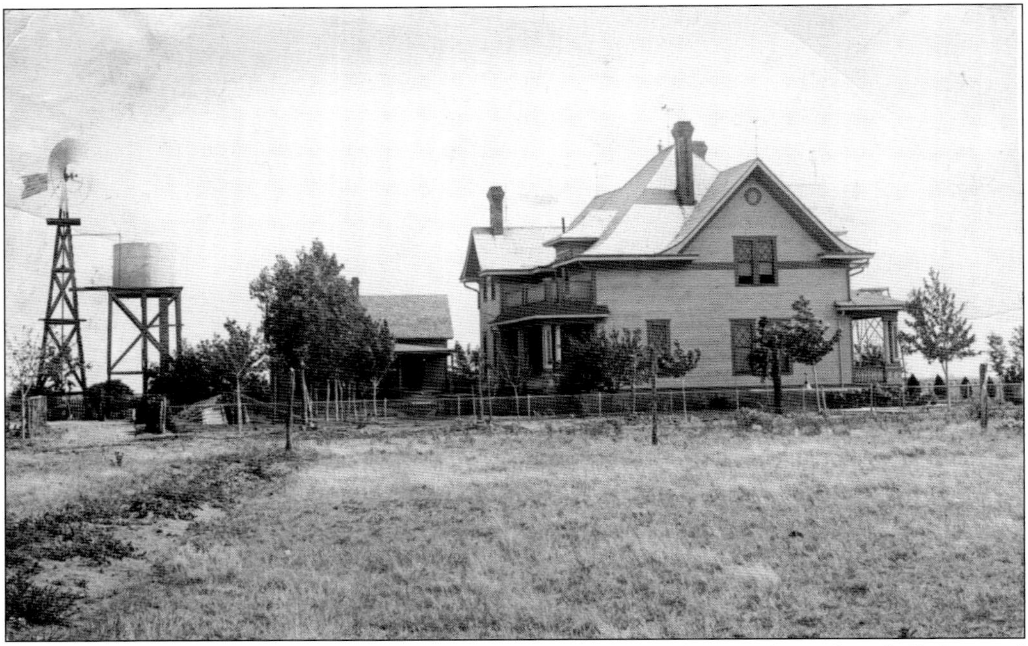

J. L. Jones was the first county clerk of Haskell County. He was later cashier of Haskell National Bank and had business ventures throughout the county. When the Kansas City, Mexico, and Orient Railroad began surveying through the county, he sold land to the land company for development of a town. Jones built this home in the eastern edge of Rule. (Courtesy of Bill Jones.)

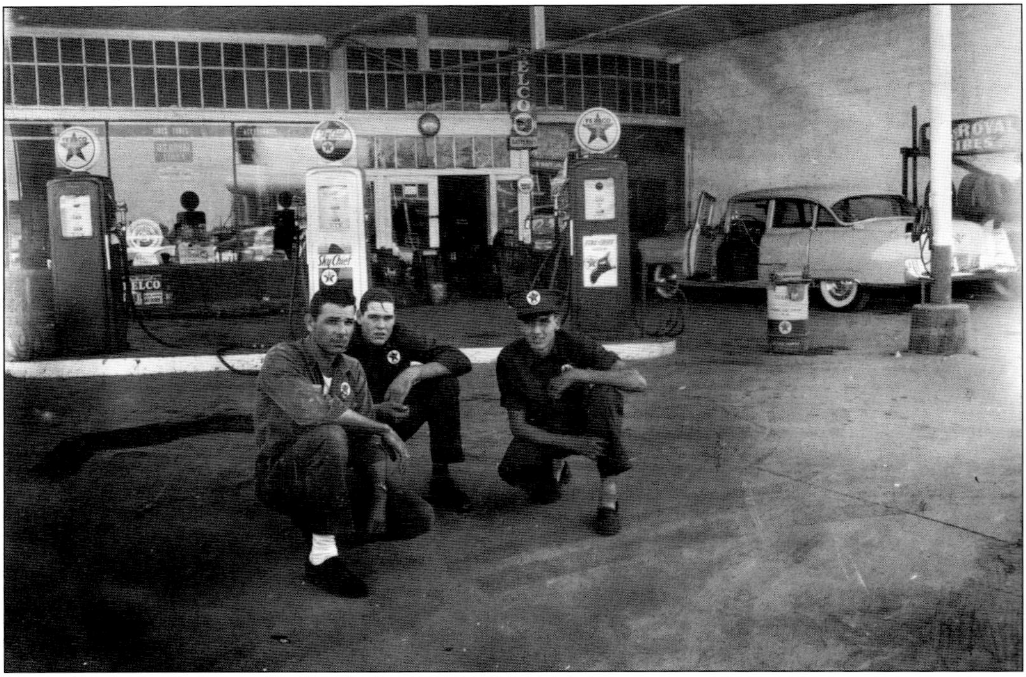

This Texaco "filling station" has occupied the same corner at Union Street and State Highway 380 in Rule for many years. There was also a Goodyear Tire business here. The young men taking a break outside the station are, from left to right, Howard Brass, Derrell Sorrells, and Jimmy Sorrells. (Courtesy of Alma Counts.)

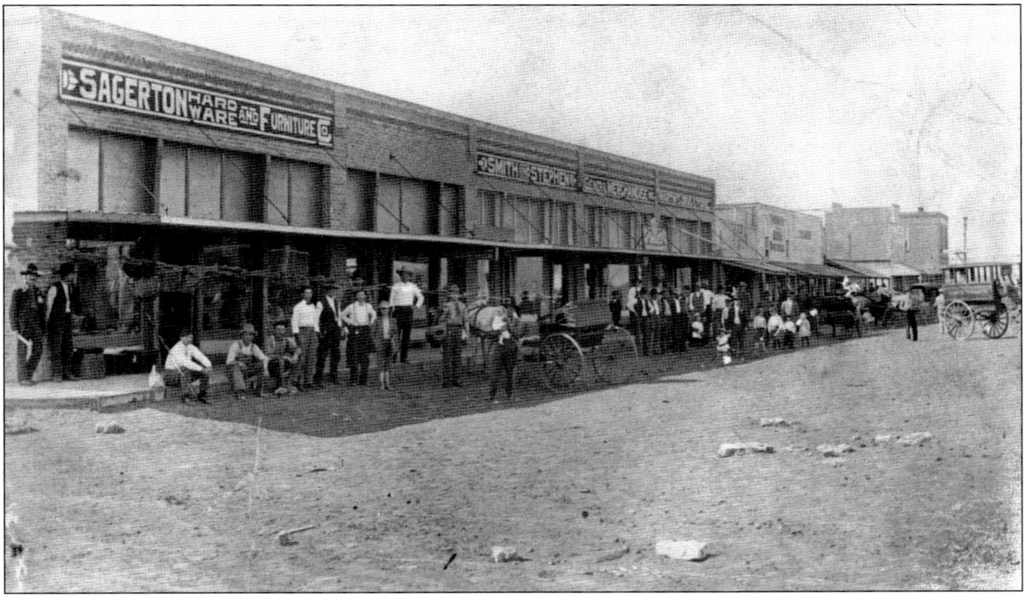

W. M. Sager settled in the southwestern corner of Haskell County about 1894. When the Kansas City, Mexico, and Orient Railroad (KCM&O) made plans to come through, Sager and M.C. Caudle sold land to the Orient Land Company for a town site. When petition was made for a post office, Sager, Texas, was taken, so Sagerton was chosen. This 1912 photograph has captured a crowd on the west side of Main Street. (Courtesy of Joyce LeFevre.)

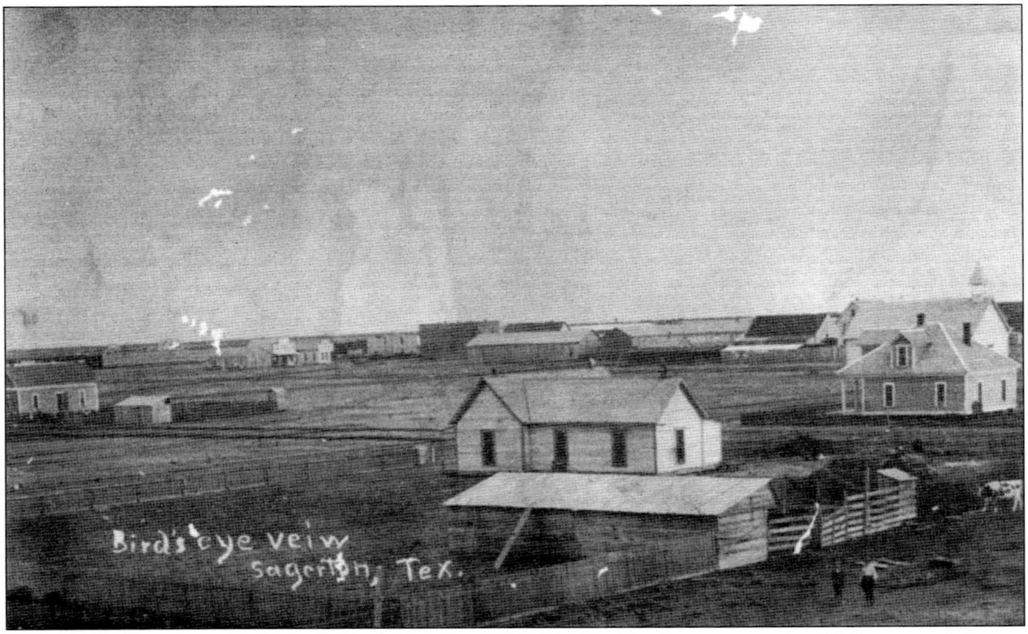

This 1908 photograph labeled "Birdseye view of Sagerton, Tex." contains the Walter Smith home in the foreground, a produce house, a telephone office, a bank building, Harris and Company Lumberyard, Moore Hotel, the Sagerton First Baptist Church, and the J. W. Martin house. Sagerton's early-day newspaper was the *Sagerton Sun*. Electricity came to town in 1927. Among Sagerton's several cotton gins was the Roy Weinke Gin, later sold to Rule-Jayton Cotton Oil Company. (Courtesy of Joyce LeFevre.)

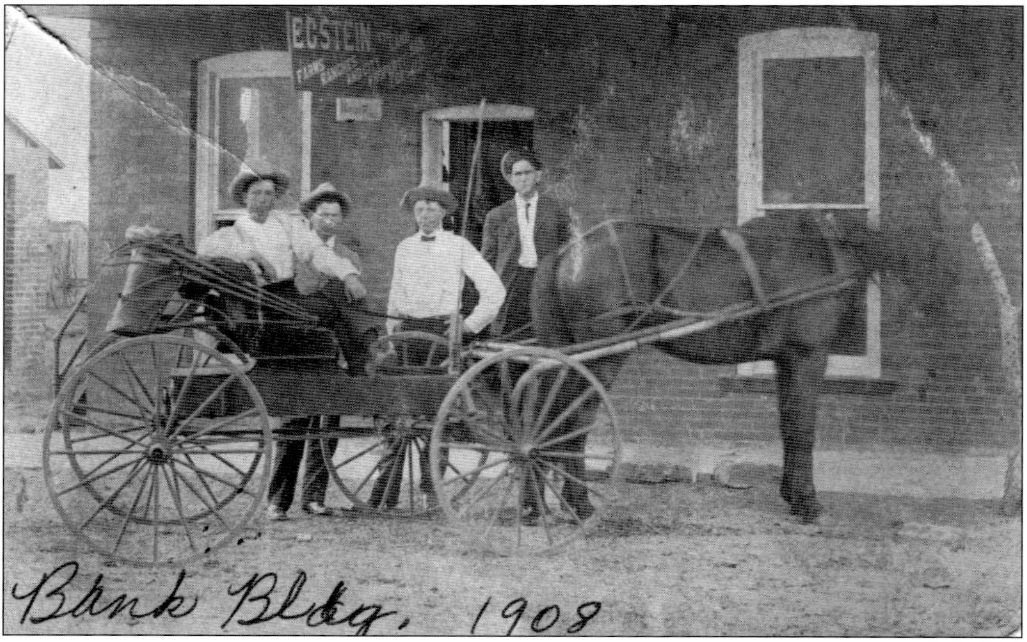

"Bank Building, 1908" is the only identification on this photograph made in Sagerton. These gentlemen stand in front of a business operated by E. G. Stein. From left to right are Tuck Davidson, Will Maddox, Mose Bryant, and Royal Tanner. The sign reads, "E. G. Stein the Land Man. Farms Ranches and City Property for Sale." Stein was a realtor, newspaper editor, justice of the peace, and bank manager. (Courtesy of Joyce LeFevre.)

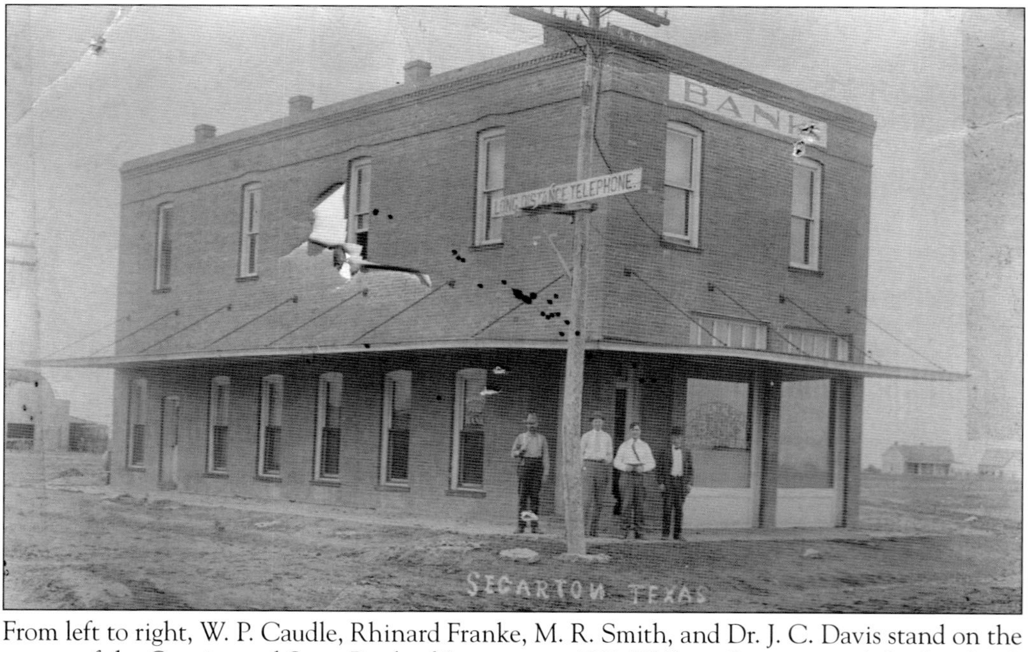

From left to right, W. P. Caudle, Rhinard Franke, M. R. Smith, and Dr. J. C. Davis stand on the corner of the Continental State Bank of Sagerton in 1911. William Sager opened the first bank in Sagerton in 1906. It operated for only two years. The Continental State Bank was formed in 1908. G. R. Couch was its last president and Paul Summers its last cashier. It closed in 1931. (Courtesy of Joyce LeFevre.)

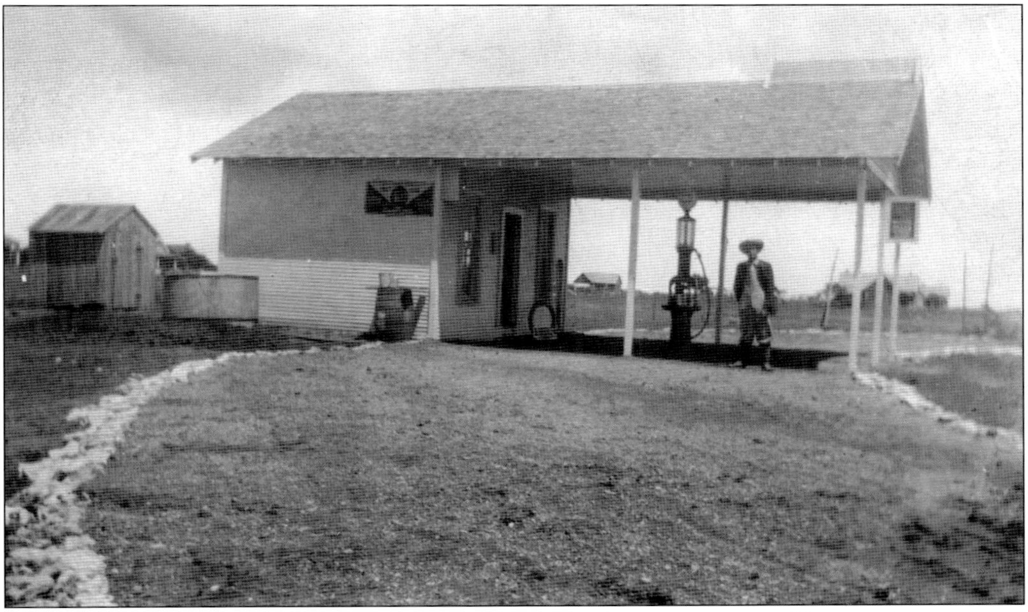

K. A. Balzer, born in Saxony, Germany, and his wife, Anna, a native of Prussia, became part of Haskell County's history in 1908 when they settled in Sagerton. K. A. Balzer operated a gin here until 1919. Will Stegemoeller is shown here beside the Balzer service station in Sagerton. Gasoline was pumped into the calibrated glass cylinder on the top of the pump and delivered by gravity into the automobile's tank. (Courtesy of Joyce LeFevre.)

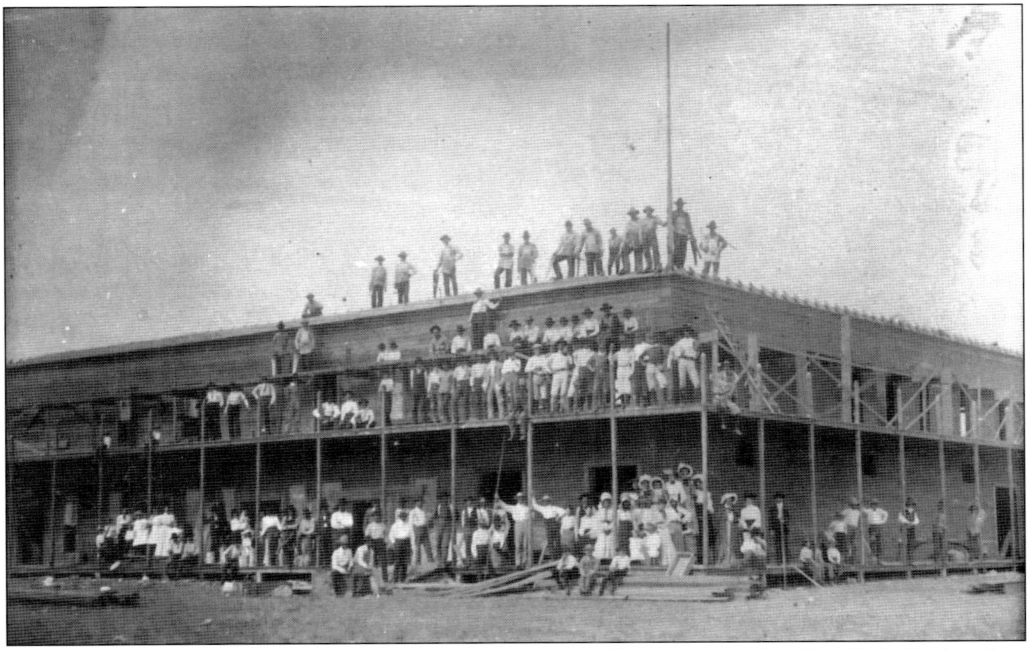

In 1902, T. G. Carney sold land in northwestern Haskell County to the KCM&O Railroad to establish a town. Originally called Carney, Texas, the name was changed to O'Brien in honor of railroad official N. J. O'Brien. T. G. Carney was instrumental in developing the new town, as is shown in this photograph of the 40-room Carney Hotel being built on the east side of town. (Courtesy of C. H. Underwood.)

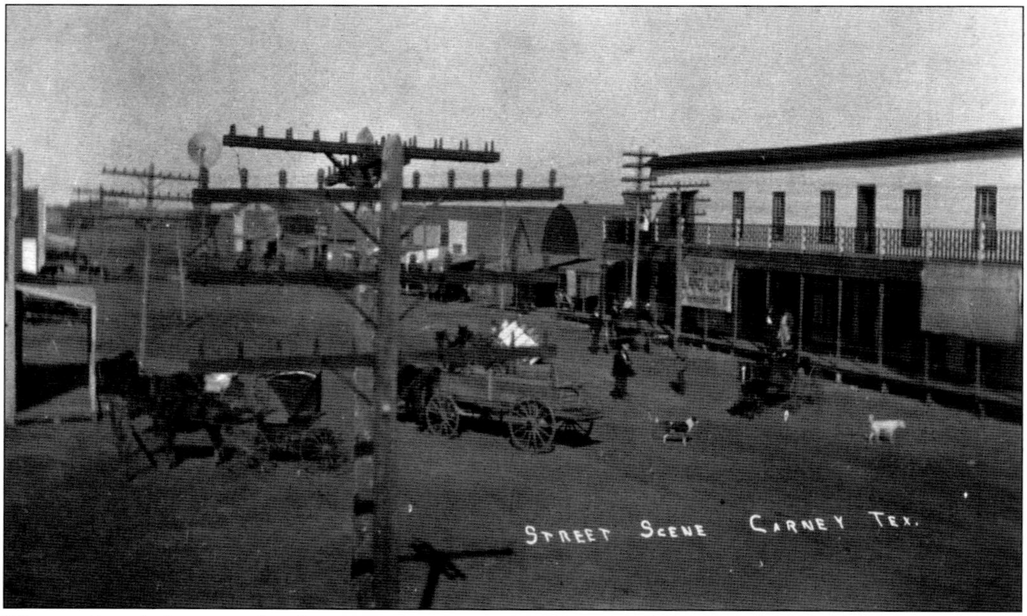

This undated photograph of a street scene in Carney, Texas, shows Haskell County in its infancy but being settled by optimistic pioneers establishing businesses on bare West Texas prairie. The sign on the large building reads, "Orient Land Loan." Once residents were assured of the railroad, the town grew rapidly to as many as 1,500 residents. Nine businesses were moved to Carney from the Cliff community. (Courtesy of C. H. Underwood.)

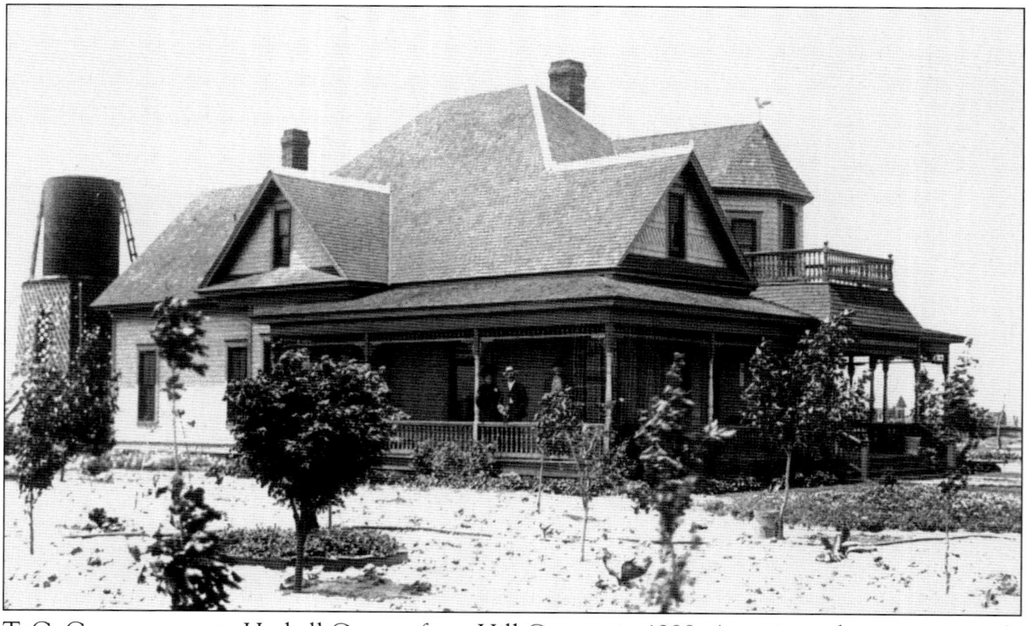

T. G. Carney came to Haskell County from Hill County in 1888. At a time when many people lived in half-dugouts, Carney traded mules for lumber and built a house. The Carney home, shown above, was built in 1905. The house had a grape arbor, goldfish pond, and sun porches. Carney sold land to the Orient Land Company upon which the town of Carney, later called O'Brien, was built. From left to right on the porch are Mrs. T. G. (Lizzie Maud) Carney, T. G. Carney, and an unidentified man. (Courtesy of C. H. Underwood.)

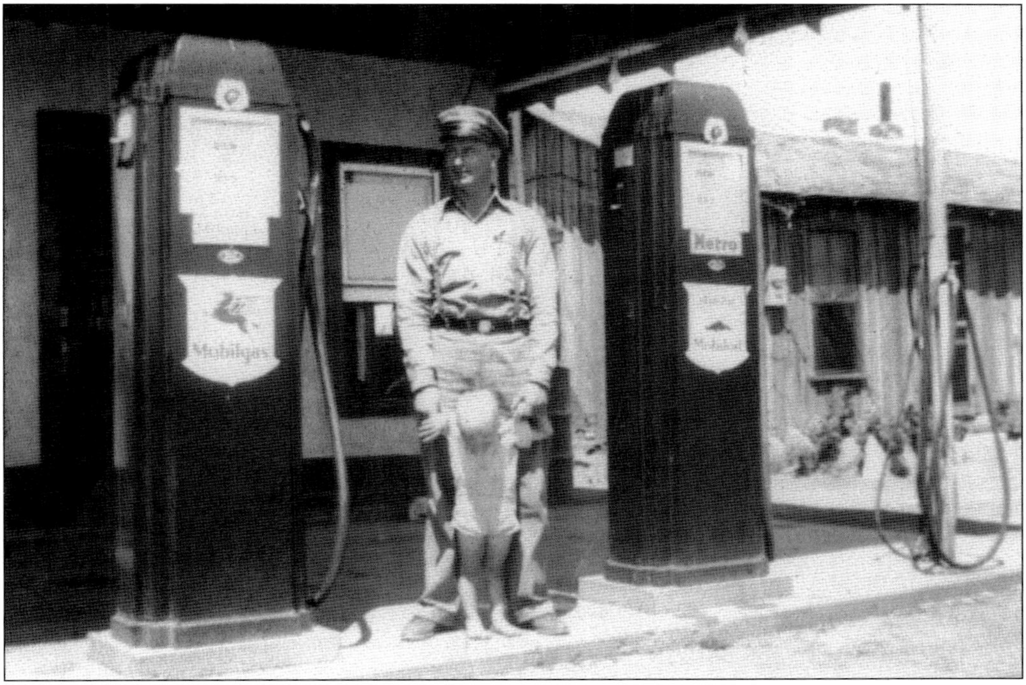

Dwight Gothard's station, at the intersection of Grand Central Avenue and Farm Road 2279, has been an O'Brien landmark since the 1950s. Even after the town had declined, Gothard's station was a familiar stop for fuel or a cold soft drink. The station closed in the 1990s. This photograph is of Gothard and his son, Paul Dean Gothard. (Courtesy of C. H. Underwood.)

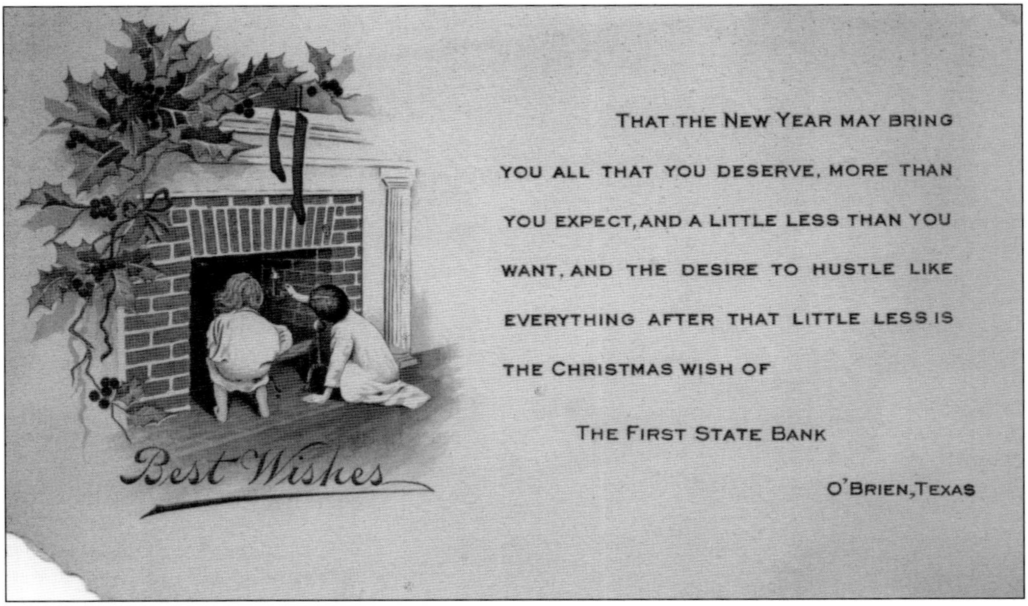

This undated postcard advertises First State Bank of O'Brien, organized about 1916. L. H. Nicks was one of the principal organizers. J. E. Pickrell was president. The bank was housed in a two-story building near a site once occupied by Barnard Grocery on the west side of Grand Central Avenue. The Woodmen of the World occupied the second floor of the building. (Courtesy of Rhonda Moeller.)

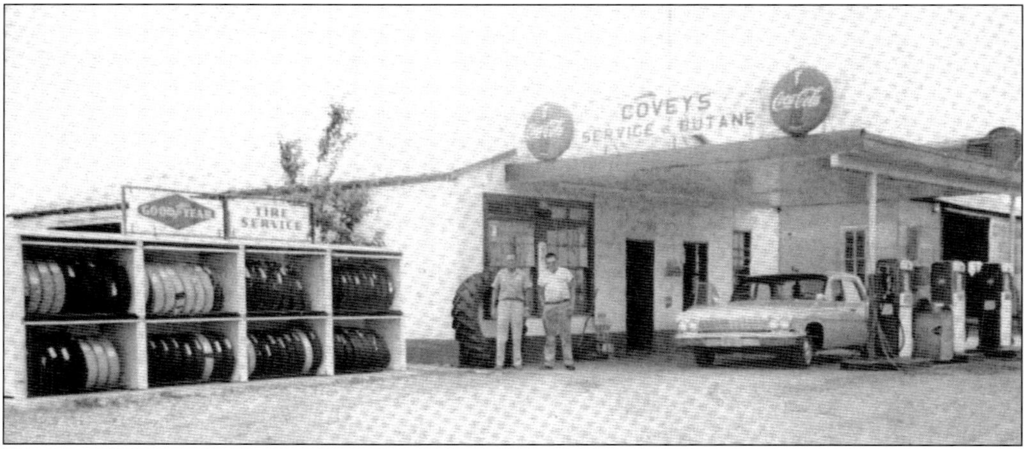

Covey's Station was a longtime business in O'Brien located on the east side of Grand Central Avenue. T. G. Carney's Hotel was just south of this building. (Courtesy of C. H. Underwood.)

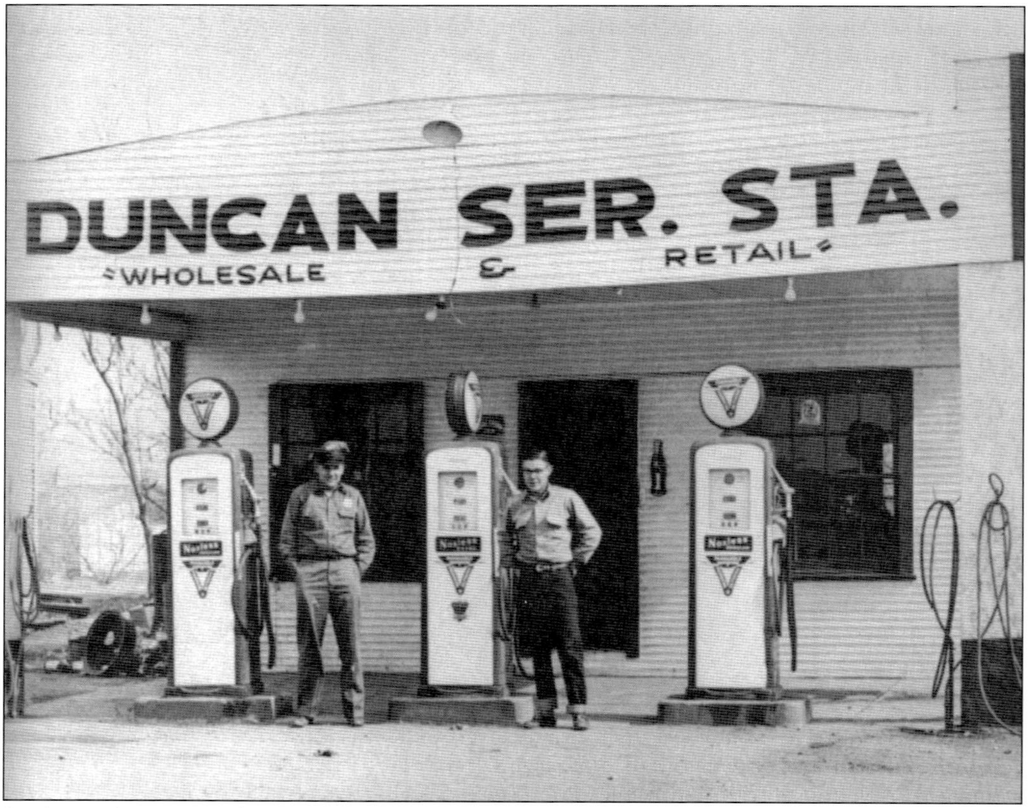

In this 1951 or 1952 photograph of Duncan Service Station are R. H. Duncan (left) and R. C. Duncan. The business, located on the east side of Grand Central Avenue (US277), dealt in Panhandle Gas and Oils. (Courtesy of Thelma Cox Burt.)

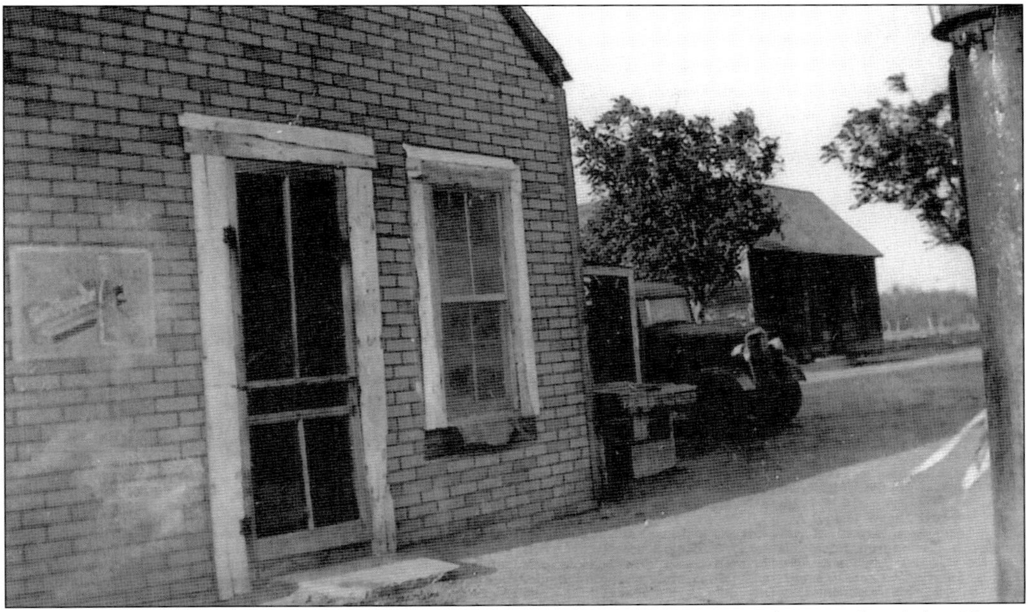

J. T. Osborn opened the Needmore store near the Brazos River 2 miles north of the Hutto Schoolhouse in 1912. It closed in 1921. The gas station and grocery store served residents of northwestern Haskell County. Summertime revivals were held at a nearby tabernacle. In the day of early automobiles, people often traveled in wagons drawn by teams to navigate the sandy roads. (Courtesy of C. H. Underwood.)

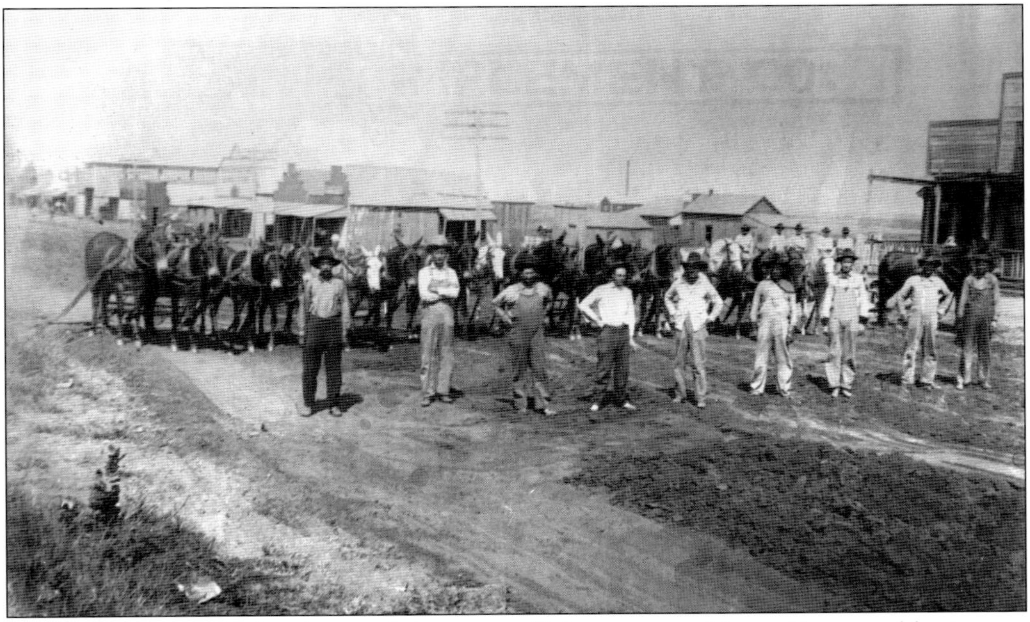

When the Orient Railroad missed the town of Marcy, most of its residents and businesses moved east to the railroad. The new town, Rochester, was established in 1906 on land given by A. B. Carothers. Pictured here from left to right are Will Wade, Mark Trimmier, Fred Hicks, unidentified, D. W. Hamilton Sr., two unidentified, Marion Hicks, and unidentified grading Rochester streets. Many of the buildings in the background were moved from Marcy. (Courtesy of Sharon Mullino.)

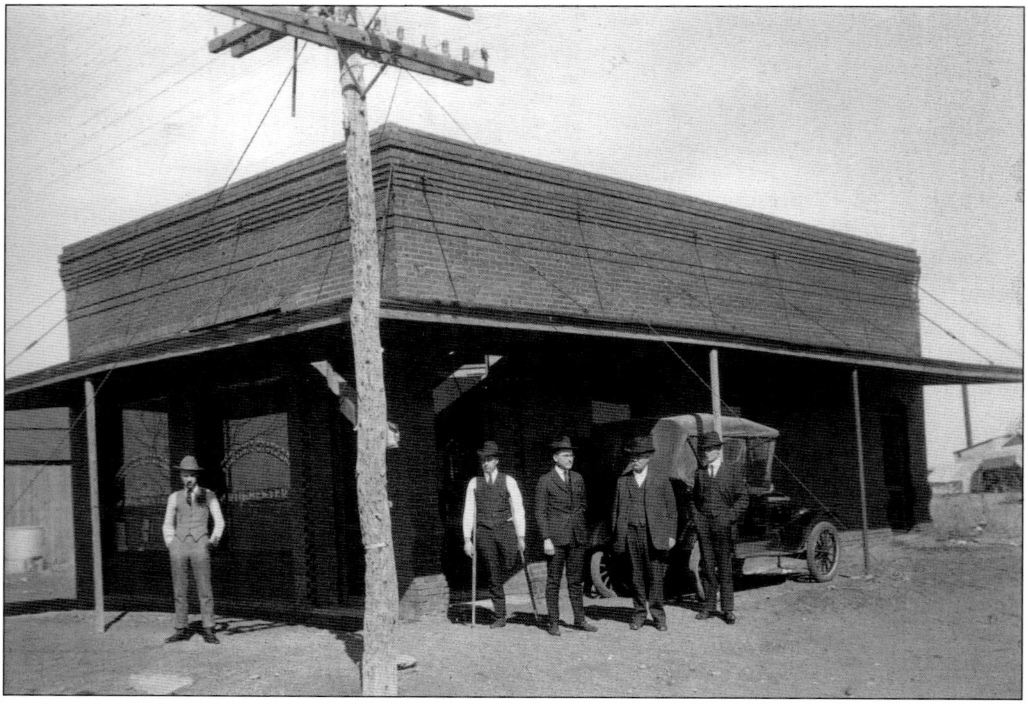

The First State Bank of Rochester was organized in September 1907 with A. B. Carothers as president and W. P. Lee as cashier. A contract was given later that year for F. W. Loerch to build a brick building on the corner of Main Street and Carothers Avenue. The bank later occupied a site at 208 Carothers Avenue. The bank was reorganized in 1932 as Home State Bank with G. F. Mullino as president. (Courtesy of Hess Hartsfield.)

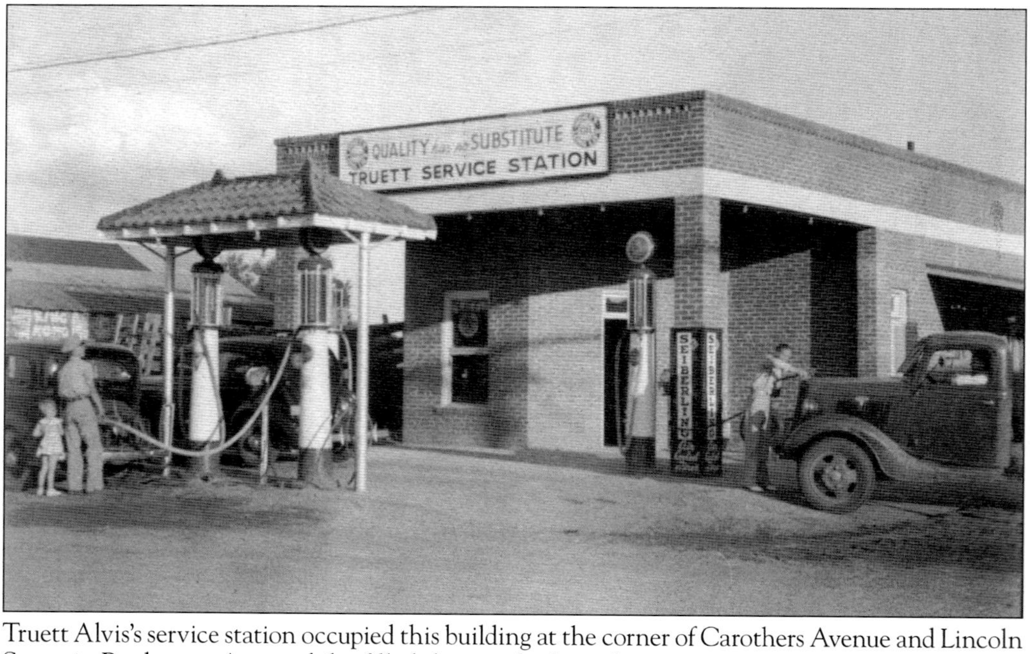

Truett Alvis's service station occupied this building at the corner of Carothers Avenue and Lincoln Street in Rochester. Automobiles filled their tanks from the gravity pumps common in that day. The building was later the site of Smith Funeral Home. (Courtesy of Sharon Mullino.)

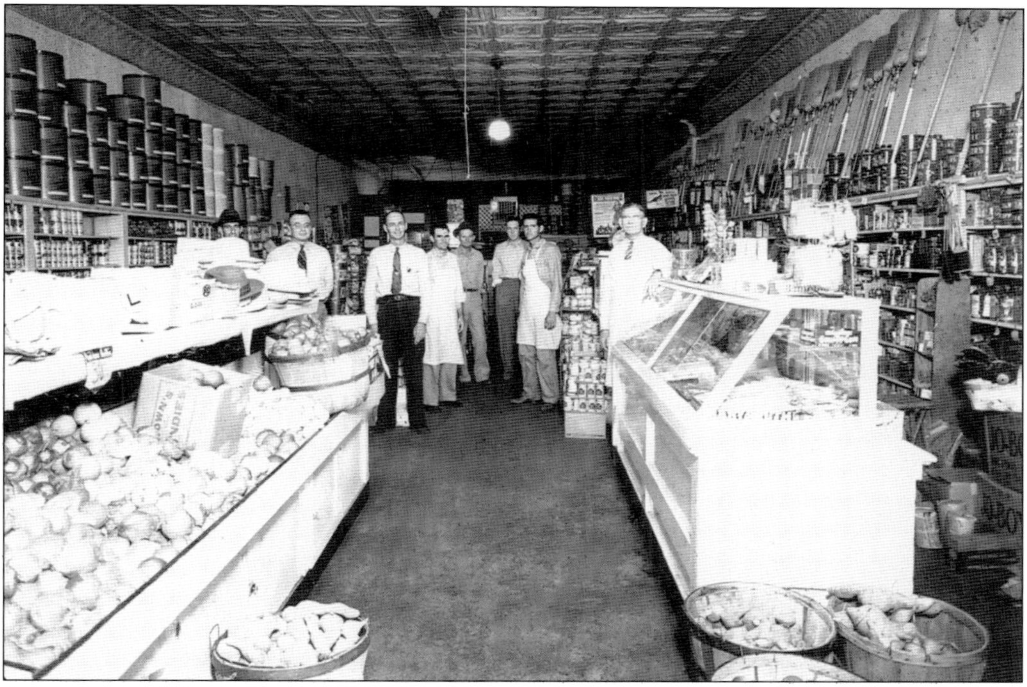

Pictured from left to right in the Bell and Speck Grocery Store in Rochester are unidentified, Bob Speck, unidentified, Pete Tanner, unidentified, Wilburn Adkins, Kenneth Tanner, and Allen Bell. The building was on the north side of Carothers Avenue. Pete Tanner later owned and operated Tanner Grocery in Rochester. (Courtesy of Haskell County Historical and Genealogical Society.)

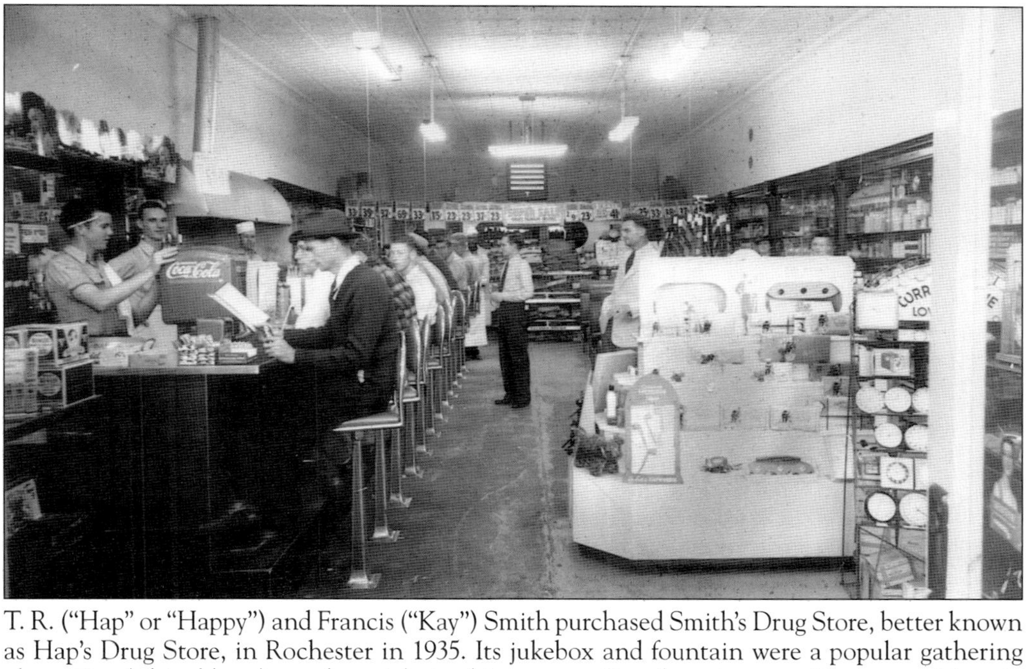

T. R. ("Hap" or "Happy") and Francis ("Kay") Smith purchased Smith's Drug Store, better known as Hap's Drug Store, in Rochester in 1935. Its jukebox and fountain were a popular gathering place. Hap (white blazer) stands at right in this store on Carothers Avenue. (Courtesy of Angela Kay Key.)

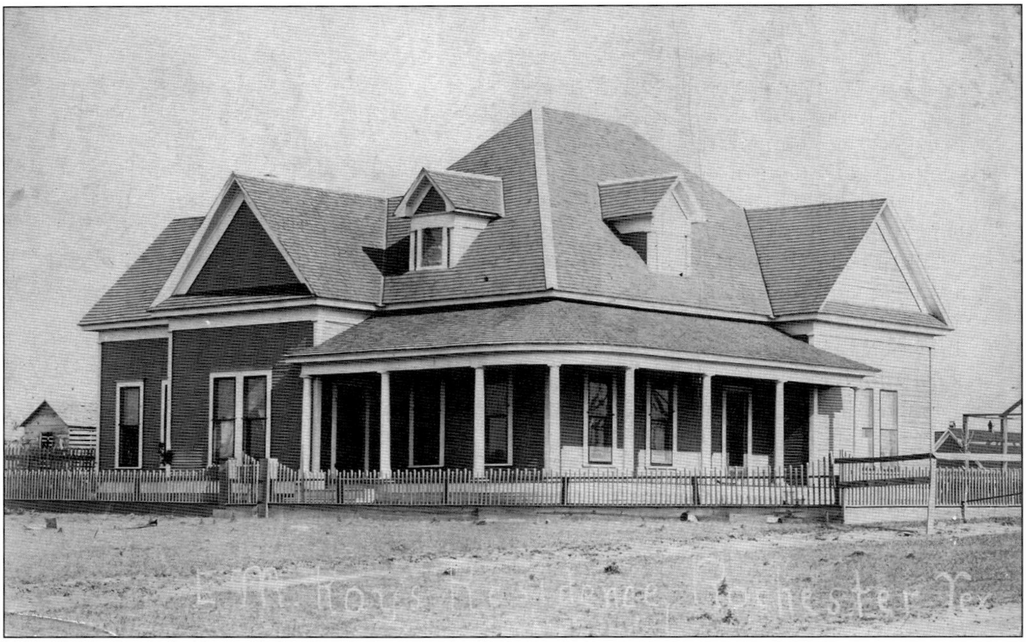

L. M. and Winnie (Bray) Kay built this house on Main Street in Rochester in 1910. L. M. Kay had owned a lumber mill in Big Sandy, and when he came to Rochester, he brought 18 boxcars of lumber with him. He operated a lumberyard in Rochester for many years. (Courtesy of Charlene Smith Voss.)

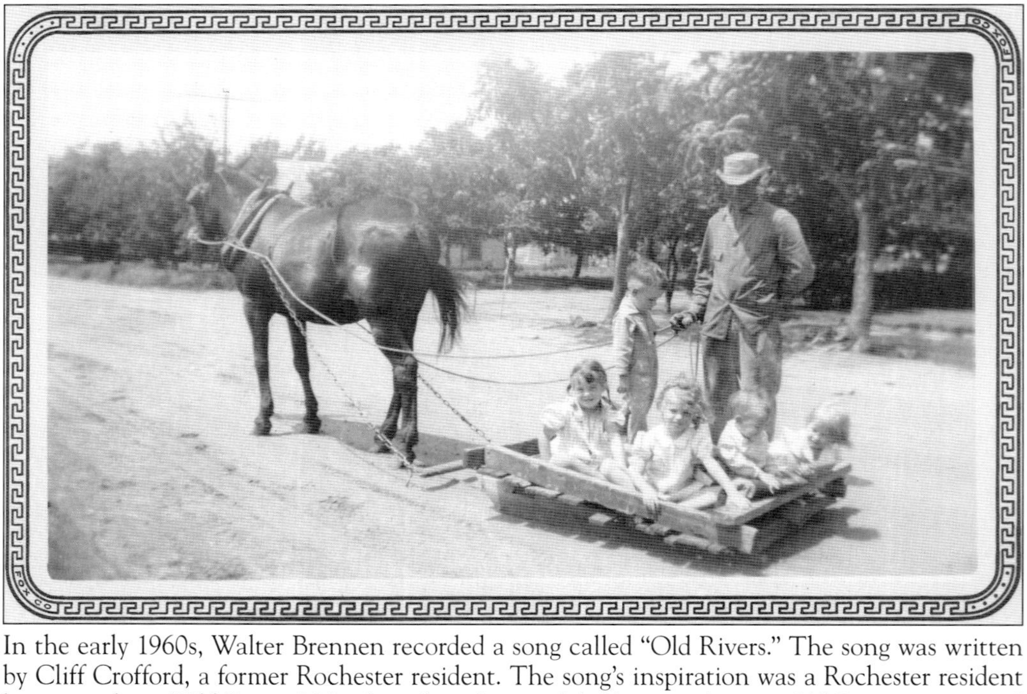

In the early 1960s, Walter Brennen recorded a song called "Old Rivers." The song was written by Cliff Crofford, a former Rochester resident. The song's inspiration was a Rochester resident known only as "Old Rivers." He plowed gardens and fields around town. Old Rivers is pictured here on an unidentified Rochester street with his mule harnessed to a sled. The children seated are the grandchildren of L. M. Kay. (Courtesy of Charlene Smith Voss.)

Four

Transportation

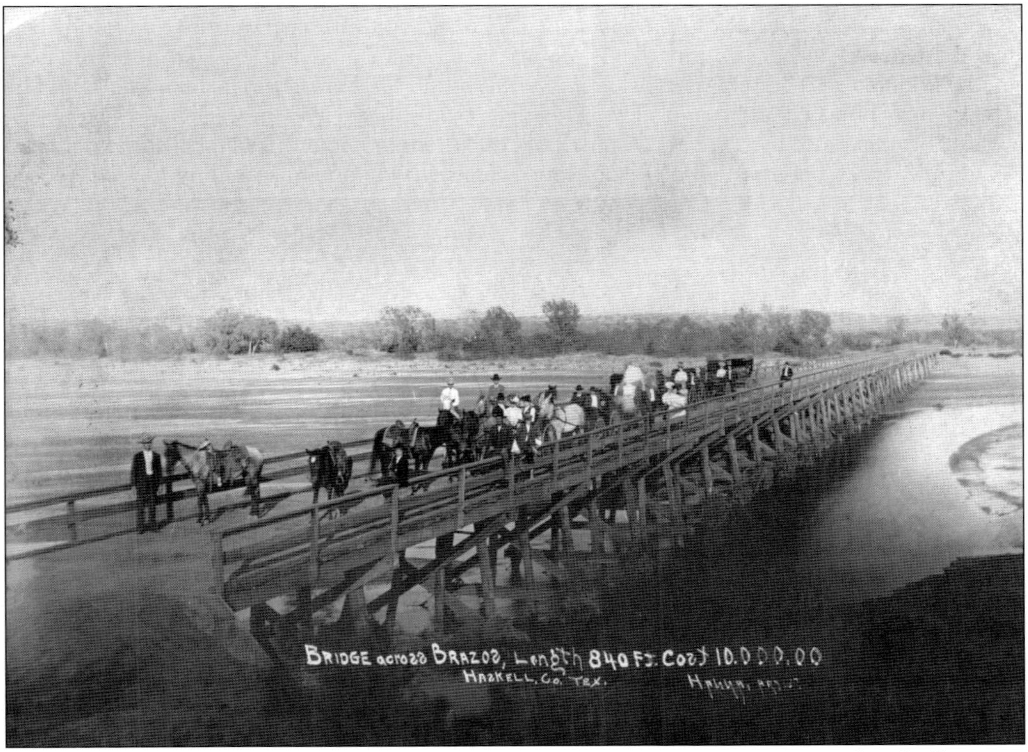

Crossing the Brazos River between Haskell and Stonewall Counties presented a challenge to early-day pioneers. Natural crossings could be unreliable, as the river, normally a quiet stream, rises suddenly during thunderstorms. The identification on this undated photograph reads, "Bridge across Brazos, Length 840 Feet Cost $10,000.00 Haskell Co., Texas." (Courtesy of Bill Jones.)

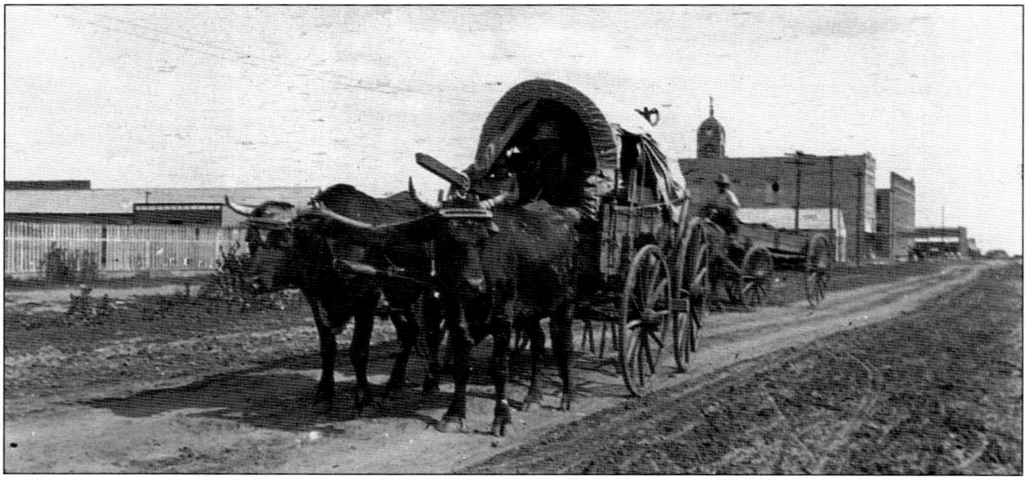

Powered by oxen, mules, or horses, covered wagons brought pioneer families to Haskell County. When railroads arrived, families rode trains to Stamford or Albany and loaded possessions in wagons to complete the trip. As communities and businesses developed, freight wagons brought supplies from as far away as Abilene and Fort Worth. Wagons also transported passengers and supplies between communities and outlying areas. When cotton production began in Haskell County, bales were freighted to Abilene for rail shipment. Depending on conditions, one could expect to travel roughly 4 miles an hour. The above photograph shows a wagon in Haskell, Texas. The clock tower on the courthouse is visible in the background. Dee Hollingsworth, sitting horseback, below, came to Haskell County from Ellis County about 1900, settling near the Jud community. This photograph was made about 1920. (Both courtesy of Haskell County Historical and Genealogical Society.)

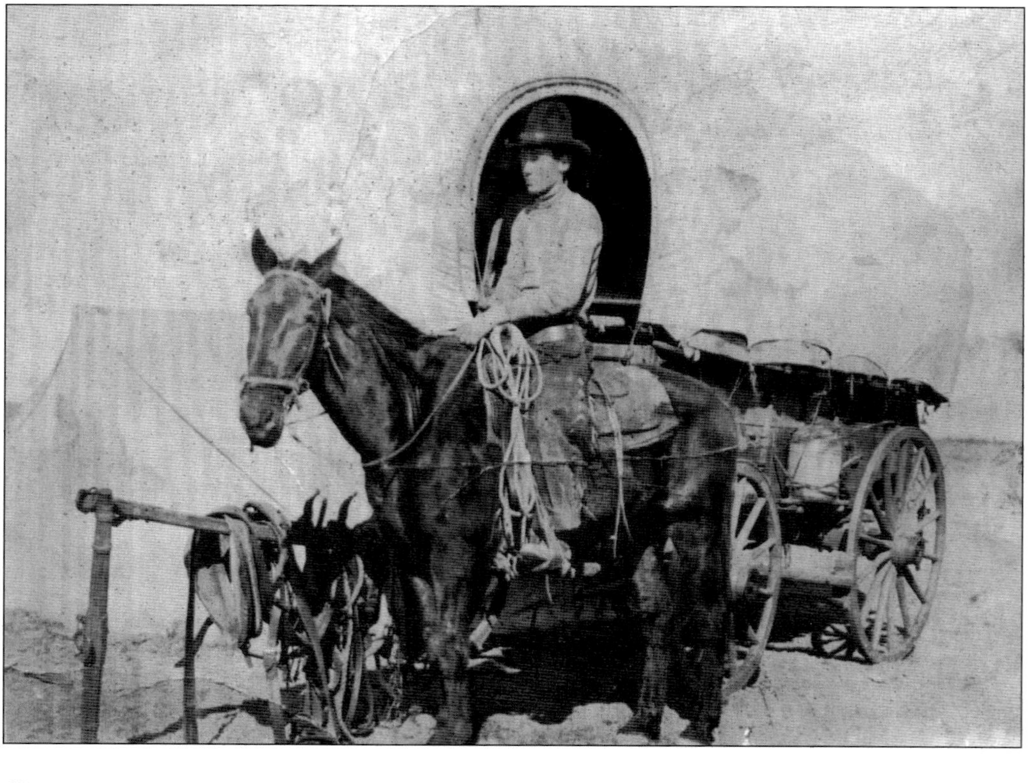

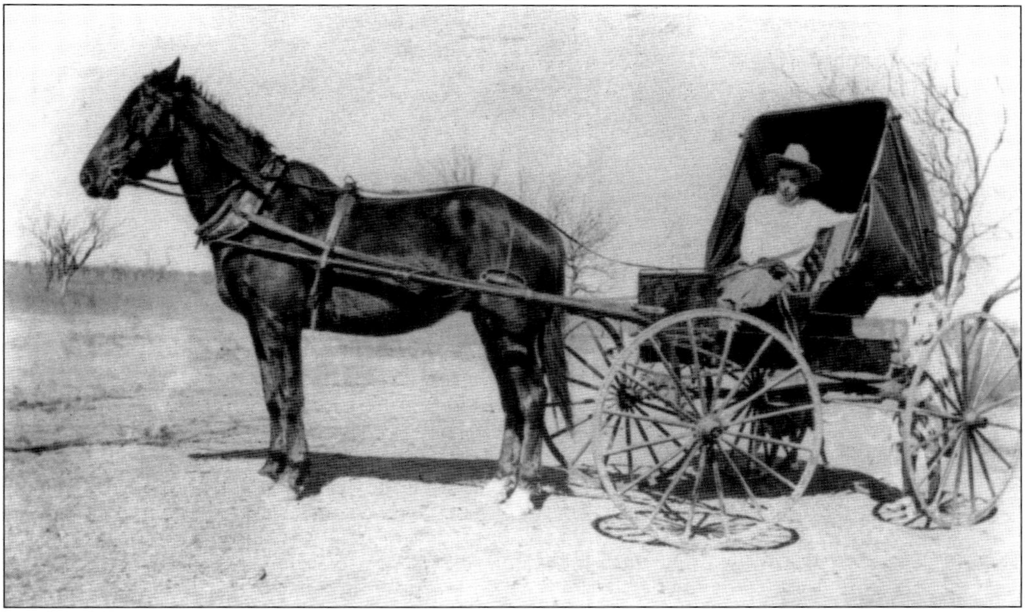

The unidentified passenger in the buggy above makes a stop near Weinert, Texas. Buggies were a relatively inexpensive, common personal conveyance on the Texas prairies, especially as roadways improved. Their light weight allowed them to travel with more speed and maneuverability than heavy wagons, and they could be drawn by a lighter horse or mule. One of the most popular styles was the piano box buggy. Buggies were more easily hitched and driven, making them more popular with women and young adults. They were widely used by doctors in making house calls and for courting. Livery stables and wagon yards rented out horses and buggies. The three couples below are dressed for a Sunday drive near Josselet Switch about 1915. (Above, courtesy of Mary Murphy; below, courtesy of Nancy Toliver.)

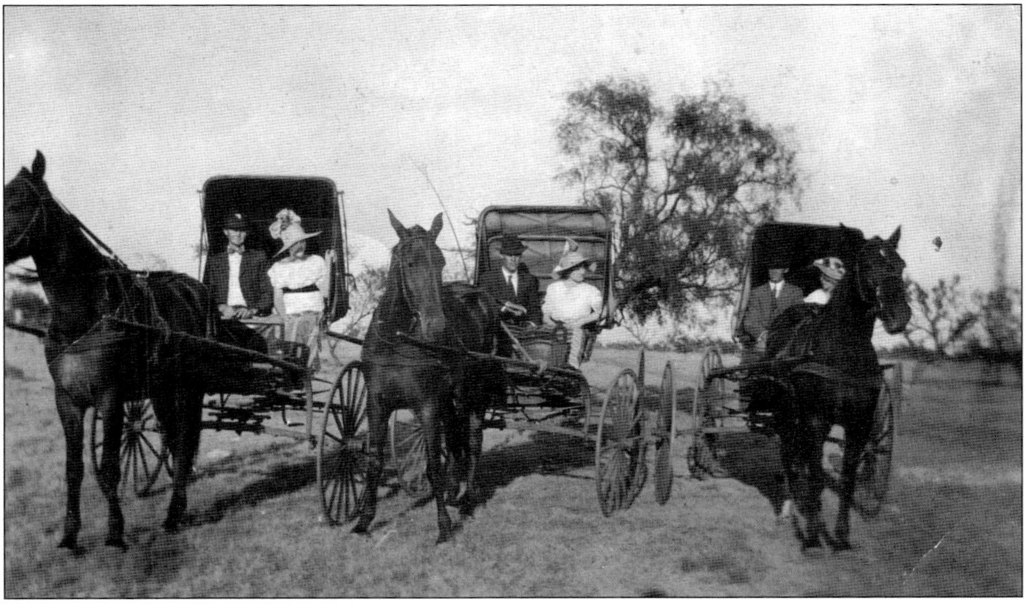

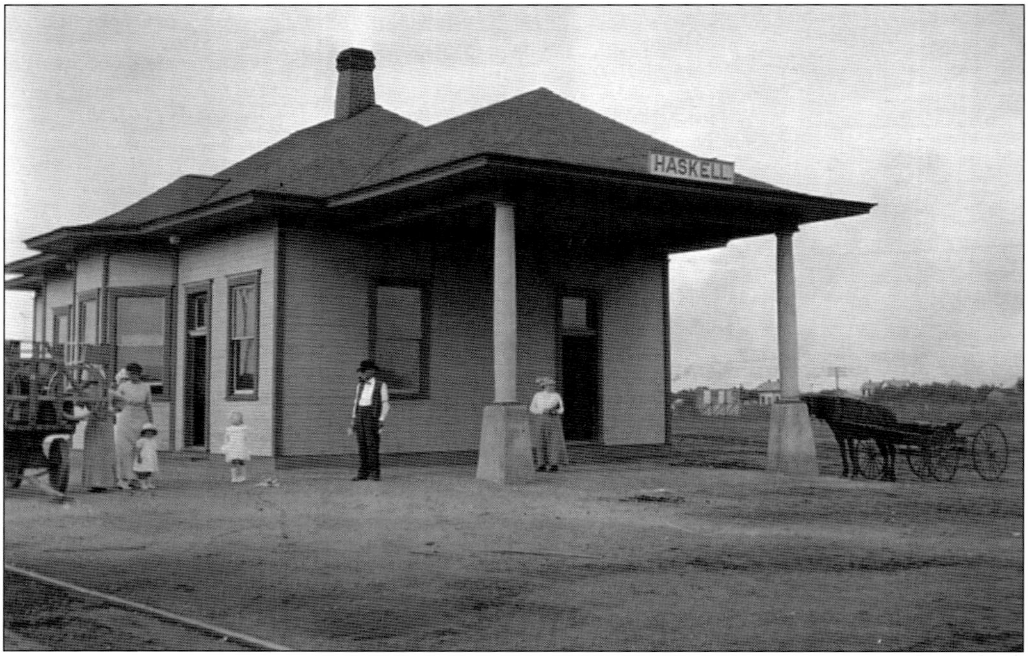

Though designated as the county seat in 1885, Haskell endured a long struggle to secure a railroad. After many years struggling and after some communities in the county already had tracks laid into them, the Wichita Valley Railroad reached Haskell in 1906. In the days before improved roads and automobiles, passenger trains had a tremendous effect on travel in the open spaces of West Texas. (Courtesy of Haskell County Historical and Genealogical Society.)

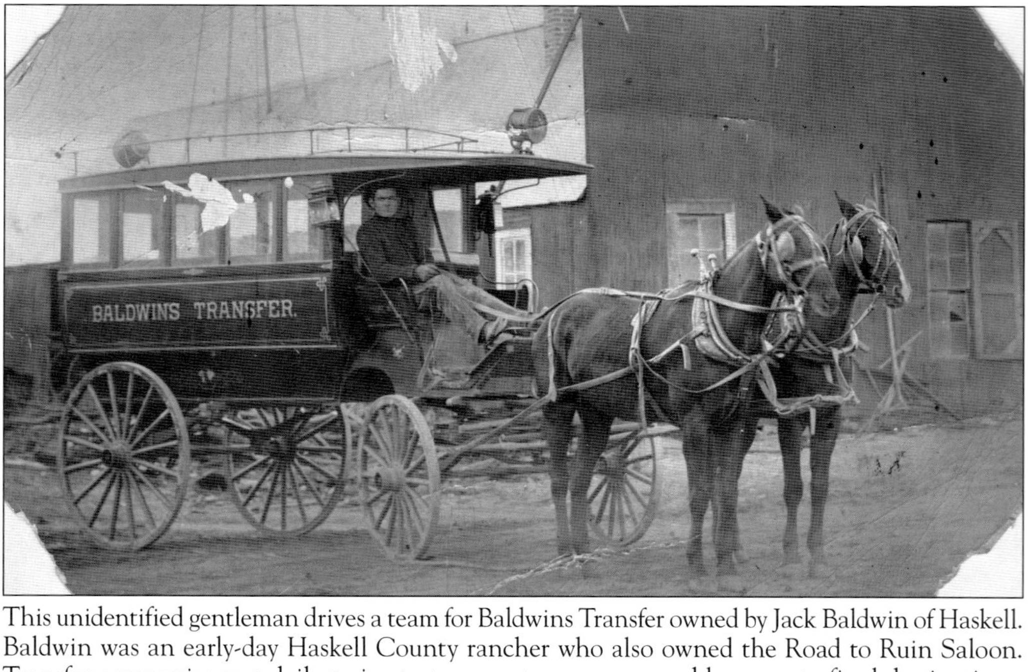

This unidentified gentleman drives a team for Baldwins Transfer owned by Jack Baldwin of Haskell. Baldwin was an early-day Haskell County rancher who also owned the Road to Ruin Saloon. Transfer companies met daily trains to transport passengers and baggage to final destinations. Before railroads came to Haskell County, passengers rode the train to Stamford or Albany and completed their journey north in buggies or hacks. (Courtesy of John Fouts.)

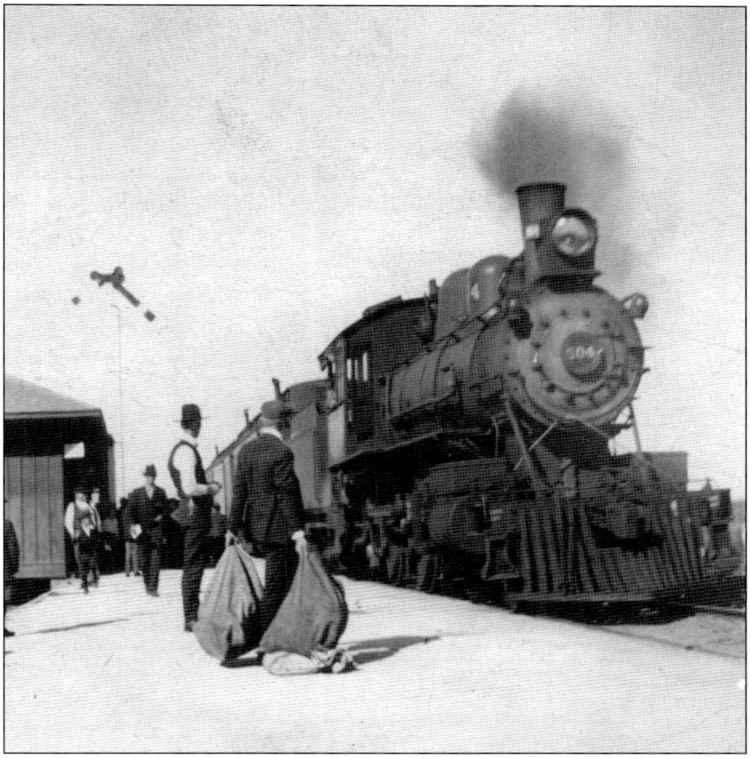

This Kansas City, Mexico, and Orient engine has pulled into Rochester. Named for Rochester, New York, hometown of railroad builder Arthur Stillwell, the town was platted on land given by A. B. Carothers. The train brought coal, lumber, kegs of Dr. Pepper and Coca-Cola, groceries, farm equipment, mules, and everything early-day settlers needed. The young man in this undated photograph prepares to pitch the mail aboard the train. (Courtesy of Alma Counts.)

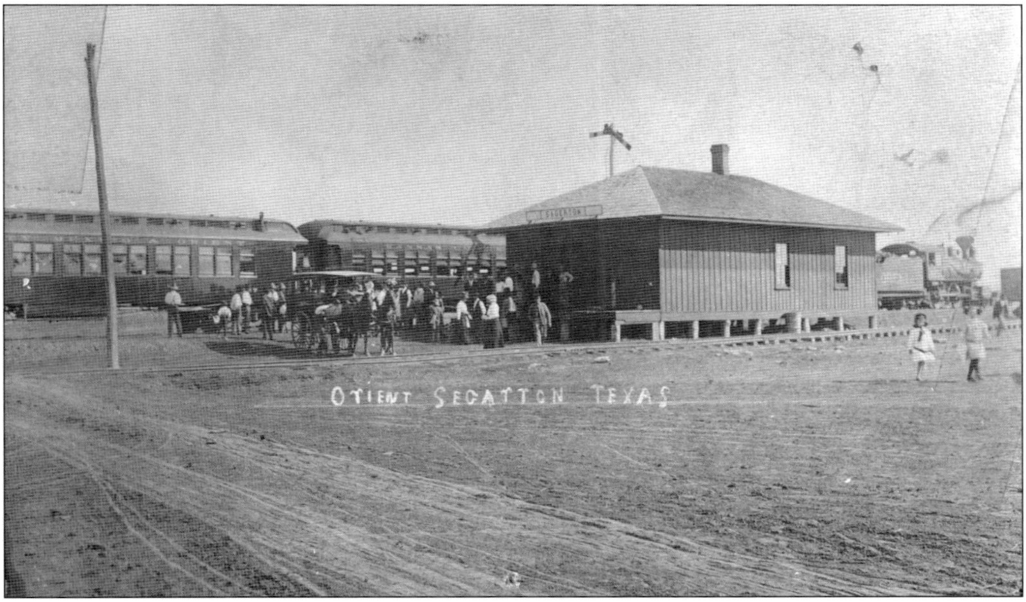

Sagerton, Texas, was the first town in Haskell County to have a railroad and the only town in Haskell County to have once had two railroads. This photograph is of the KCM&O depot. Originating in Kansas, the railroad had a planned but elusive destination on the Pacific coast of Mexico, accessing Orient seatrade. It was sold to Santa Fe in the 1930s, then to shortline operators, and salvaged about 1996. The Orient line's legacy is West Texas communities that sprang up along its path. (Courtesy of Joyce LeFevre.)

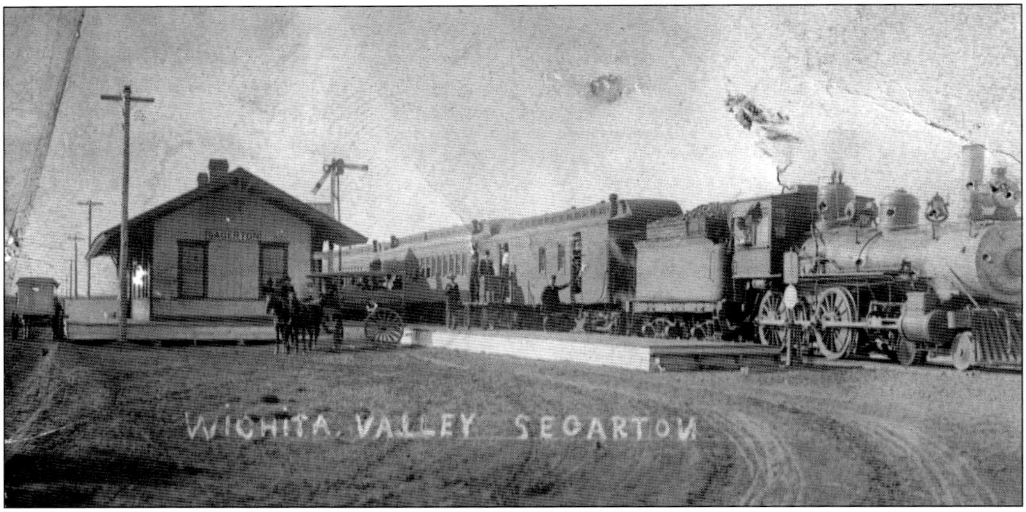

The Stamford and Northwestern Railroad arrived in Sagerton in 1909. It was leased to the Wichita Valley in 1910 and merged with the Fort Worth and Denver in 1952. In this *c.* 1910 photograph, Moore's Transfer has loaded passengers arriving in Sagerton, and freight is loaded onto a baggage cart. The train carries coal to fire its steam locomotive. While the railroads once were the lifeblood of communities, better roads and automobiles eventually lessened their patronage. (Courtesy of Joyce LeFevre.)

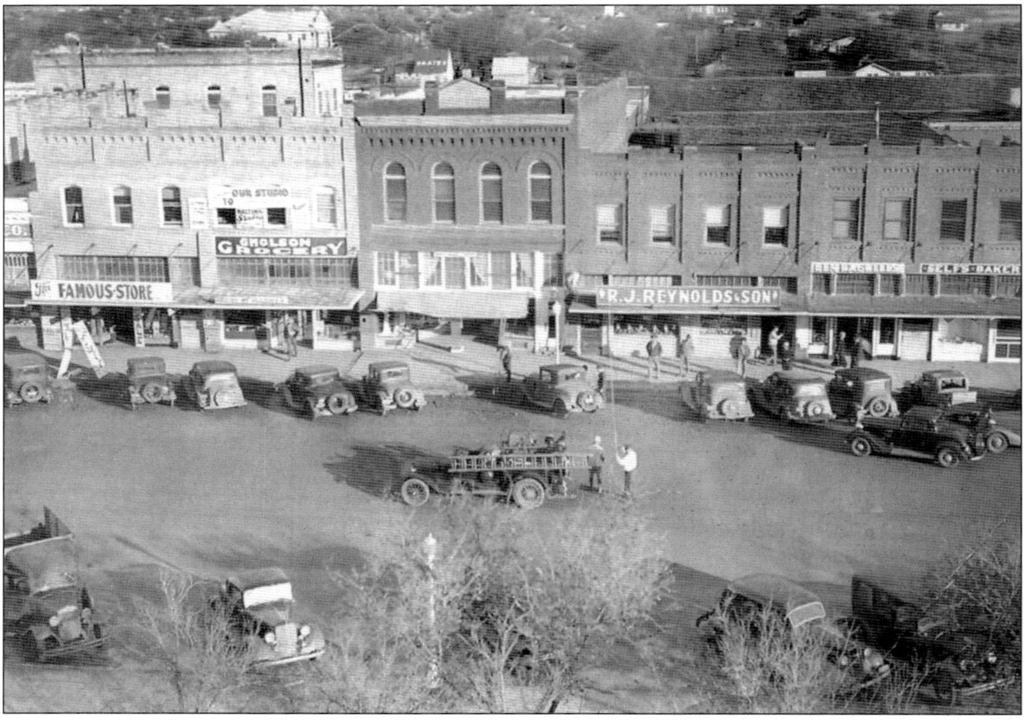

The Haskell Volunteer Fire Department was organized about 1906. R. E. Sherrill was appointed the first fire marshal in 1910. This photograph made in the early 1930s shows a variety of vintage automobiles, trucks, and an early fire truck. Looking north across what is now North First Street, the original Haskell Free Press building and First Baptist Church may be seen. (Courtesy of Hess Hartsfield.)

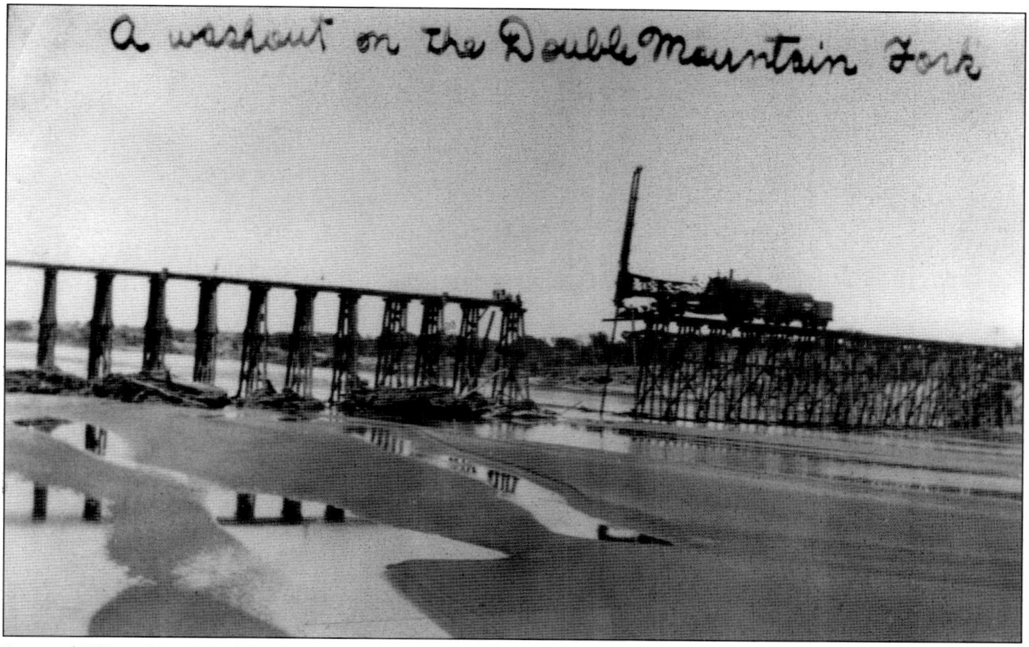

In arid West Texas, the Brazos River can become a raging torrent during thunderstorms over its watershed. When the river comes down, a wall of water carries large trees and other debris violently downstream. Here railroad crews repair damage from a washout. According to residents of Sagerton, this was a common scene in the days of wooden bridges. (Courtesy of Joyce LeFevre.)

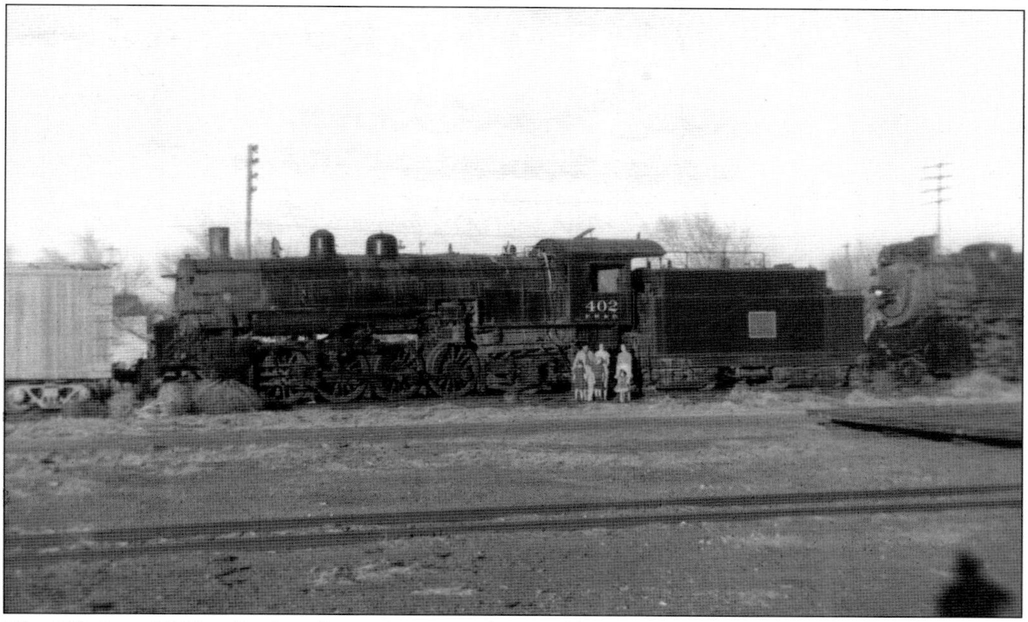

The Wichita Valley Railroad ran from Wichita Falls to Abilene, Texas, beginning in 1906, providing service to Weinert and Haskell. It later merged with the Fort Worth and Denver, then the Burlington Northern, and was no longer in service by the mid-1990s. In this undated photograph, J. L. Toliver Jr. (second row, left) shows this Fort Worth and Denver locomotive to his wife, Martha, and daughters Trisha and Karen. Toliver was with the railroad from 1954 until 1986. (Courtesy of Nancy Toliver.)

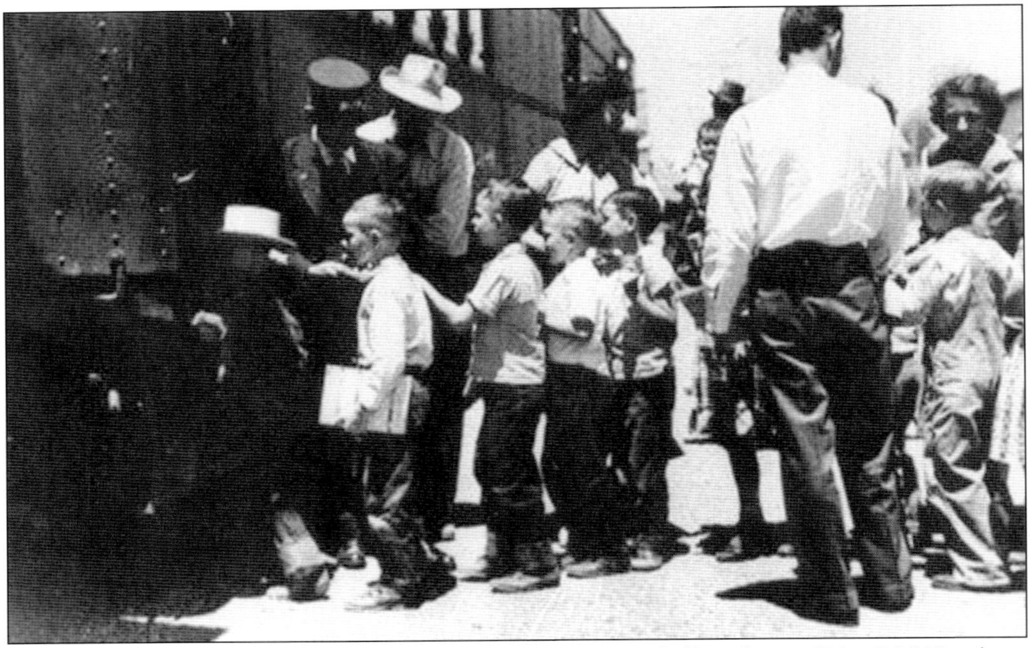

Passengers boarding the train in this 1947 photograph are Haskell students of Mrs. J. V. Vaughter. In an earlier day, children might have taken excursions on Haskell's streetcar. In 1909, a 10¢ fare bought a seat on a gasoline-powered streetcar traveling on a 3-mile track. The car met daily trains and kept an hourly schedule. The route ended north of Haskell near what became the country club. (Courtesy of Hess Hartsfield.)

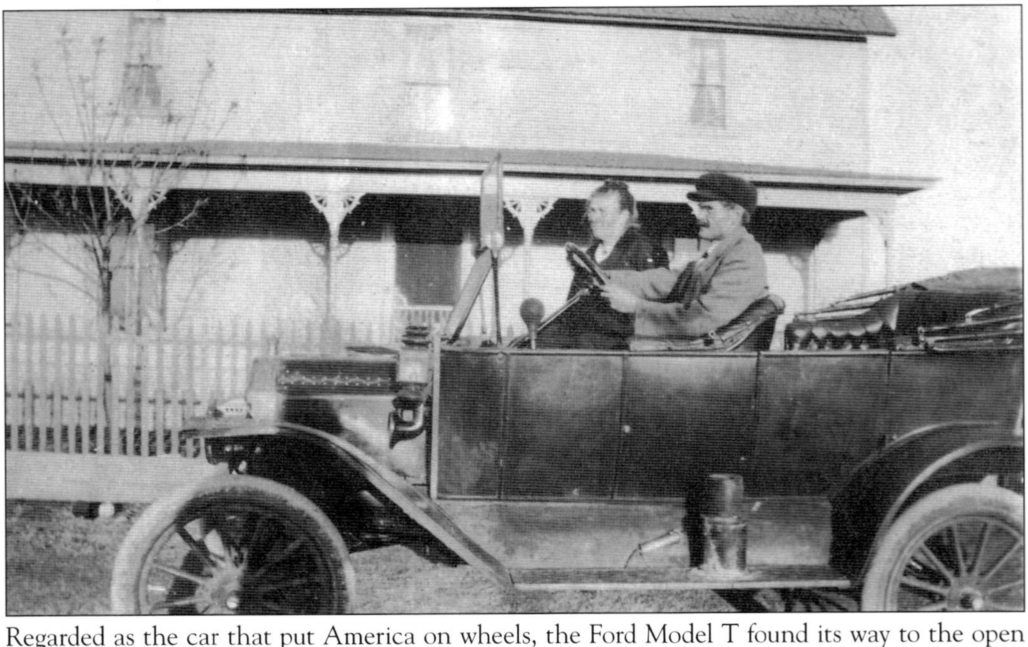

Regarded as the car that put America on wheels, the Ford Model T found its way to the open prairies of Haskell County. The Model T fuel tank design often meant backing the automobile up steep hills to keep fuel flowing. This was not a significant issue in the flatlands of Haskell County. K. A. Balzer had the first car in Sagerton. He is shown here with his wife, Anna. (Courtesy of Joyce LeFevre.)

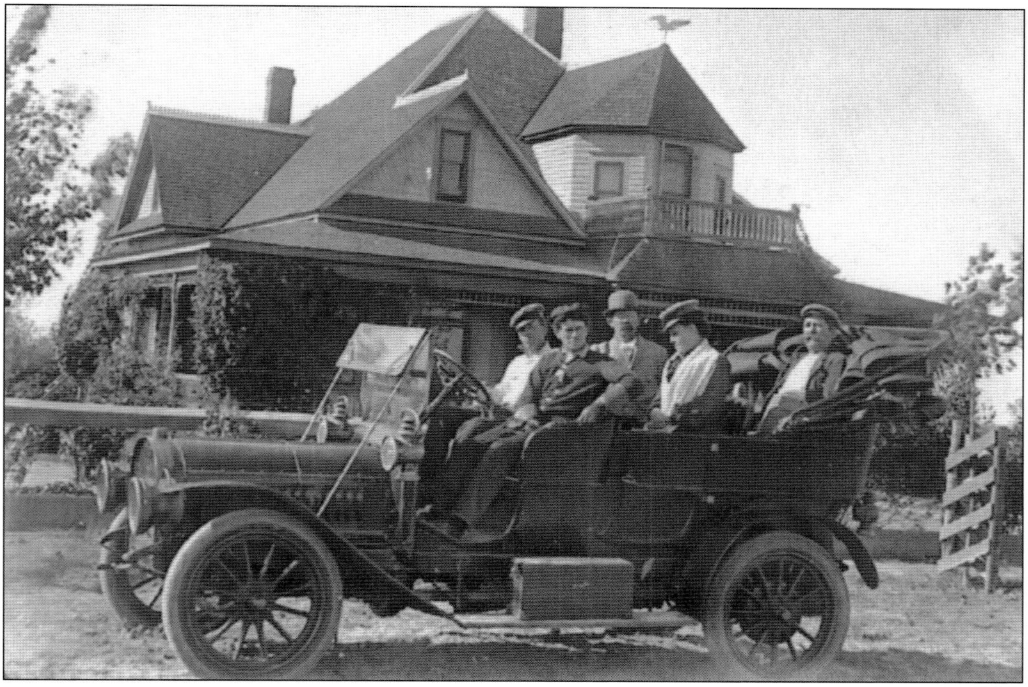

The unidentified passengers in this automobile pause on a street in Carney (O'Brien), Texas. The home of T. G. Carney, founder of the community, is in the background. Unusual for West Texas was a fig tree in the backyard of this home. (Courtesy of Hess Hartsfield.)

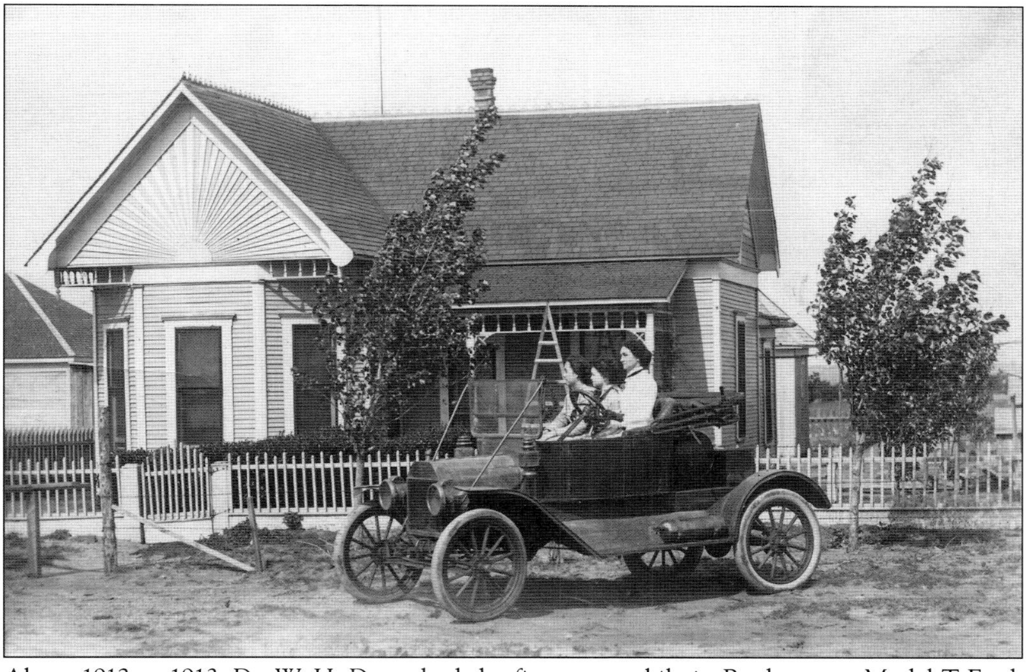

About 1912 or 1913, Dr. W. H. Dunn had the first automobile in Rochester, a Model T Ford. Because it belonged to Dr. Dunn, people ignored the commotion it caused. Mrs. Dunn is seated at the wheel in front of their home at 600 Main Street, accompanied by her daughters. Dr. Dunn also operated a drugstore in town. (Courtesy of Charlene Smith Voss.)

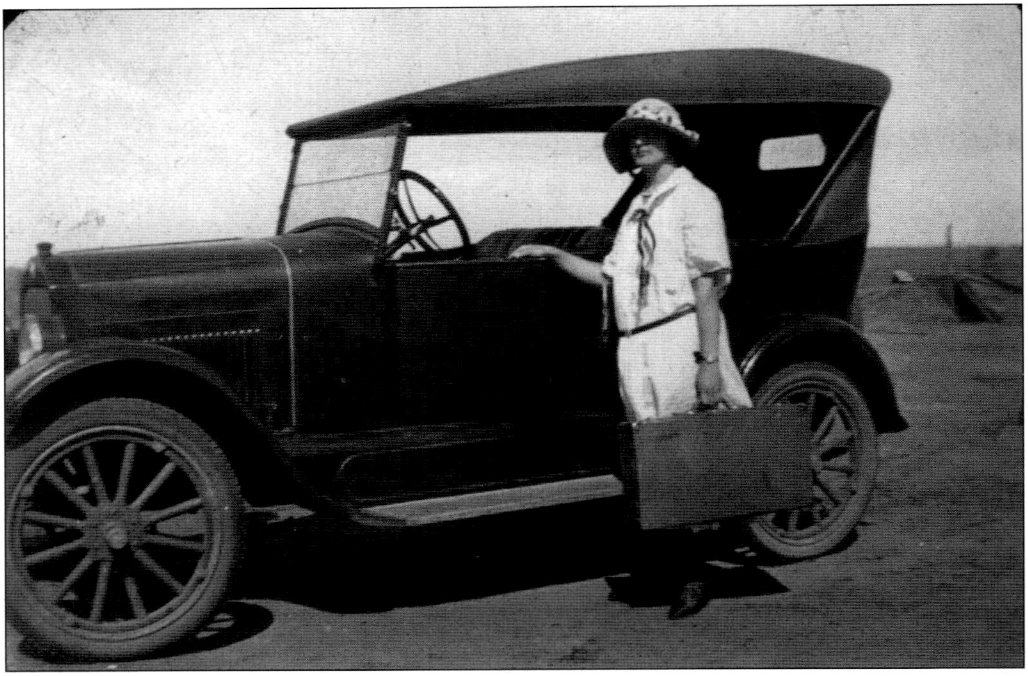

Myrtle Johnston is pictured here beside this Ford Model T. Johnston grew up northwest of Rule and was known for her skills as a nurse and midwife. By 1918, half of all automobiles produced in the United States were Ford Model Ts. (Courtesy of Alma Counts.)

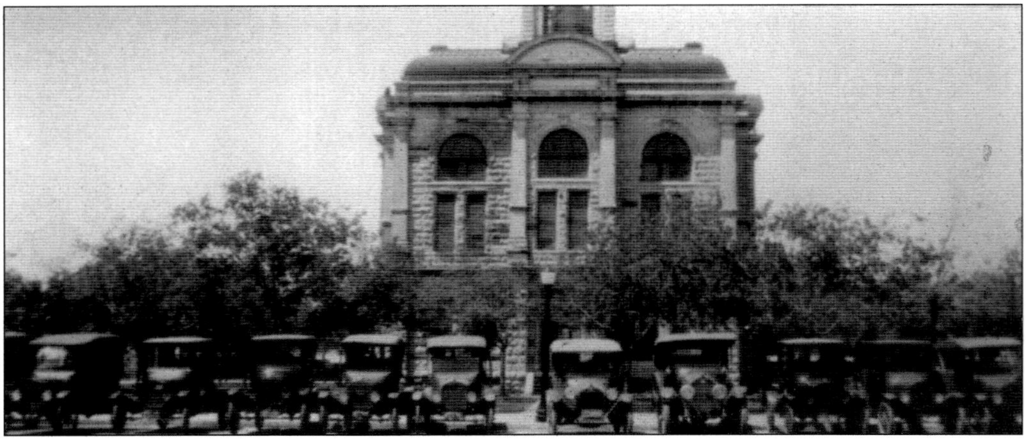

Once mass production started, a Ford Model T could be assembled in just over 90 minutes, with a car coming off the line every 3 minutes. The Model T has been called the most influential car of the 20th century. Lynn Pace of Haskell established the first motor company in Haskell, Pace Ford. (Courtesy of Haskell County Historical and Genealogical Society.)

M. E. ("Gene") Overton sits on the bumper of this early-day automobile. Overton came to the Post community in 1917. Like thousands of others, he left his rural West Texas home and served his country during World War II. He returned to the Paint Creek area to farm following the war. (Courtesy of Wallar Overton.)

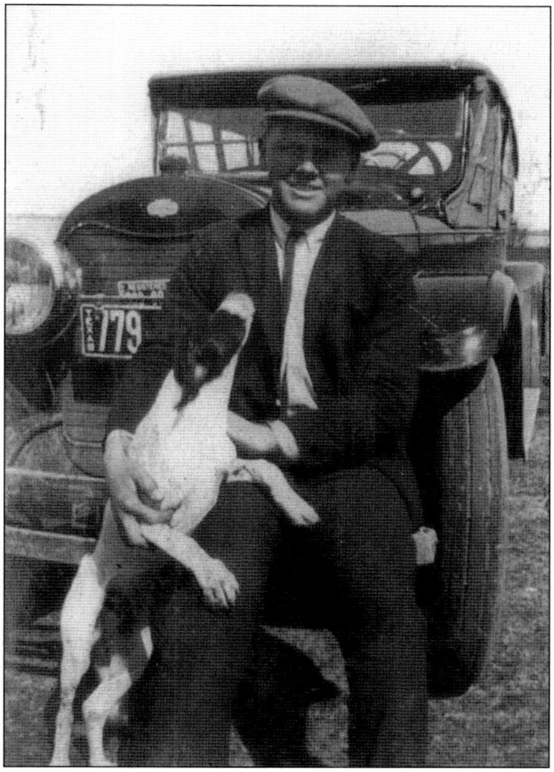

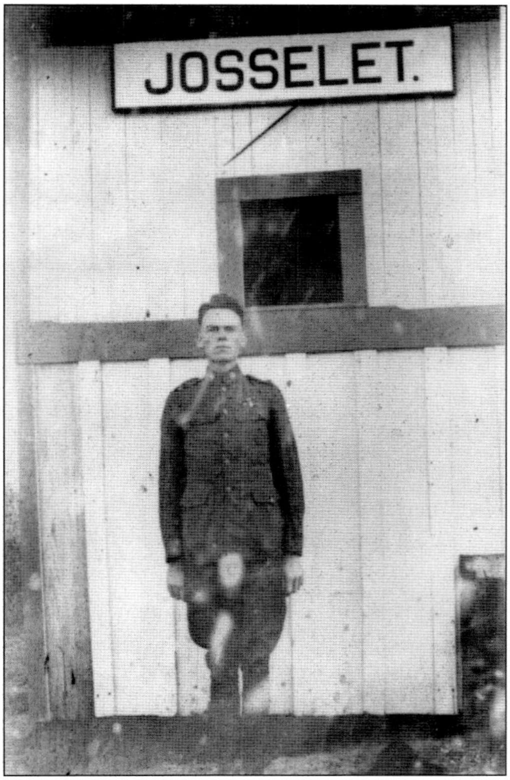

This 1918 photograph shows Homer Turnbow arriving by train at Josselet Switch following World War I. In addition to Wichita Valley depots in Weinert and Haskell, there were train stops at Josselet Switch north of Haskell and McConnell Switch, 7 miles south of Haskell. Passengers, cattle, and farm products shipped through these points. Homer Turnbow built a store near Josselet called Honeycutt. Several businesses and a school were located at McConnell. (Courtesy of Doris Reeves.)

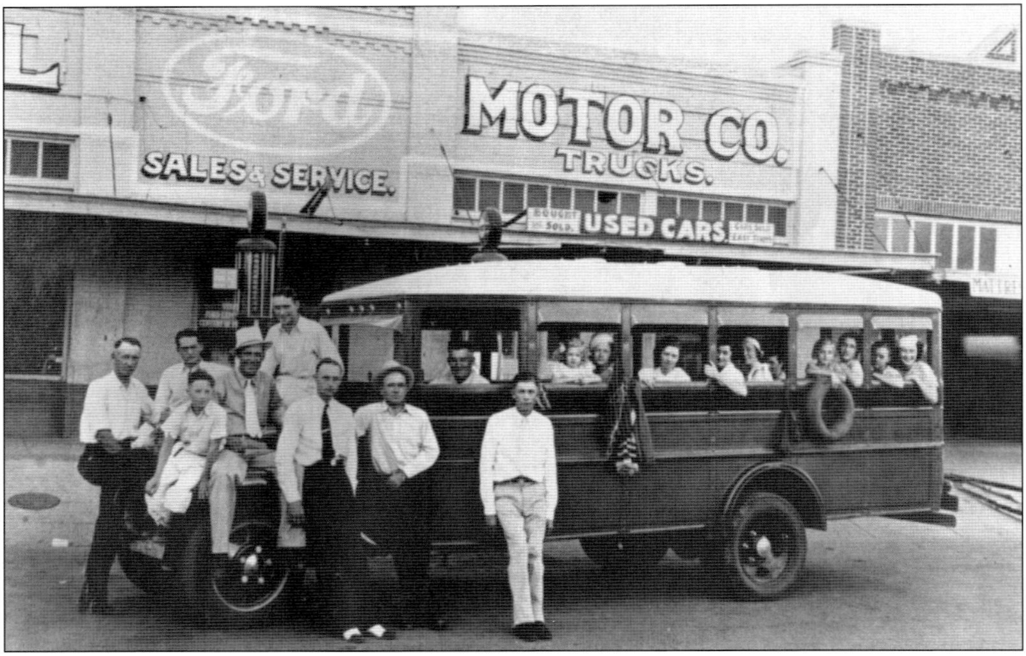

In the early days of Haskell County, schools were located in such a way that children did not usually have to walk more than a mile or two. In the 1930s, many country schools throughout the county began consolidating into centralized schools. School buses were purchased to transport children over large areas of the county. This is one of the first school buses in Haskell County. (Courtesy of Haskell County Historical and Genealogical Society.)

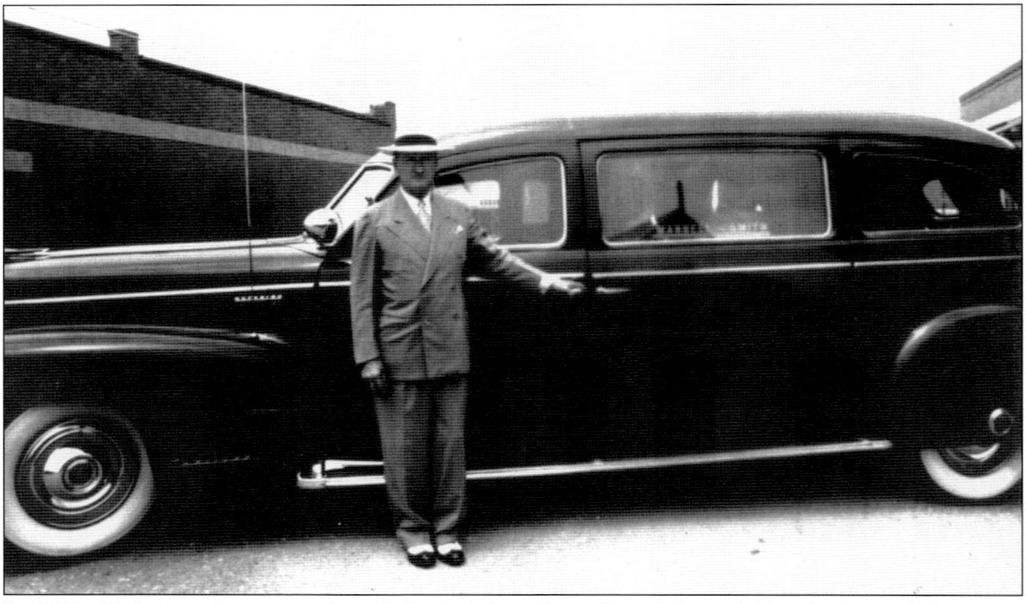

In 1933, Hob Smith partnered with P. A. Mansell to form Mansell Smith Funeral Home in Rochester. Smith purchased this hearse in the 1930s for $3,600. The hearse was also used as an ambulance for many years. Smith was a licensed funeral home director in Haskell County until the 1990s. His family continues to operate Smith Funeral Home in Rochester. (Courtesy of Martha Sue Smith McCurly.)

Five

Activities and Recreation

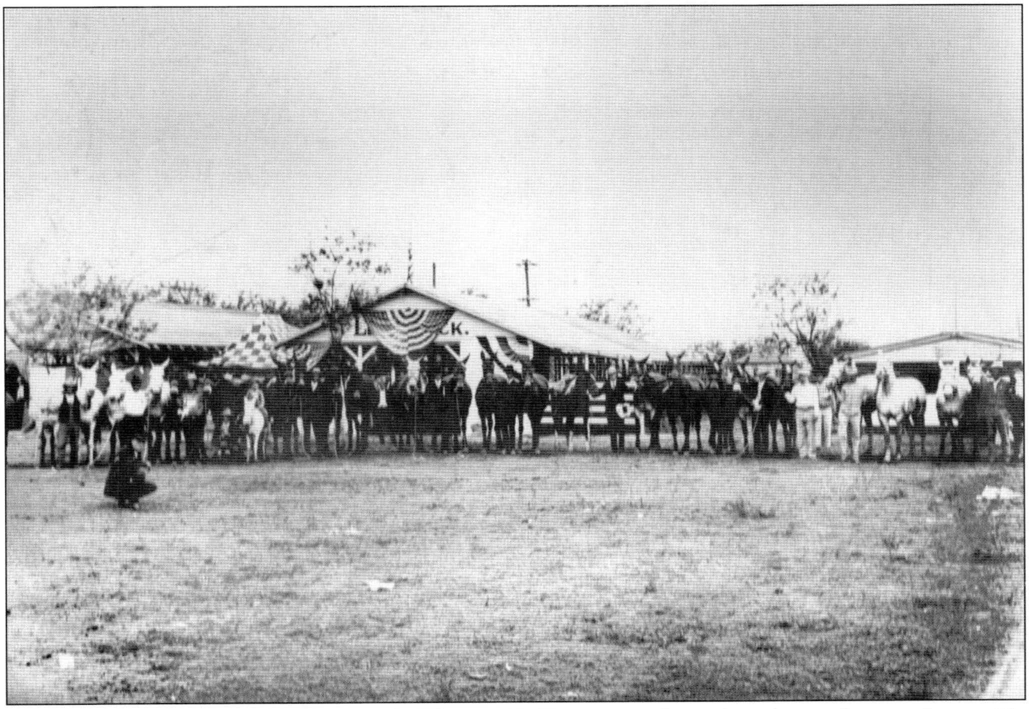

The first fair in Haskell County was held in 1903. Farmers and ranchers have always taken pride in livestock, so vital to their livelihood, and are glad to put them on display. Third from left is Knott Ballard of Rochester. According to the *Haskell Free Press*, the fair that year featured a "fine display" of horses, mules, hogs, cows, and poultry, and crops produced in Haskell County. A women's department was added in 1904. (Courtesy of Marguerite Gauntt.)

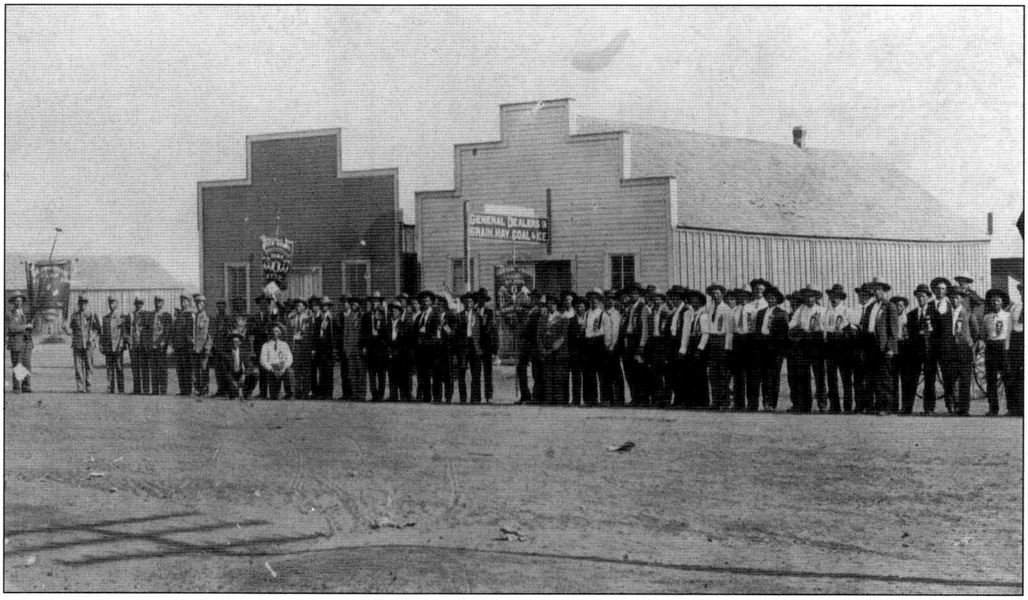

This photograph, probably made before 1920, is of a gathering of members of the Woodmen of the World, a fraternal organization. The county had chapters in several communities. The banners identify each group. The banners read, from left to right, "Haskell," "Rule," and "Center Point." The location is unidentified. (Courtesy of Alma Counts.)

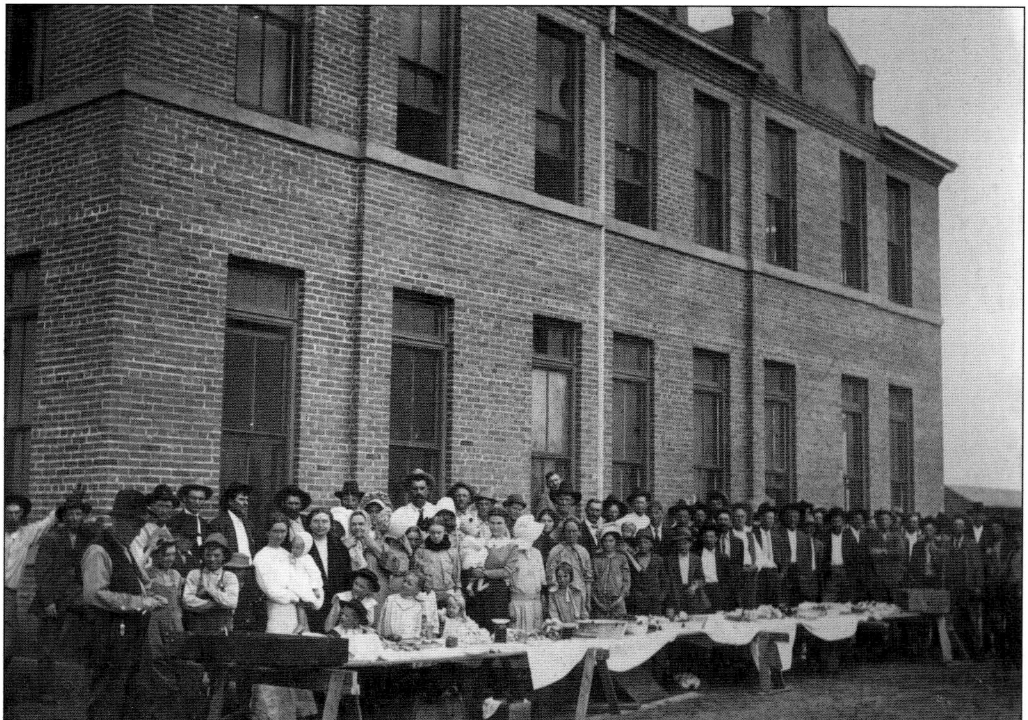

All ages of the Rochester community have gathered at the Rochester school building for a town picnic. The meal is spread on cloth-covered wooden planks. The crowd appears to be trying to stay within the confines of shade provided by the building. (Courtesy of Sharon Mullino.)

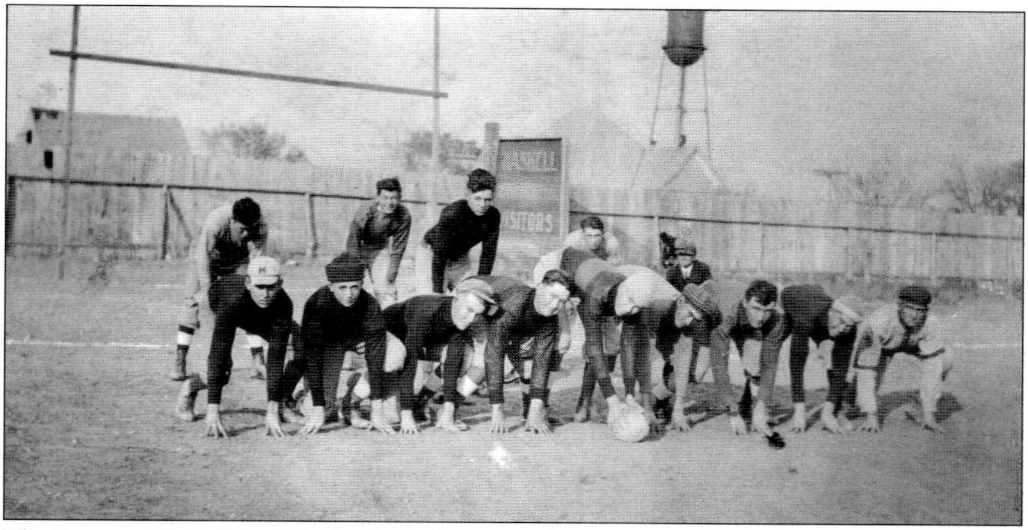

The Sagerton High School Eagles football team is about to take the field for a game with Haskell about 1916. The scoreboard behind reads "Haskell" and "Visitors." Team members are, from left to right, (first row) Floyd Smith, Mason Martin, Ray Martin, Pernie Burrow, unidentified, Aubrey Pilley, two unidentified, and Clarence Pilley; (second row) four unidentified players and Prof. T. R. Havins. In later years, the Eagles were at one time coached by Irene Stewart, an icon in Haskell County history and education. (Courtesy of Joyce LeFevre.)

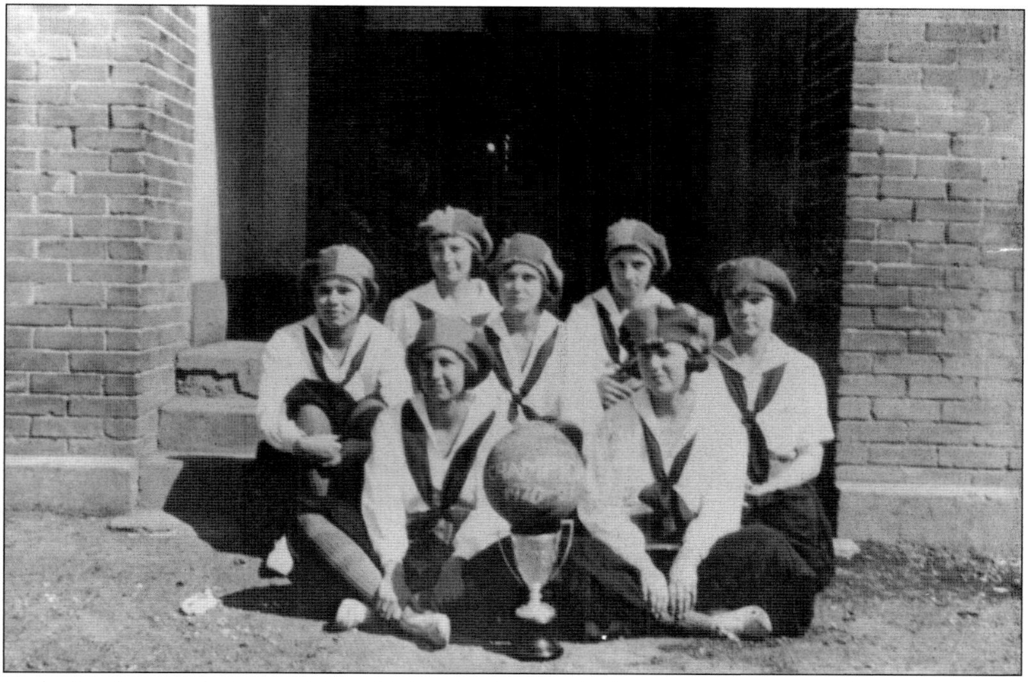

Girls first began playing in Texas high school basketball tournaments in 1906. By 1910, high school girls could advance to regional playoffs. This Rochester girls basketball team poses with their 1920 unidentified championship trophy. Uniforms featuring bloomers, stockings, long sleeves, and matching scarves were typical of the era. From left to right are (first row) Lois Mansell Smith and unidentified; (second row) Louise Mullino, Hazell Mullino Cluck, and unidentified; (third row) two unidentified. (Courtesy of Sharon Mullino.)

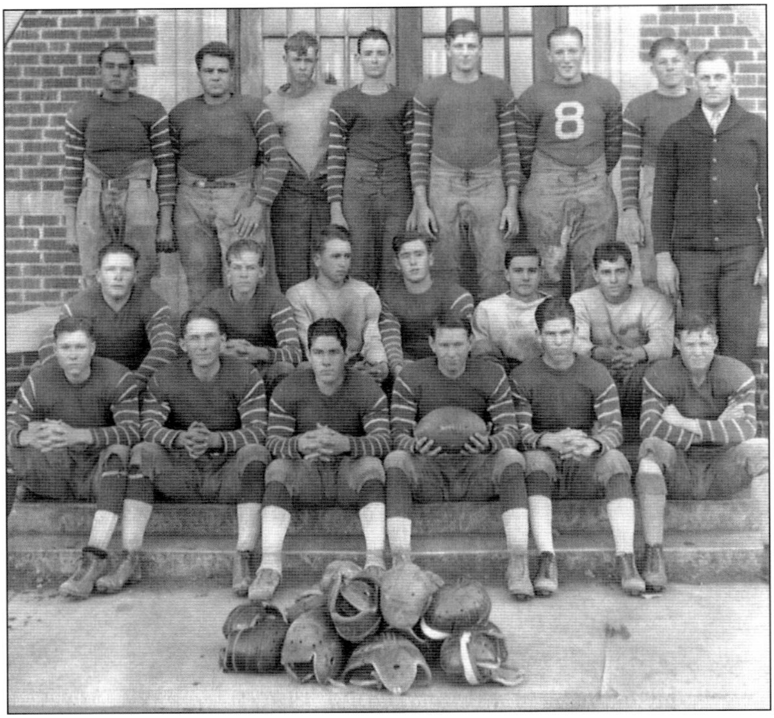

This Rule Bobcat football team is suited up in front of the Rule school about 1929 or 1930. Leather helmets are in the foreground. From these early beginnings, the Rule Bobcats went on to field outstanding football teams in both 11-man and 6-man football. The 1973–1974 Bobcats advanced to state playoffs in 11-man football. The 2006 and 2007 teams advanced to state playoffs in 6-man football. (Courtesy of Village Primitives Antiques.)

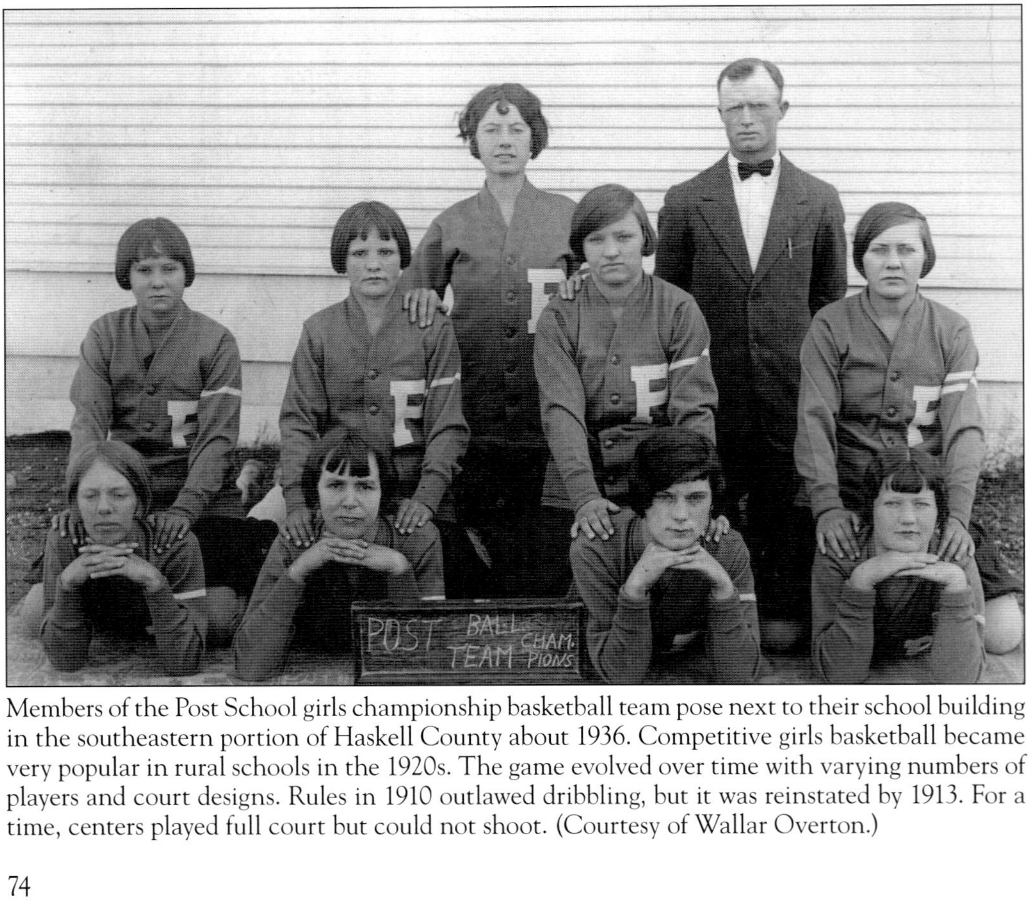

Members of the Post School girls championship basketball team pose next to their school building in the southeastern portion of Haskell County about 1936. Competitive girls basketball became very popular in rural schools in the 1920s. The game evolved over time with varying numbers of players and court designs. Rules in 1910 outlawed dribbling, but it was reinstated by 1913. For a time, centers played full court but could not shoot. (Courtesy of Wallar Overton.)

In this photograph, members of the 1937 Weinert High School girls basketball team pose in front of their school. Wearing the blue and white uniforms of the Weinert Bulldogs are, from left to right, Junita, Opal, and Estella Dunnam. (Courtesy of Wanda Dunnam Ham.)

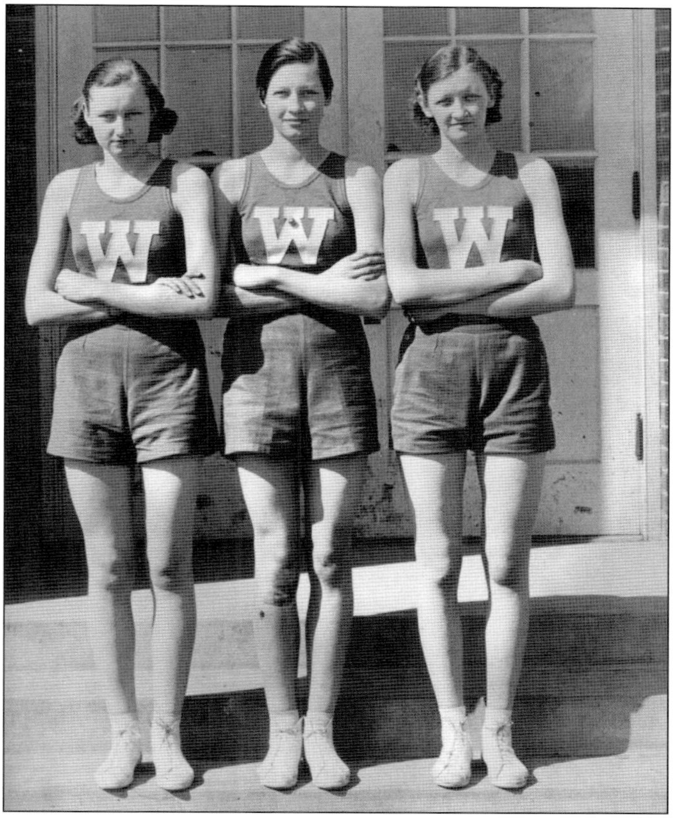

Country baseball teams were a common pastime in early-day Haskell County. This team is suited up for O'Brien. Towns, schools, and even churches formed baseball teams for recreation. In the photograph are two men from the Barnard family. (Courtesy of Haskell County Historical and Genealogical Society.)

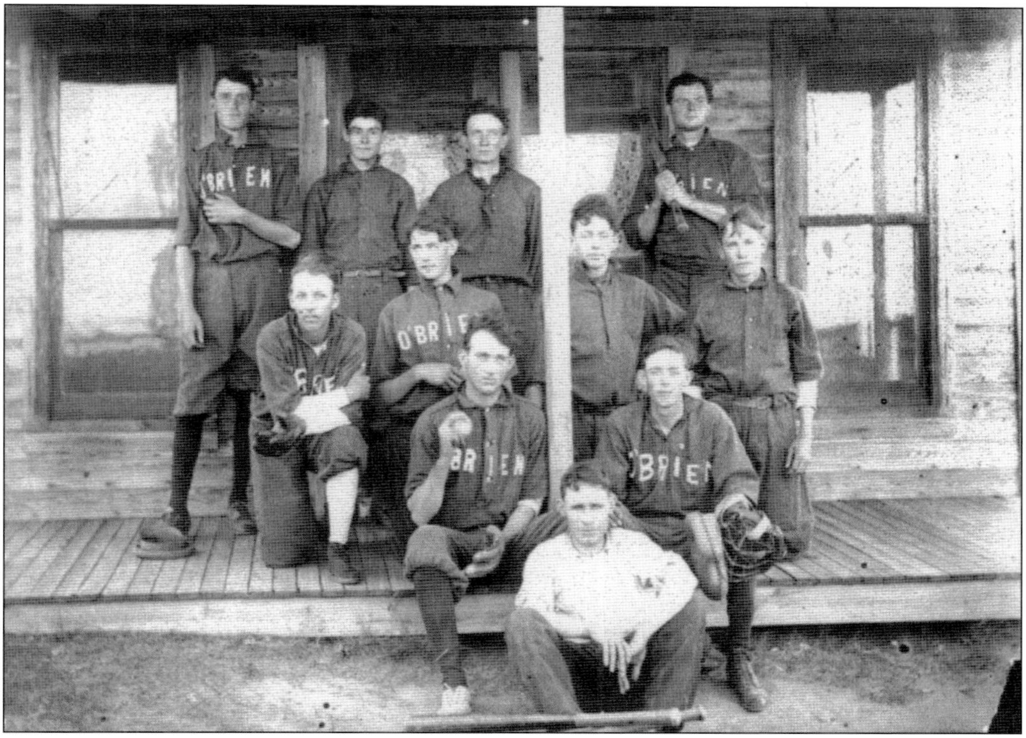

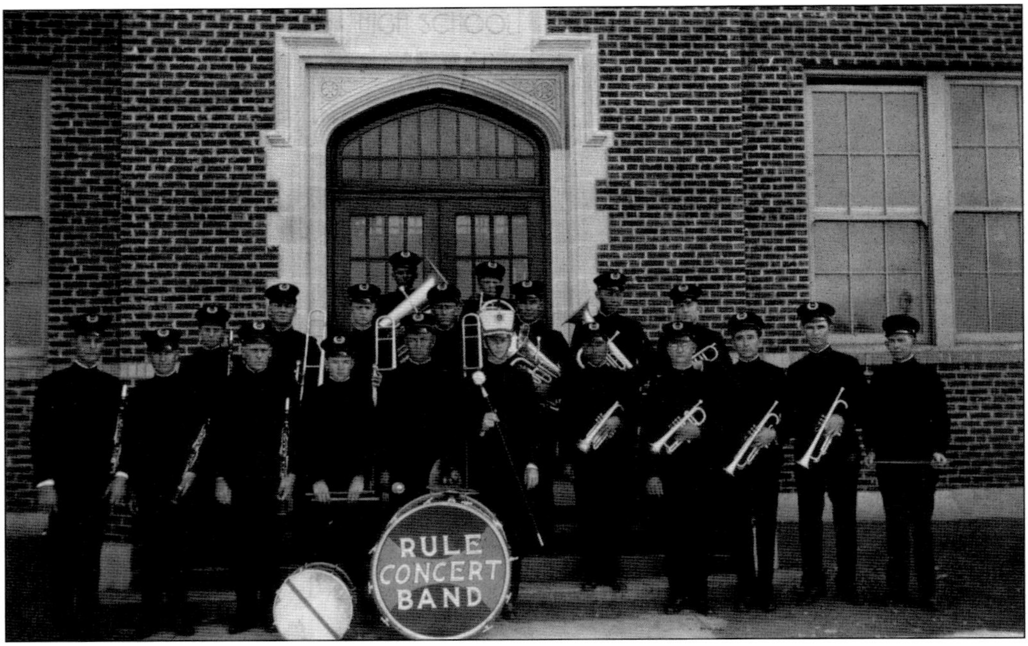

This 1923 photograph is of the Rule Concert Band. Early-day musicians gathered in homes for musical entertainment. Often it meant carrying an instrument across the field to meet with neighbors after work. Community bands were organized, complete with uniforms, and traveled to perform at special events. (Courtesy of Linda Lane-Bloise.)

The Haskell Magazine Club was organized in 1902. Its purpose was to "secure . . . magazines, follow a general course of reading, and to study literary, social, moral and economic questions." The club provided educational development and championed civic causes. The club met in this building, which was available for social functions and served as a library. (Courtesy of Hess Hartsfield.)

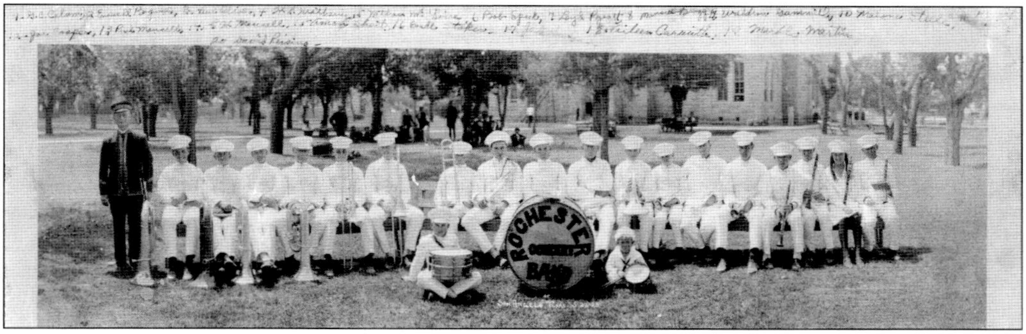

The Rochester Concert Band is seen in this 1923 photograph made in San Angelo, Texas. Members identified are, from left to right, band director G. C. Colum, Ewell Bagwell, Paul Oliver, H. L. Matheny, Nathan McGuire, Bob Speck, Lloyd Pyeatt, Mansell Bragg, Waldron Gammill, Malone Steele, Hobart Reising, Joe Cooper, Paul Mansell, C. H. Mansell, Amon Short, Earl Stoker, Jack Huntsman, Aileen Carruth, and Marable Martin. David Reising (left) and Son Reising are seated in front. (Courtesy of Rochester Heritage Museum.)

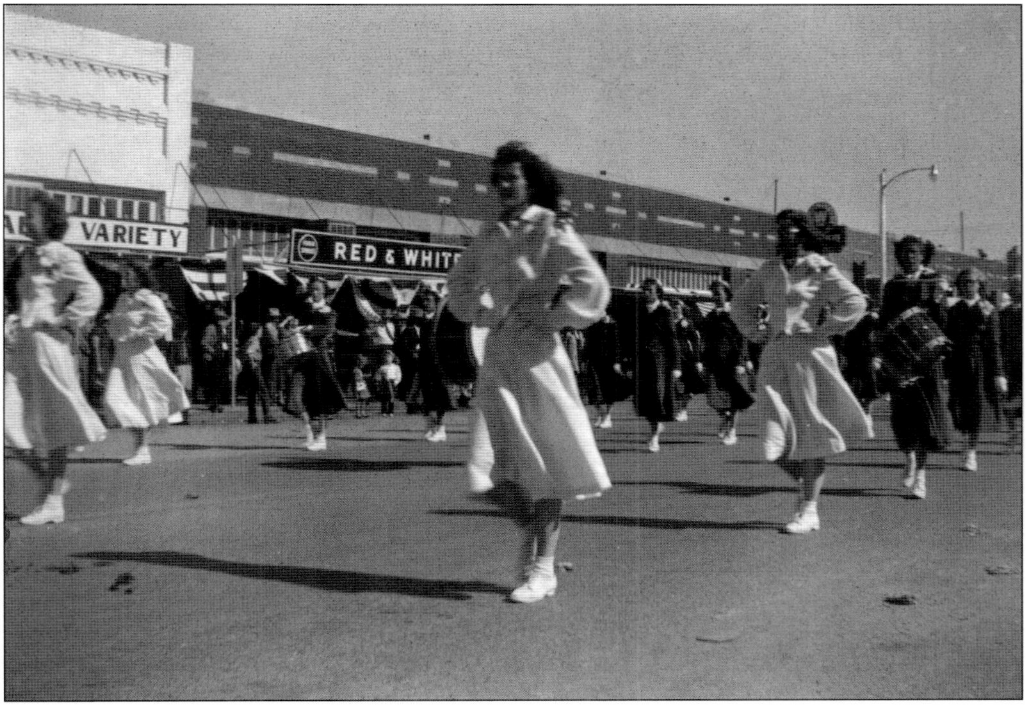

In this undated photograph, members of the Rule High School Pep Squad march in a parade in Rule. The town held a Veterans Day parade for many years. Businesses visible on Fifth Street, the main city thoroughfare, are McAdoo Variety Store and the Red and White Grocery Store. (Courtesy of Alma Counts.)

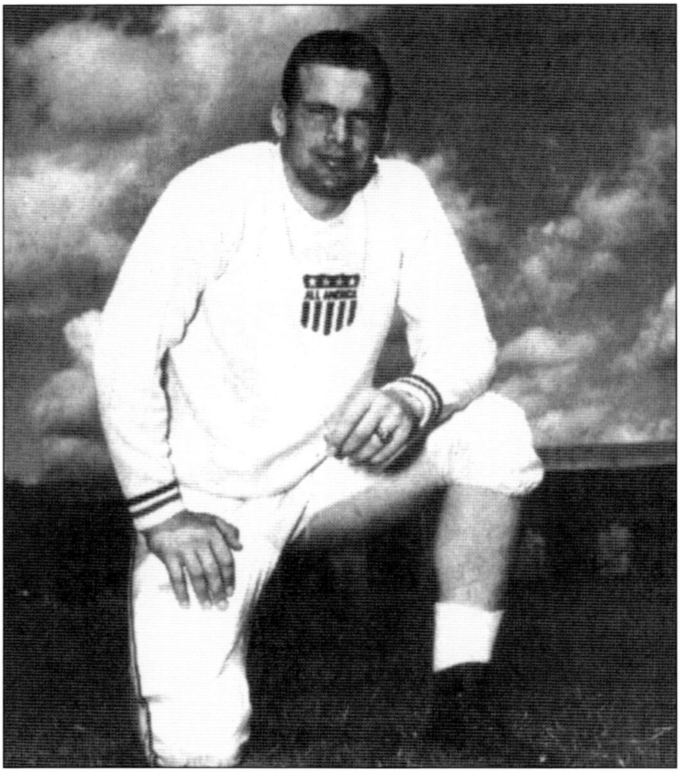

The "Haskell Hurricane," John Kimbrough, was one of the most renowned football stars of all time. Born in Haskell, Texas, in 1918, "Jarrin' John" was the most valuable player of the 1939 Texas A&M National Championship football team. He was named All-American in 1939 and 1940 and was twice nominated for the Heisman. Following service in World War II, he played professional football and was inducted into the National Football Hall of Fame. (Courtesy of Barbara Kimbrough.)

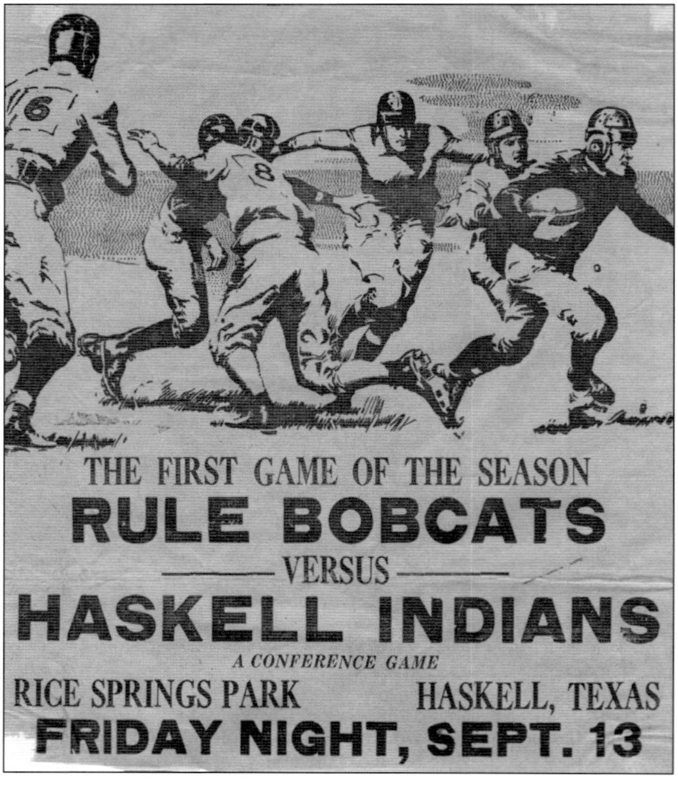

This undated newspaper item advertises a game between the Haskell Indians and Rule Bobcats. Accompanying the advertisement is a list of "tentative" starters: S. A. Moser or ? Henshaw; Weldon Smith or Robert Thompson; Lloyd McMillian or Eugene Rose; Ernest McMillian, Bill Reeves, Robert Wheatley, or Marvin Huff; James Roy Akins or Thomas Kaigler; and quarterback Jack Kimbrough. (Courtesy of Village Primitive Antique Store.)

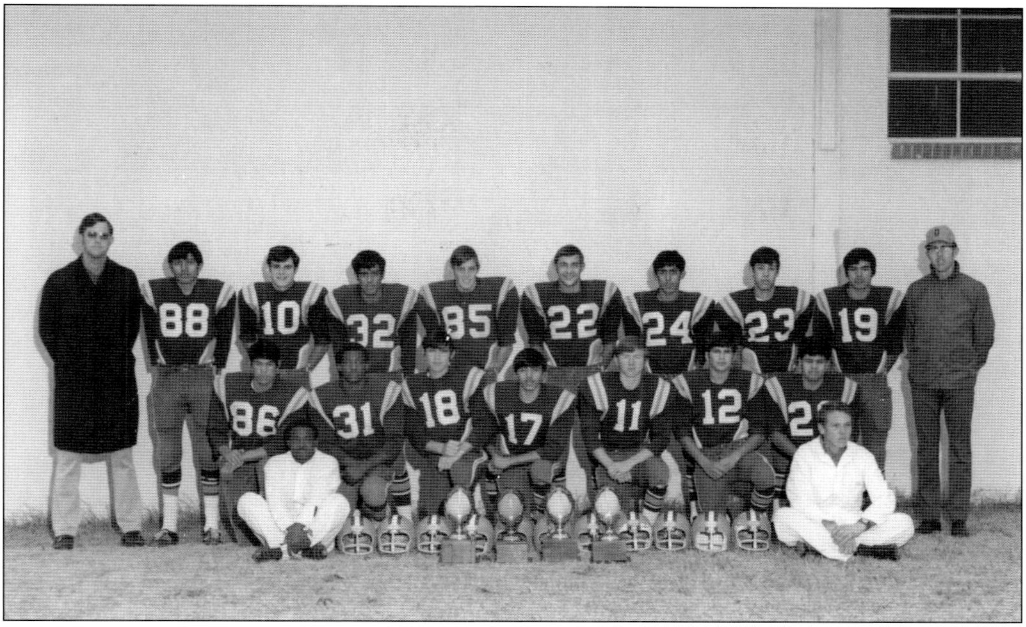

In 1972, the undefeated O'Brien Bulldogs won Texas's first UIL State Championship for six-man football. From left to right are (first row) managers James Washington and Don Brothers; (second row) Tony Alsides, Henry Washington, Randy Watson, Steve Rojas, Sammy Jackson, Bert Gutierrez, and Charles Casillas; (third row) assistant coach Benny Grill, Louis Rojas, Louis Conn, Mague Rocha, Arly Watson, Rayland Hayes, Jamie Rocha, Eulalio Garcia, Danny Del Hierro, and coach C. H. Underwood. (Courtesy of C. H. Underwood.)

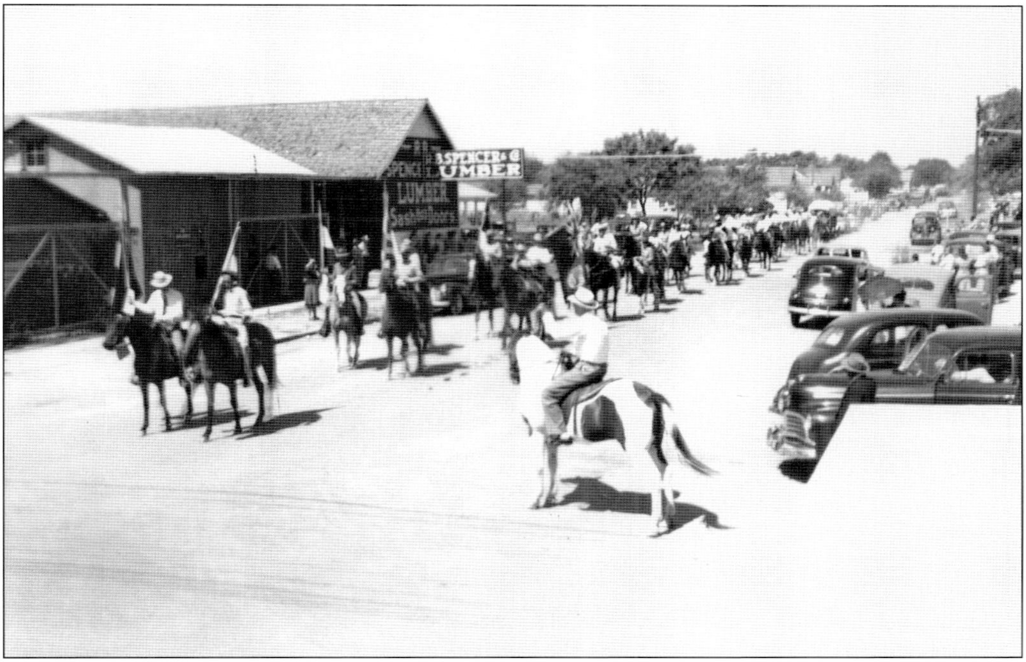

This 1940s parade is moving south down Avenue D in Haskell. Haskell County's ranching heritage is shown in the large number of horses in the parade. Spencer and Company Lumber is shown in the background. (Courtesy of Hess Hartsfield.)

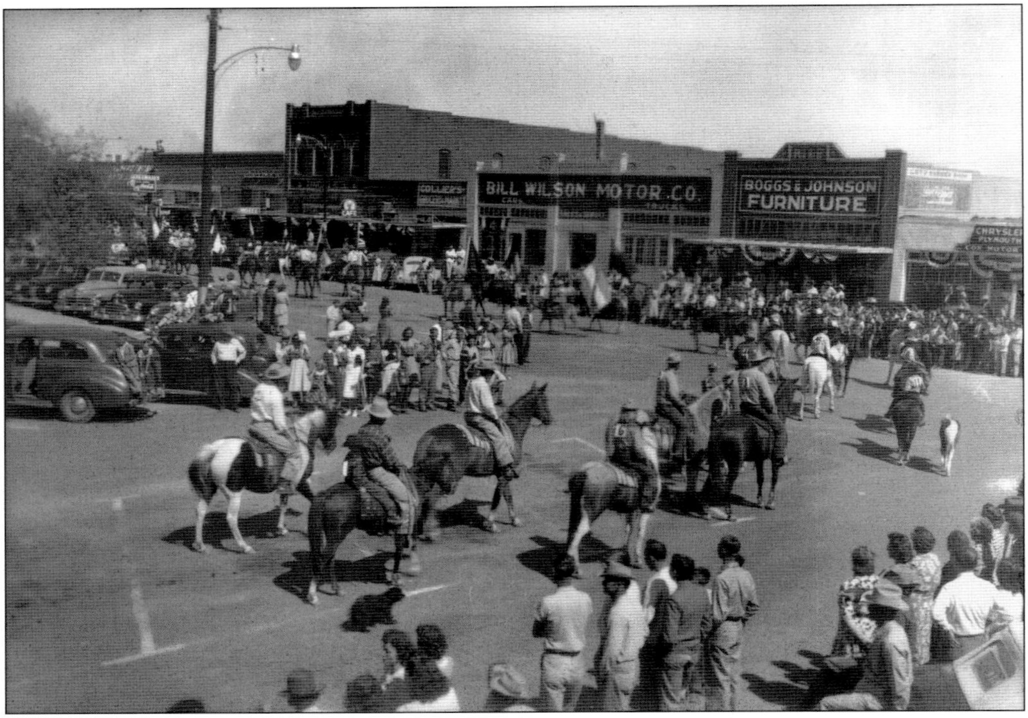

Riding clubs have long been a part of Haskell County history and always made a colorful addition to parades. The Haskell Sheriff's Posse club, with their trademark red shirts and Palomino horses, traveled to parades throughout West Texas. Unidentified riders in this parade photograph prepare to turn north onto Avenue D. Businesses in the background include Bill Wilson Motors and Boggs and Johnson Furniture. (Courtesy of Hess Hartsfield.)

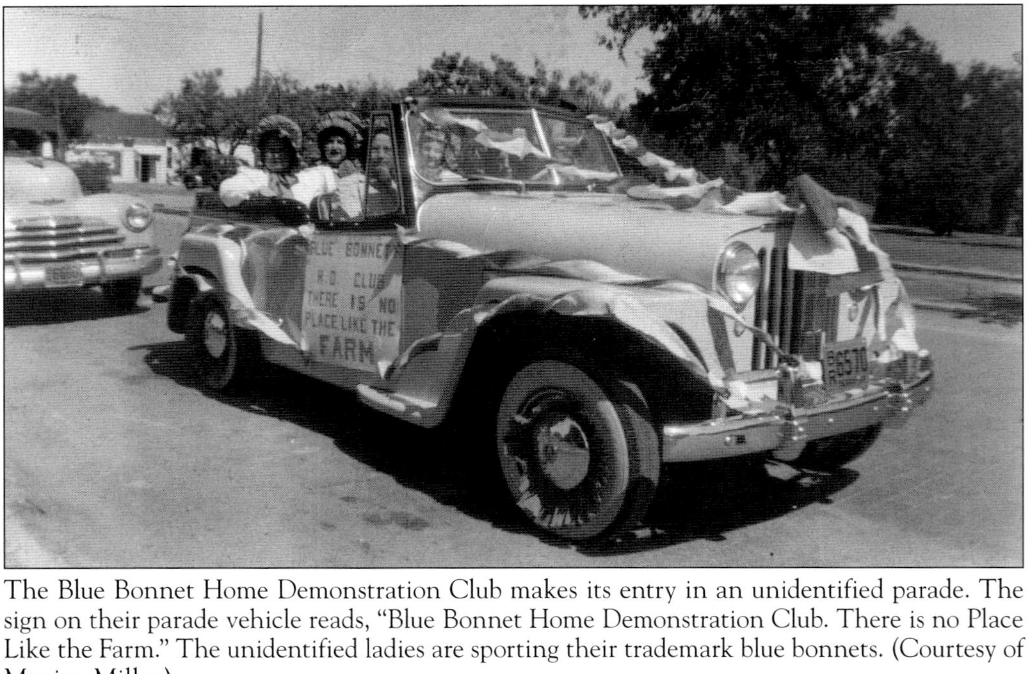

The Blue Bonnet Home Demonstration Club makes its entry in an unidentified parade. The sign on their parade vehicle reads, "Blue Bonnet Home Demonstration Club. There is no Place Like the Farm." The unidentified ladies are sporting their trademark blue bonnets. (Courtesy of Maxine Miller.)

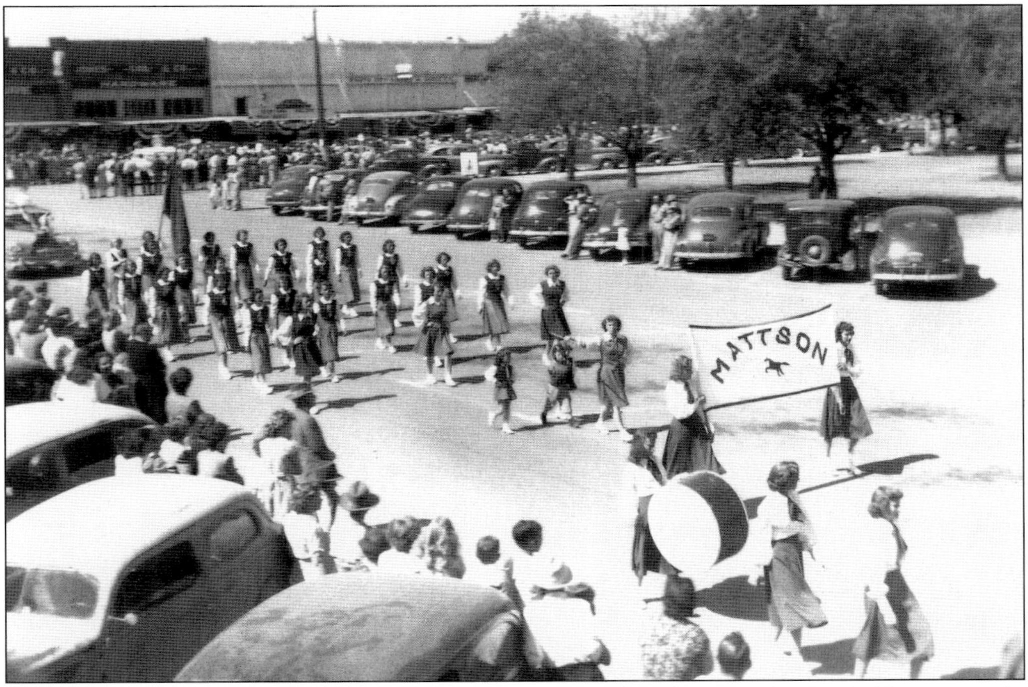

The Mattson High School Pep Squad is represented in this photograph of a 1940s-era parade in Haskell. Mattson Rural High School was formed when several country schools in the county consolidated. Their football team was known as the Mattson Mustangs. This view looks west down South First Street in Haskell. Banners decorate storefronts along Avenue E behind the parade. (Courtesy of Hess Hartsfield.)

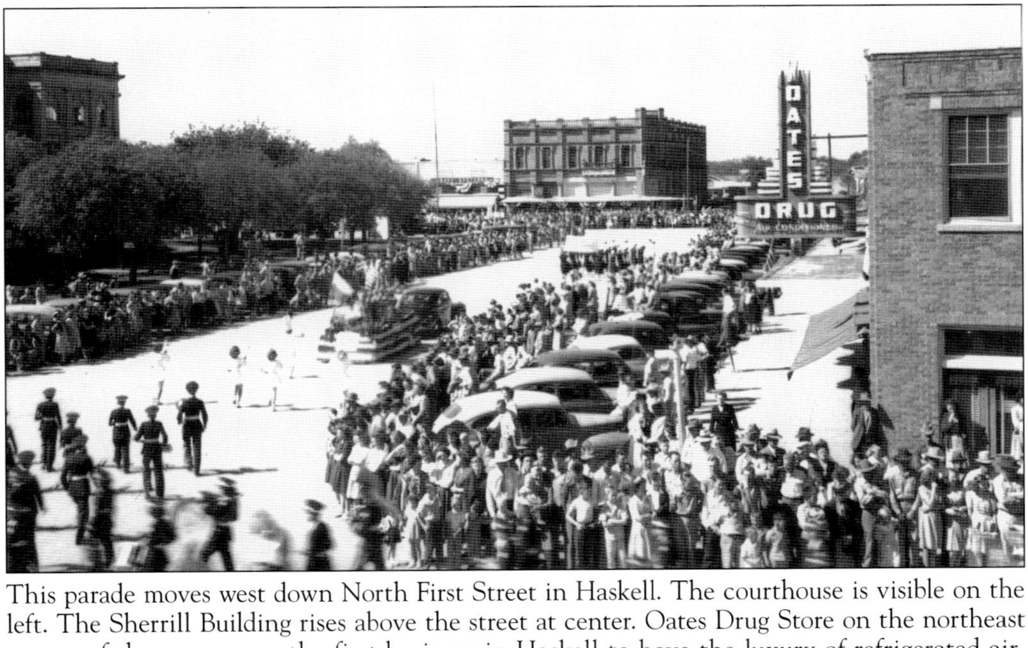

This parade moves west down North First Street in Haskell. The courthouse is visible on the left. The Sherrill Building rises above the street at center. Oates Drug Store on the northeast corner of the square was the first business in Haskell to have the luxury of refrigerated air-conditioning. Customers were served at one of the most modern fountains of the era. (Courtesy of Hess Hartsfield.)

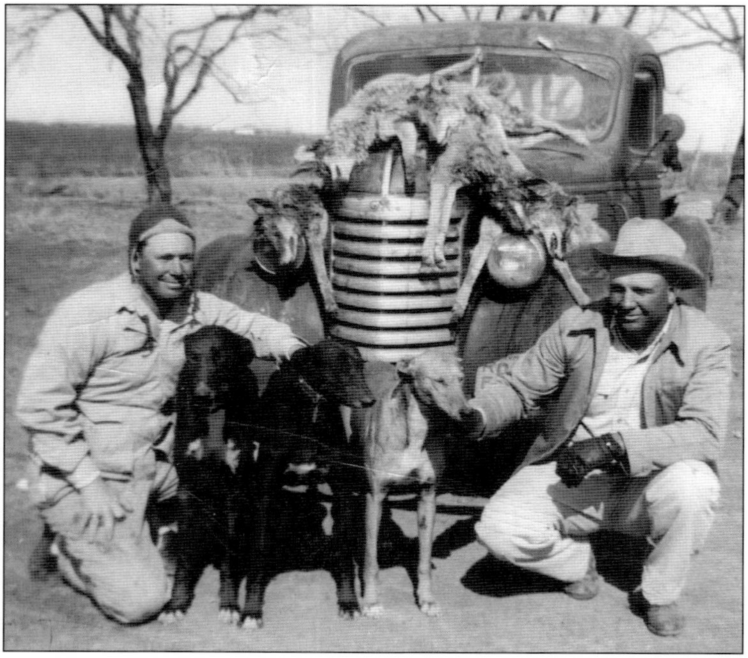

Bill Reeves (left), former Haskell County clerk and county auditor, poses with his unidentified hunting partner. The automobile was a *c.* 1936 model coupe stripped down for hunting. Hunting has long been a part of the heritage of local residents. In the 1990s, recreational hunting became a significant economic development. Visitors travel to Haskell County to hunt a variety of game, including geese and wild boar. (Courtesy of Doris Reeves.)

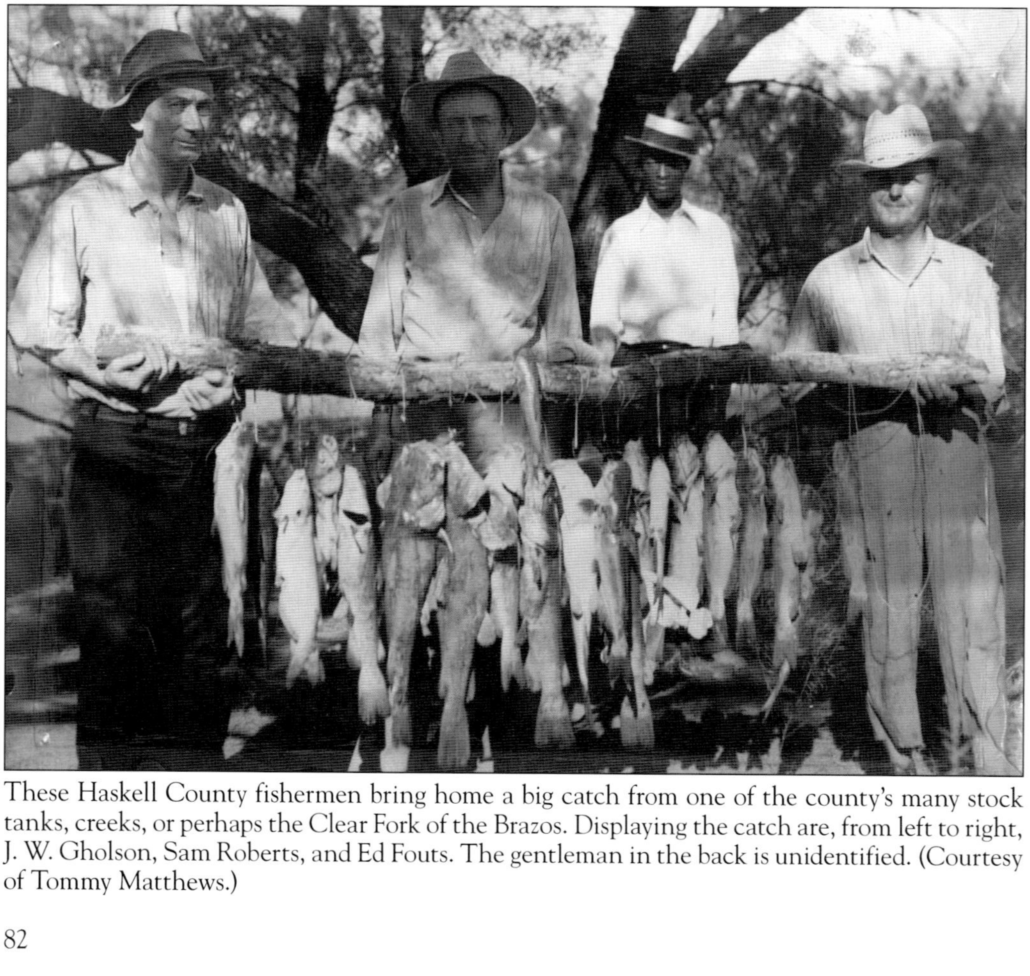

These Haskell County fishermen bring home a big catch from one of the county's many stock tanks, creeks, or perhaps the Clear Fork of the Brazos. Displaying the catch are, from left to right, J. W. Gholson, Sam Roberts, and Ed Fouts. The gentleman in the back is unidentified. (Courtesy of Tommy Matthews.)

Six

SACRED SCENES

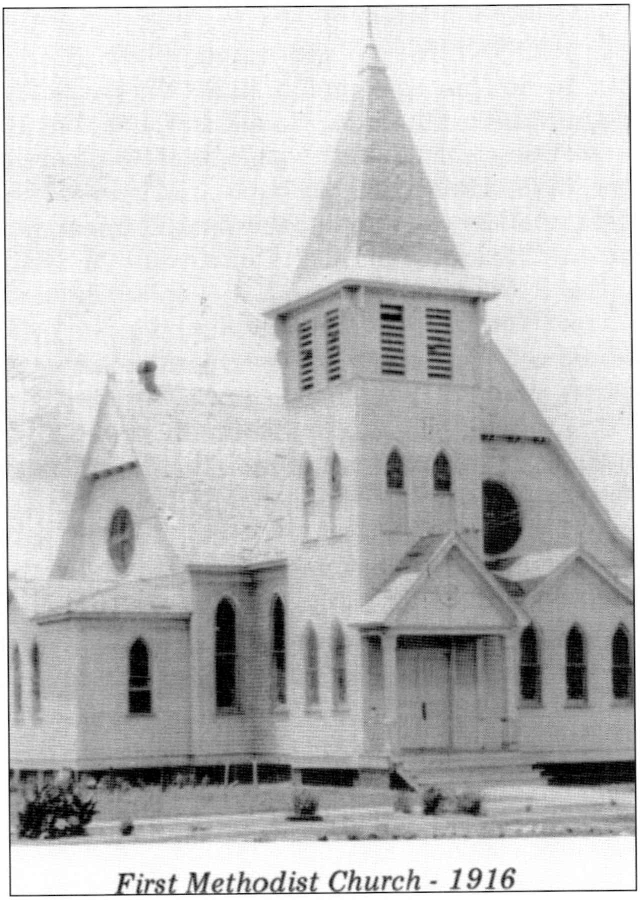

The First Methodist Church of Rule was organized in 1902 by Rev. I. L. Mills, onetime pastor of Pinkerton Methodist Church. Worship services were held in a school building until the purchase of the lot on Union Avenue. Services here were held in a tabernacle for a time. The first building, seen in this 1916 photograph, was completed in 1908. (Courtesy of Myrtle Kutch.)

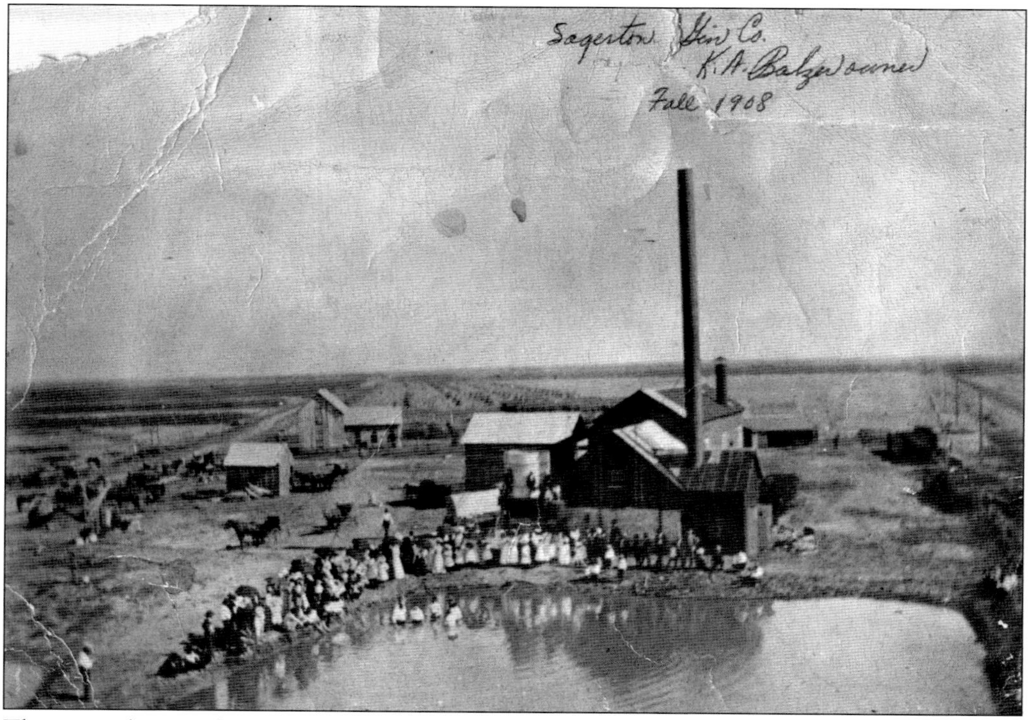

This scene depicts a baptismal service in the fall of 1908 by members of the First Baptist Church of Sagerton. The tank was adjacent to a gin north of Sagerton owned by K. A. Balzer. The congregation's first Sunday school had been organized in July of that year. (Courtesy of Joyce LeFevre.)

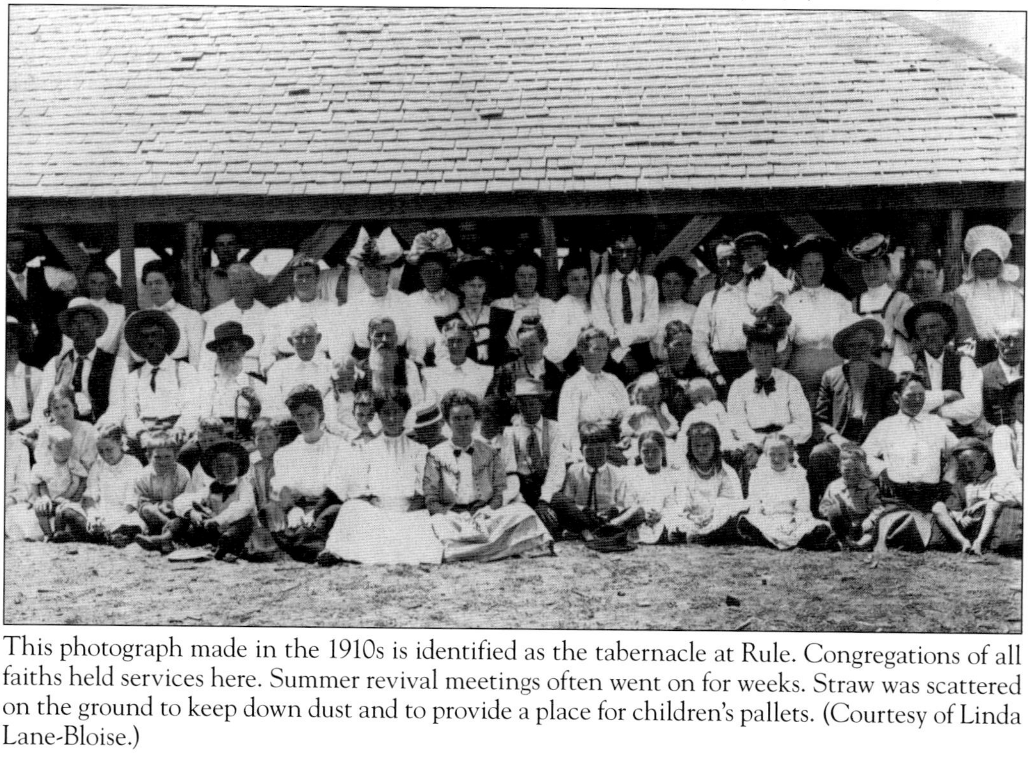

This photograph made in the 1910s is identified as the tabernacle at Rule. Congregations of all faiths held services here. Summer revival meetings often went on for weeks. Straw was scattered on the ground to keep down dust and to provide a place for children's pallets. (Courtesy of Linda Lane-Bloise.)

A Methodist church was organized at Marcy and moved in 1906 to Rochester when the railroad came through. The big event each year was a summer revival. All denominations attended, coming by foot, wagon, buggy, and automobile. A tornado damaged the church building in April 1907. The Rochester First Methodist Church seen in this 1919 photograph of Tempie Bell Alvis was completed in 1917. (Courtesy of Jimmy Alvis.)

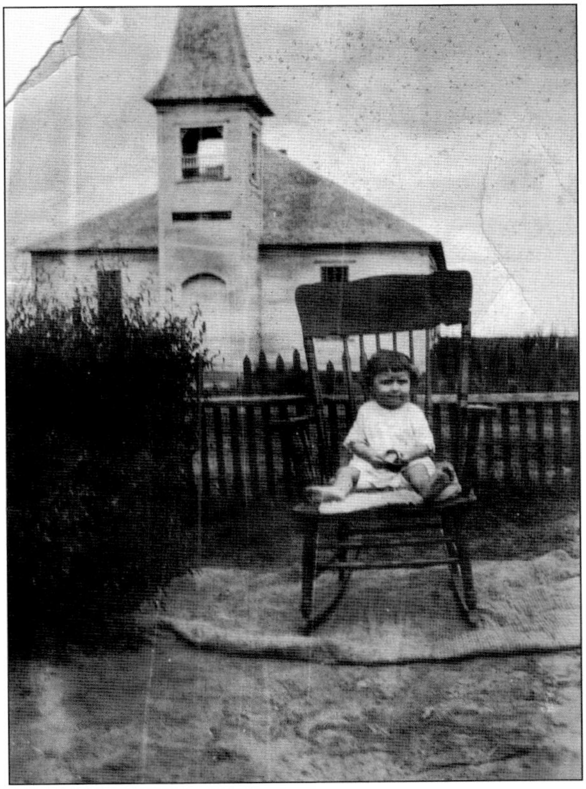

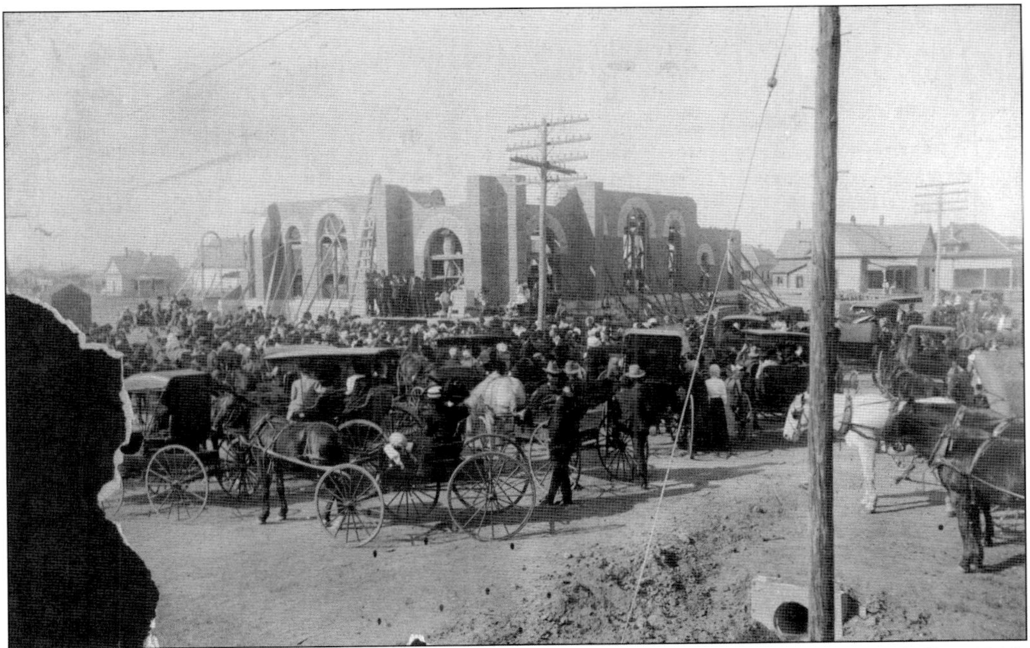

The first church organized in Haskell County was the First Methodist Church of Haskell in 1885. Members met in homes until a building was completed about 1890. Lumber was hauled by wagon from Abilene. In 1910, the present building was begun. It is pictured here, under construction, during a dedication ceremony. (Courtesy of Wallace Cox.)

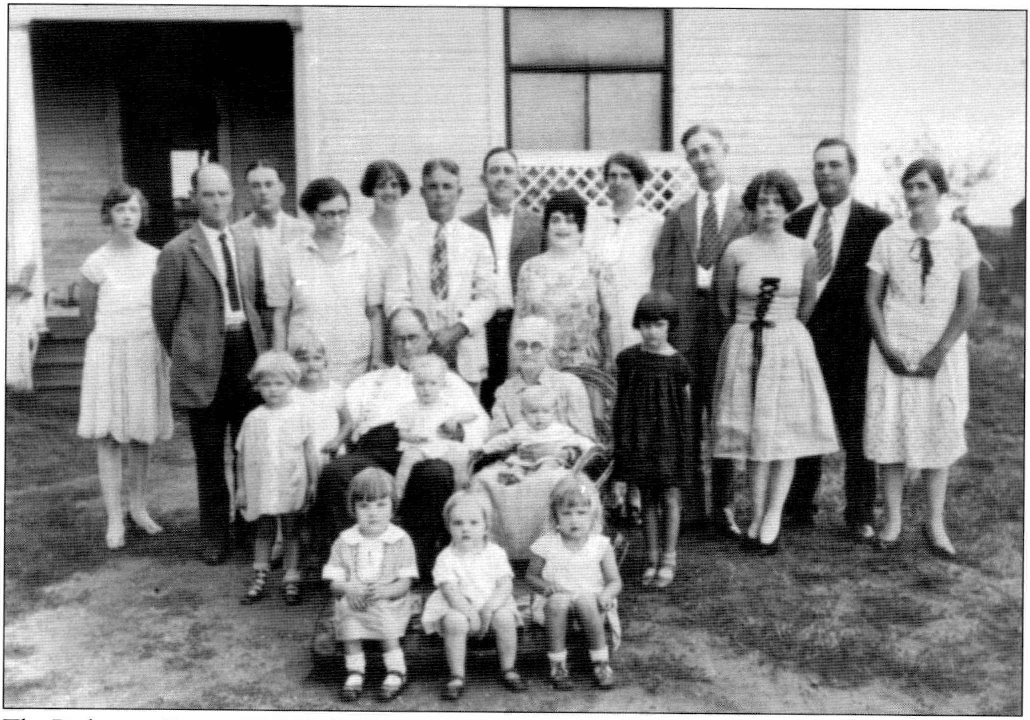

The Pinkerton Baptist Church, between Haskell and Rule, organized in 1891 through an evangelist who often preached to cowboys under the trees. The church was named Prairie Dale in the beginning. Pinkerton had the Pinkerton First Methodist Church, a grocery store, post office, blacksmith, doctor, two gins, and a school. The community of Prairie View, also known as Wild Horse Prairie, was later named for John F. Pinkerton, whose family is pictured here. (Courtesy of Haskell County Historical and Genealogical Society.)

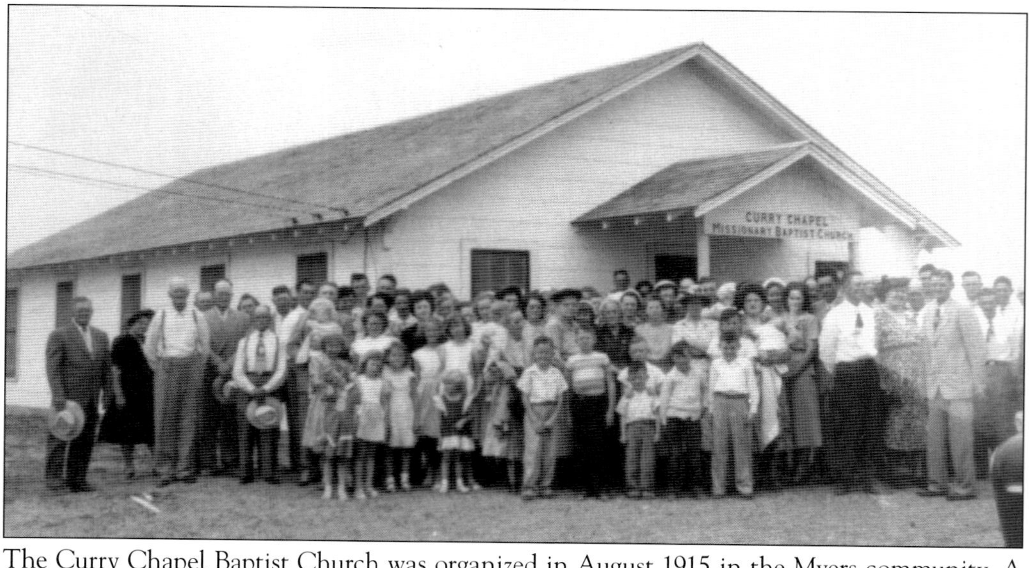

The Curry Chapel Baptist Church was organized in August 1915 in the Myers community. A one-room building was constructed on land donated by I. R. Grindstaff. J. W. Reed was the first pastor. Summer revivals were preached in a brush arbor near the building. (Courtesy of Haskell County Historical and Genealogical Society.)

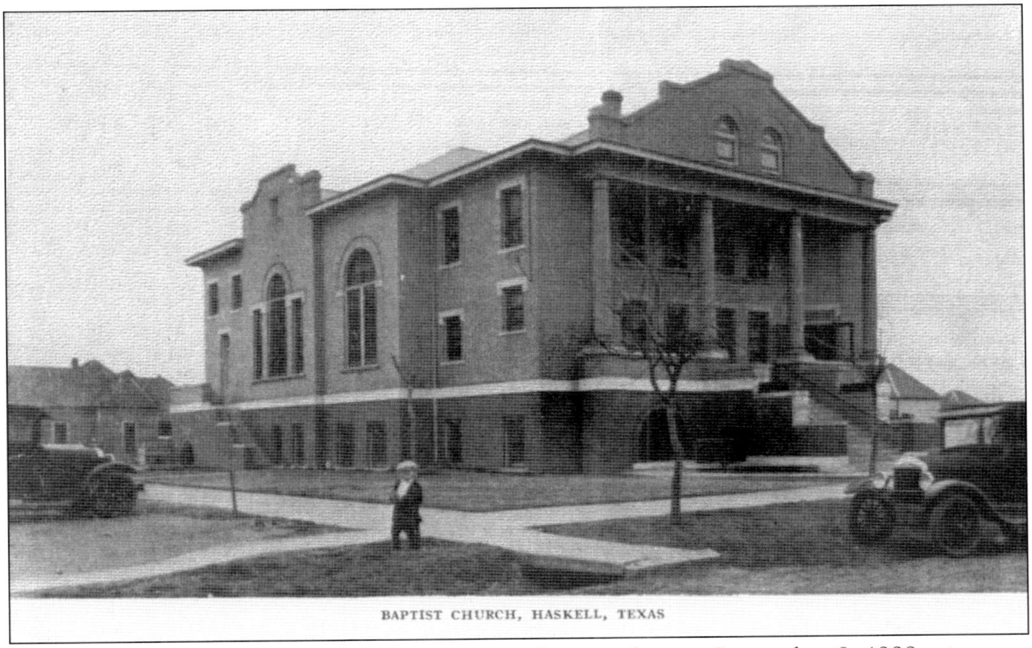

In 1885, Baptists near Haskell held services in the courthouse. September 8, 1888, nineteen charter members gathered in a schoolhouse on the south side of town to organize the First Baptist Church of Haskell. S. H. Blair was the first pastor. In 1892, the church dedicated a new building three blocks north of the square. Increased membership called for a larger brick building, pictured here, completed in 1915. (Courtesy of Hess Hartsfield.)

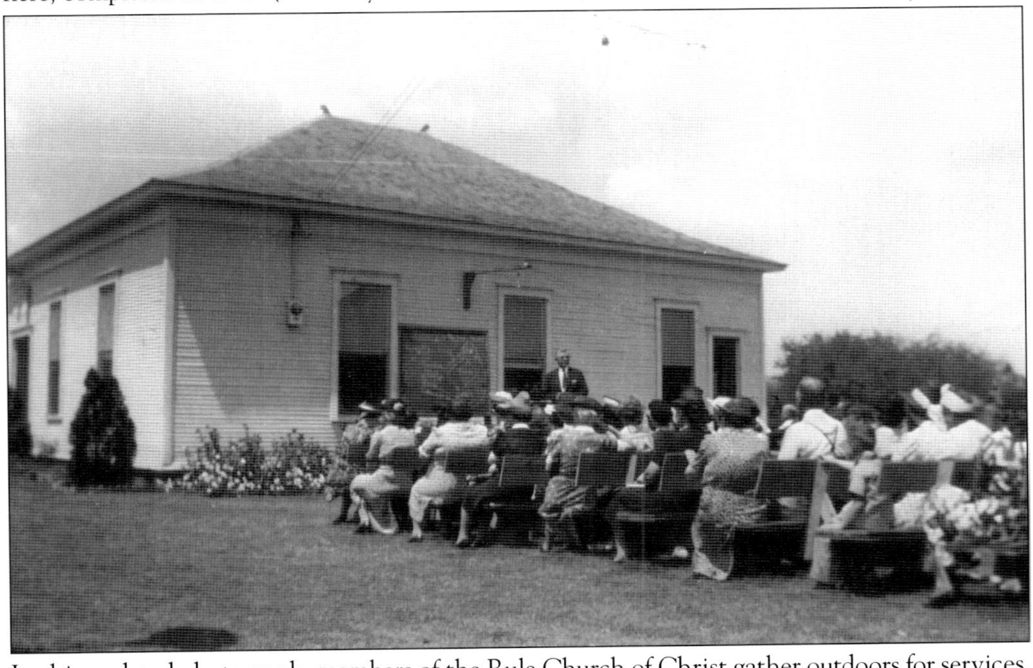

In this undated photograph, members of the Rule Church of Christ gather outdoors for services, a common practice in days before air-conditioning. The church was organized very early in the history of Rule. In 1915, its first church building was erected on the site of the church's present Union Avenue location. (Courtesy of John Greeson.)

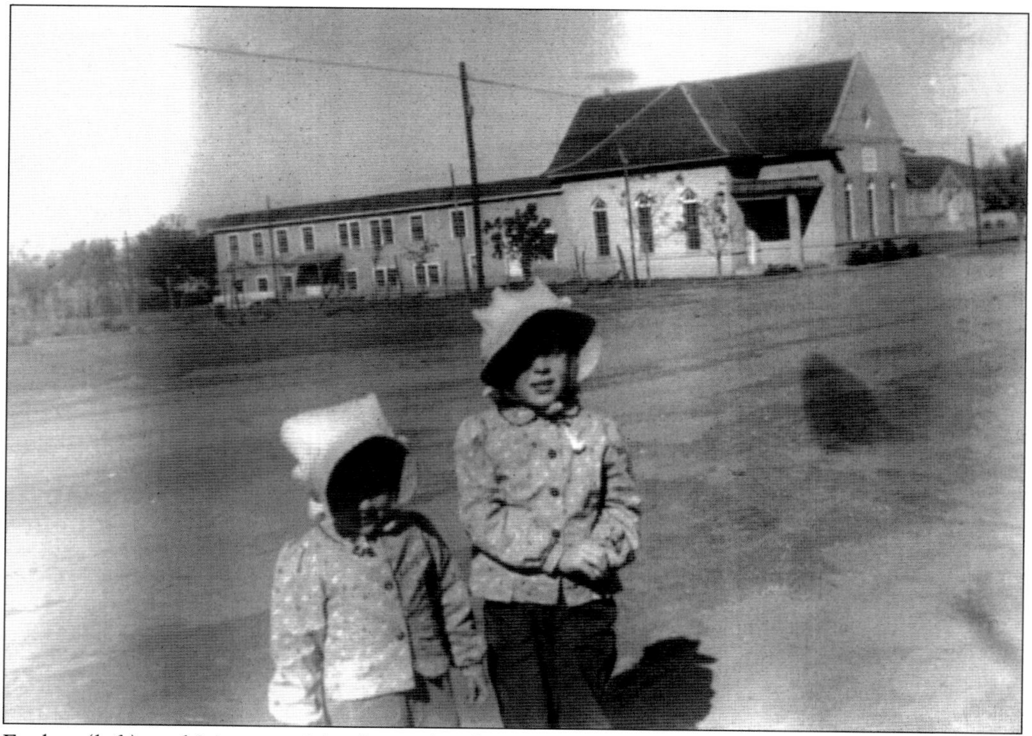

Evelyn (left) and Margaret Meadows, daughters of pastor Cecil Meadows, pose in this 1950s photograph of Rochester First Baptist Church. The congregation was organized at Marcy in 1899. It moved to Rochester in 1906, first locating on the north side of town. The church moved to this Main Street location in 1911. The building shown here was replaced in 1957. The photograph looks west from the parsonage on Main Street. (Courtesy of Evelyn Meadows McAnelly.)

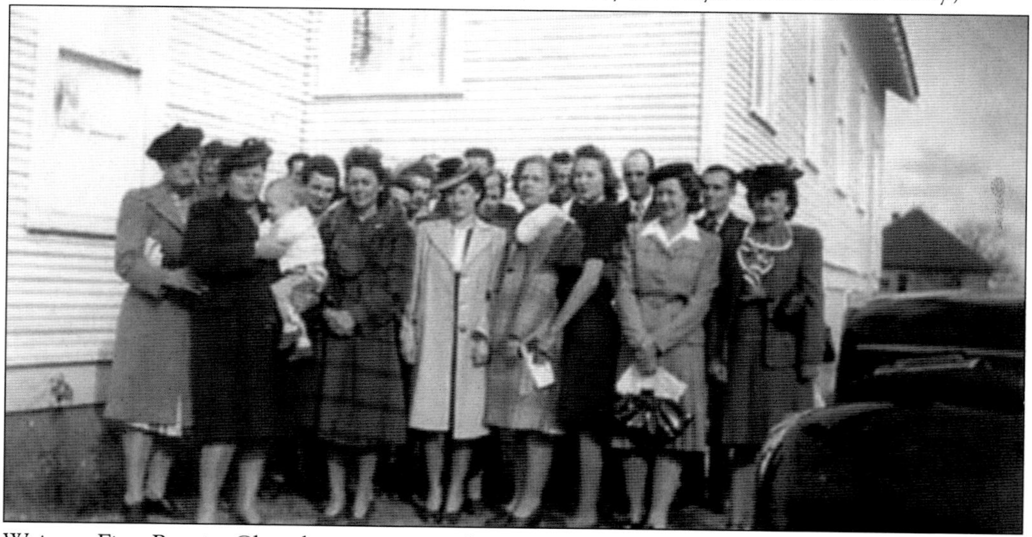

Weinert First Baptist Church was organized in August 1908. Services were held in the Weinert schoolhouse and in the Union Hall. About 1910, the Weinert Presbyterian Church building was purchased, then a new building was constructed in 1929. For a time, baptisms took place in area stock tanks and creeks. In this 1950s photograph, members of the Weinert First Baptist Church stand next to their building. (Courtesy of Mary Murphy.)

Following the 1937 formation of Paint Creek High School from among five rural schools, Methodist congregations at Ketron Chapel and Morris Chapel joined together to organize Paint Creek Methodist Church near the new school. The Morris Chapel building was moved to the new location and became the sanctuary. Lumber from Rose School was used to build Sunday school rooms. The building was finished with native rock. (Courtesy of Susan Turner.)

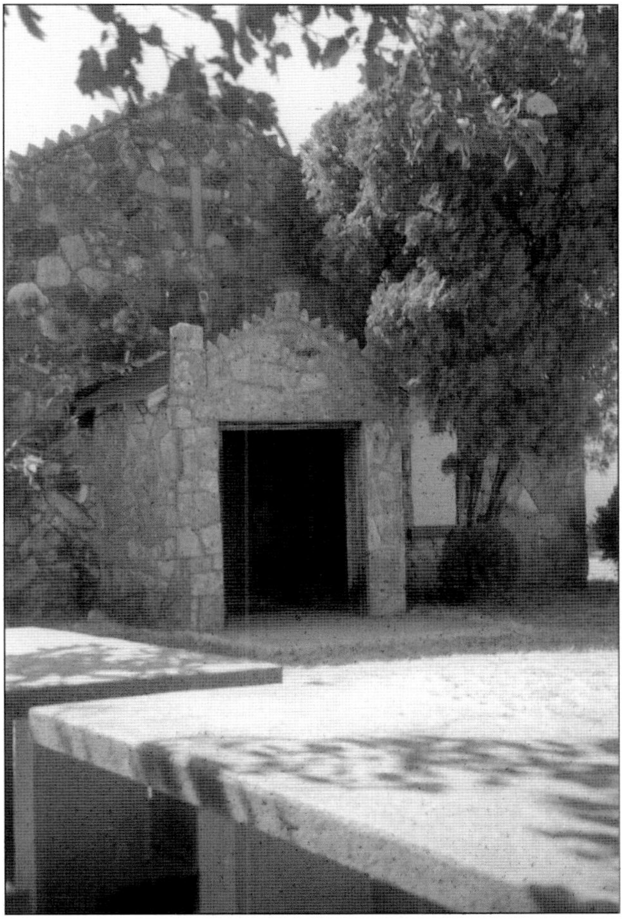

In 1905, families of the Lutheran faith began meeting in the Tanner Paint schoolhouse. This congregation became known as St. Paul's Lutheran Church. Zion Lutheran Church organized in 1906, with first services held in members' homes. These congregations merged in 1967 to form Faith Lutheran Church. (Courtesy of Dorothy Toney.)

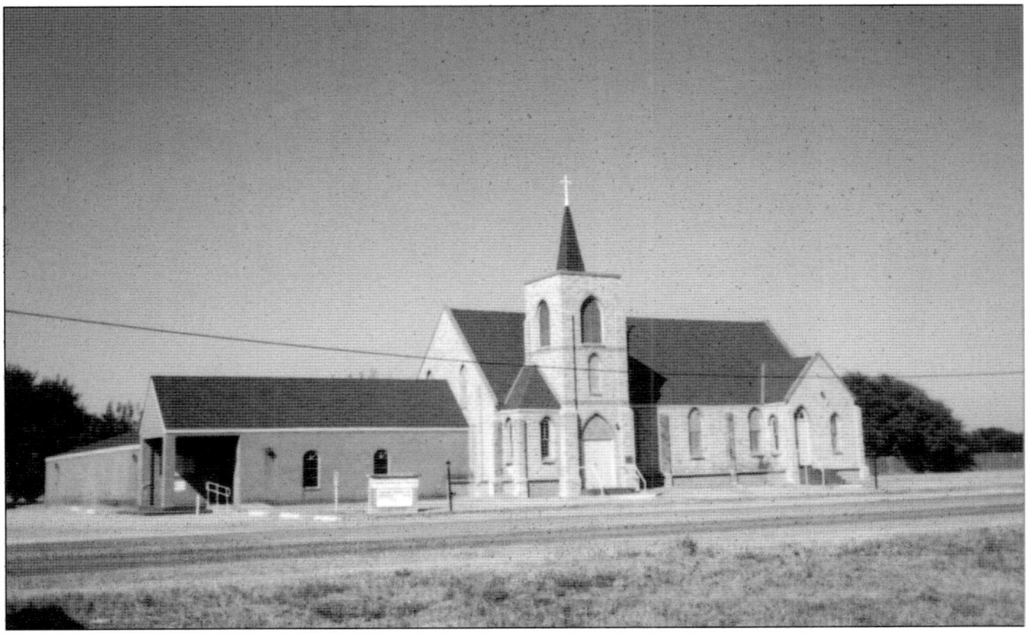

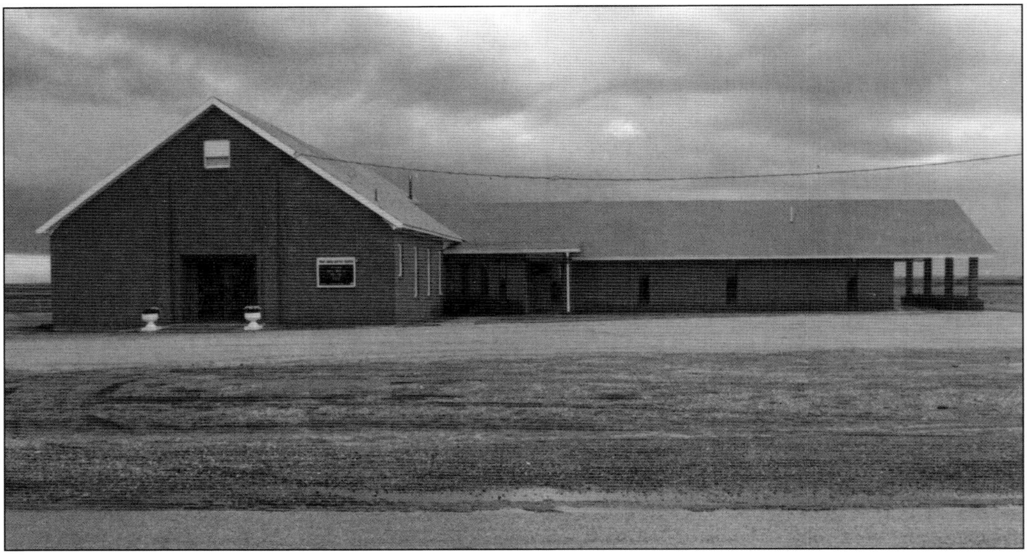

Paint Creek Baptist Church organized south of the tributary of the Brazos Clear Fork called Paint Creek in 1890. The church reorganized in 1901 and met in Curtis Chapel. In 1917, the location changed and the name became Post Baptist Church. Post later consolidated with Howard Baptist Church, organized in 1902. Howard and Post combined to form Paint Creek Baptist Church near the Paint Creek School in 1938. (Courtesy of Ruby Middlebrook.)

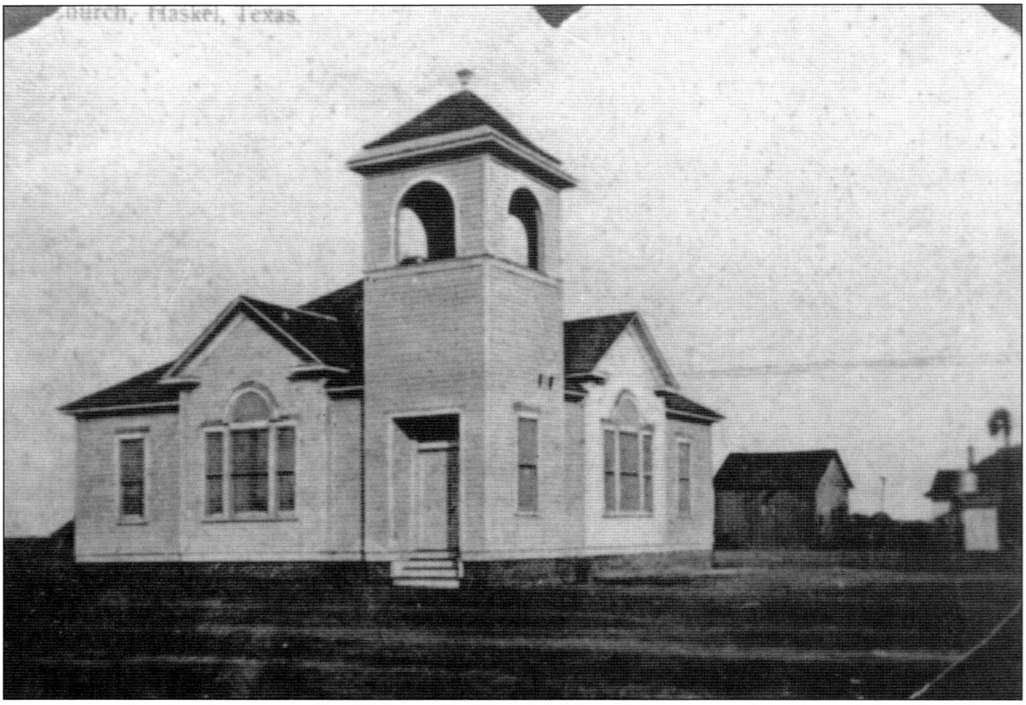

The Haskell Church of Christ was organized in January 1888. The church was reorganized in 1890 when the county population increased. A building was constructed around this time with lumber hauled from Abilene. The church began holding singing conventions about 1965. Attendees from throughout the United States stay in Haskell County homes during the weeklong schools. (Courtesy of Haskell County Historical and Genealogical Society.)

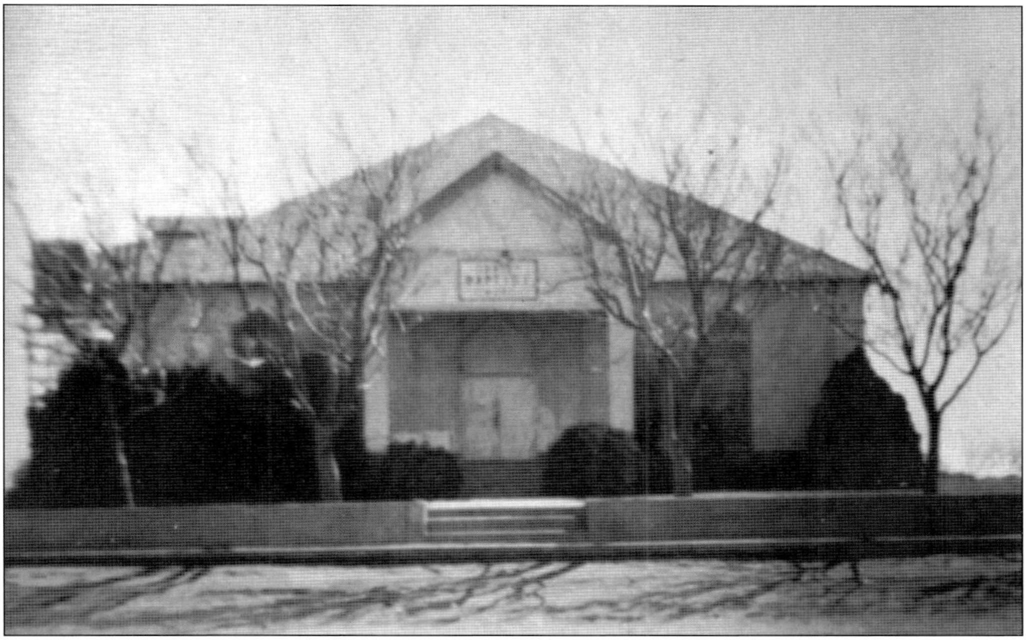

Carney (O'Brien) was established in 1905. Soon after, O'Brien First Baptist Church organized. The congregation built a church, pictured here, at Park Avenue and Seventh Street. A new building was dedicated in 1957 at the corner of Grand Central Avenue and Farm Road 2229, the former site of a stone building owned in 1908 by founder T. G. Carney. The steps and sidewalk of the Park Avenue building are still visible. (Courtesy of Thelma Cox Burt.)

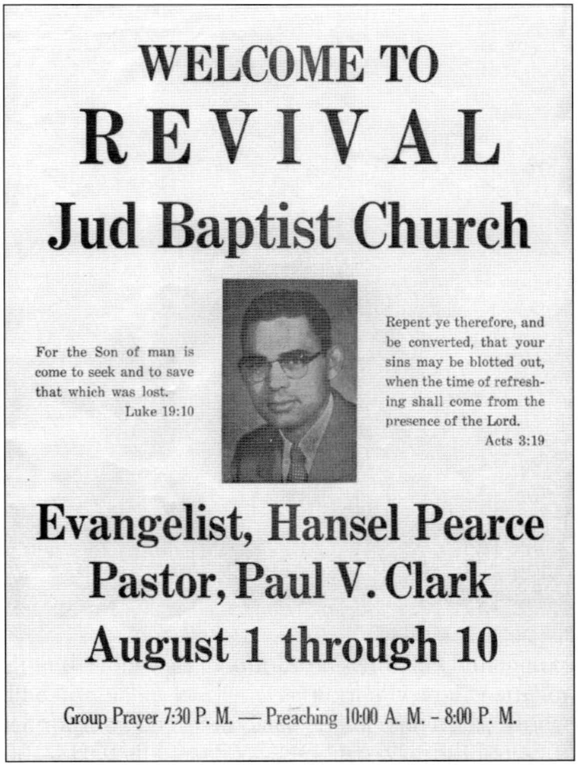

Jud, Texas, established near the Salt Fork of the Brazos River in 1895, had both Methodist and Baptist congregations. There was a tabernacle at Jud where summer revivals were held. This undated flyer advertises revival services at Jud Baptist Church. Services were held in the Jud Baptist Church until 1969. Br. Randolph Wilson was the last pastor to serve the Jud congregation. (Courtesy of Village Primitive Antique Store.)

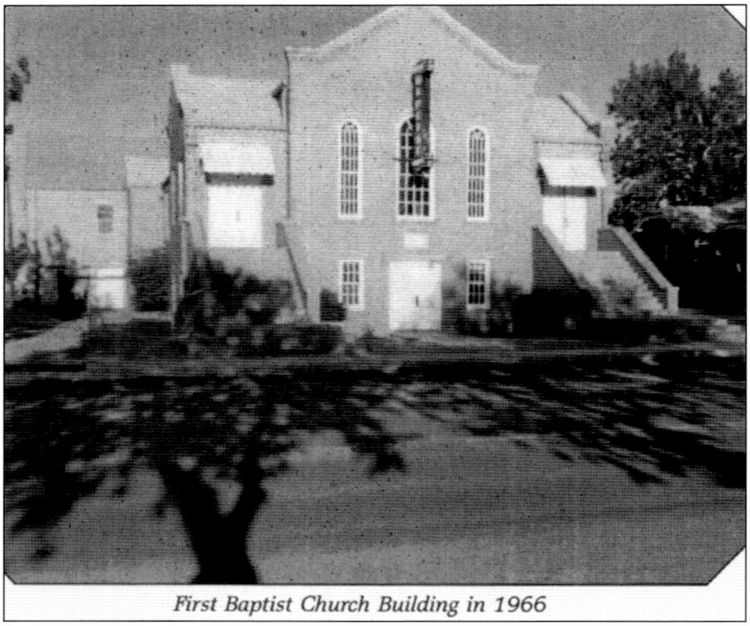

First Baptist Church of Rule was organized in a schoolhouse in the southwest part of Rule. The congregation worshipped in the First Christian Church building for a time. The first church building constructed for the Baptist congregation was a wooden frame building on Union Avenue. In 1925, members moved into this brick building on Union Avenue. (Courtesy of Rule First Baptist Church.)

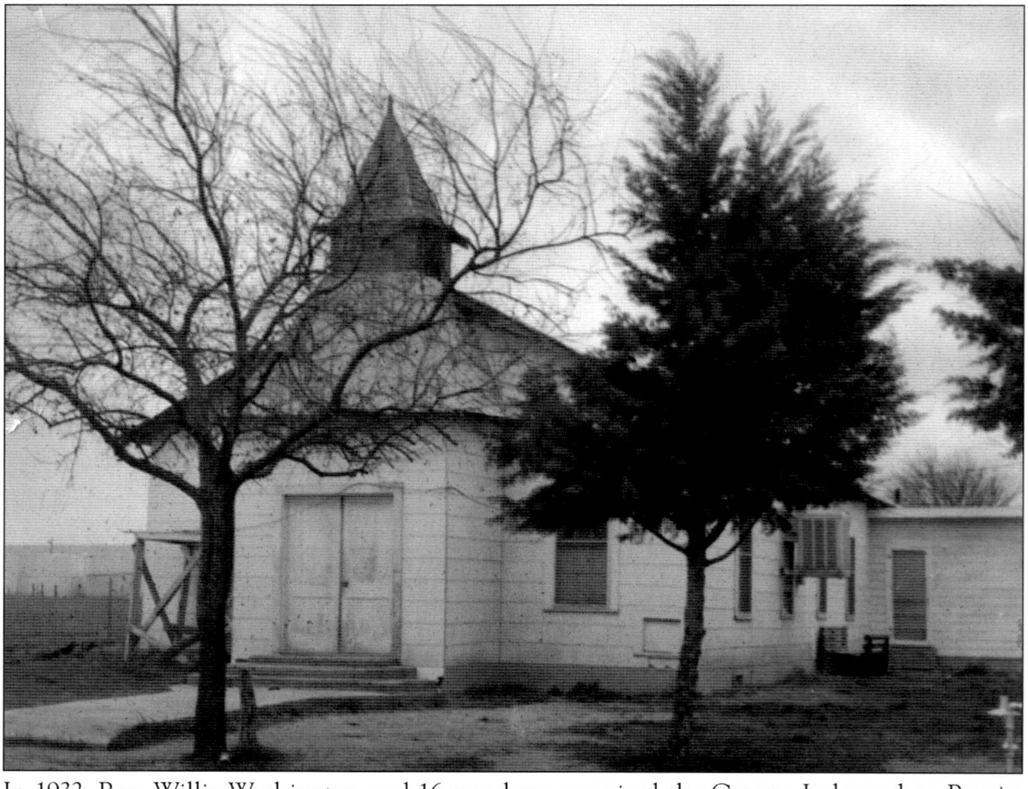

In 1932, Rev. Willie Washington and 16 members organized the Greater Independent Baptist Church in a house south of Haskell. More members soon joined. Later, members tore this building down and built the small church pictured here at 1500 North B Street. Rev. J. L. Maxwell was pastor. Under the pastorate of Rev. F. E. Chenault, the church relocated to its present site at 301 North Third Street. (Courtesy of May Lou Yelldell.)

Seven

School Days

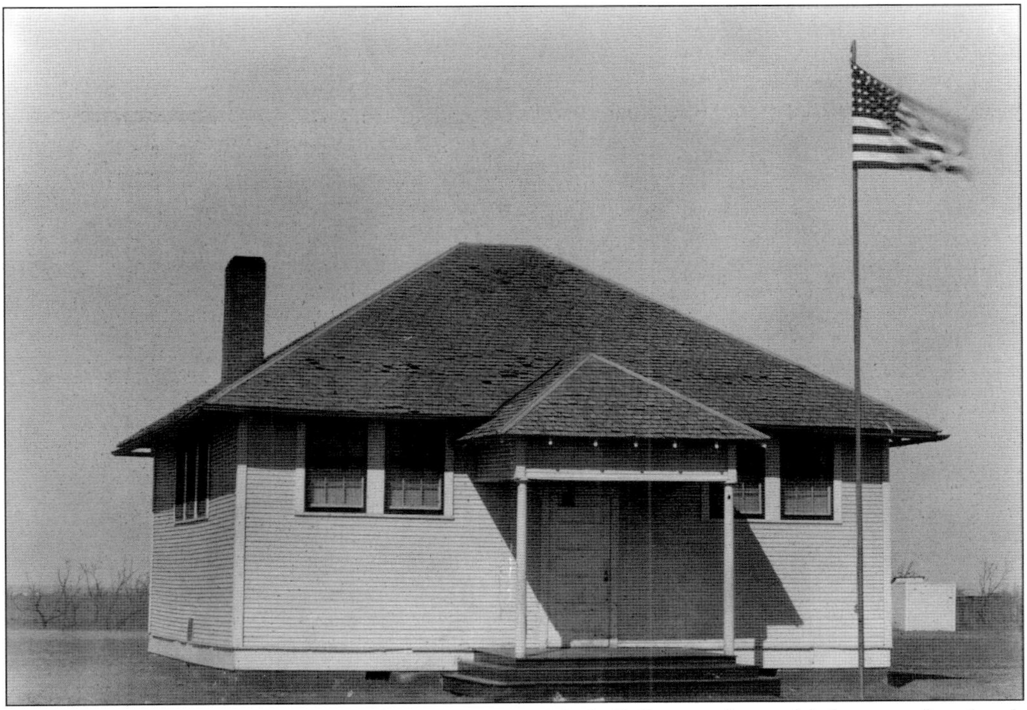

William Ward sold land in the Ward community to Haskell County for establishment of a school. The site was approximately 13 miles southwest of Haskell. In 1889, the building was moved to a new site on land given by A. R. Davis. In 1890, forty-one students enrolled. The last Ward School, built in 1921, was 2.5 miles northeast of Stamford. In 1939, Ward contracted its students to Paint Creek Rural School. (Courtesy of Bonnie Adkins Fouts.)

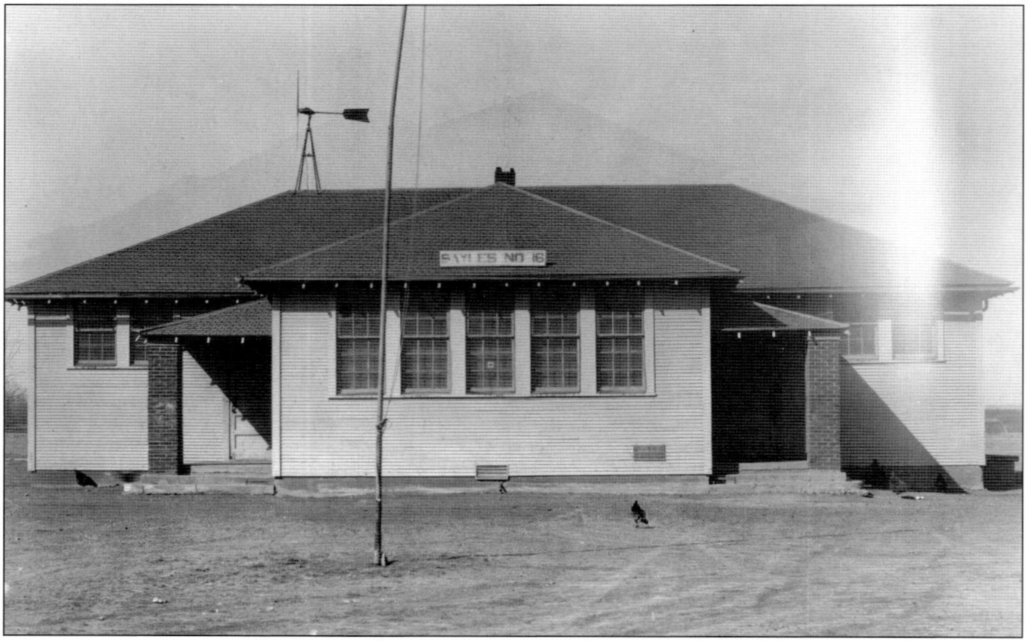

In 1904, A. H. Storrs deeded land in the southern part of Haskell County to the Sayles community for a school. In 1907, the schoolhouse was moved to a more central location. As was typical, school did not start until November to allow children to pick cotton. Sayles consolidated with Haskell in 1949. (Courtesy of Bonnie Adkins Fouts.)

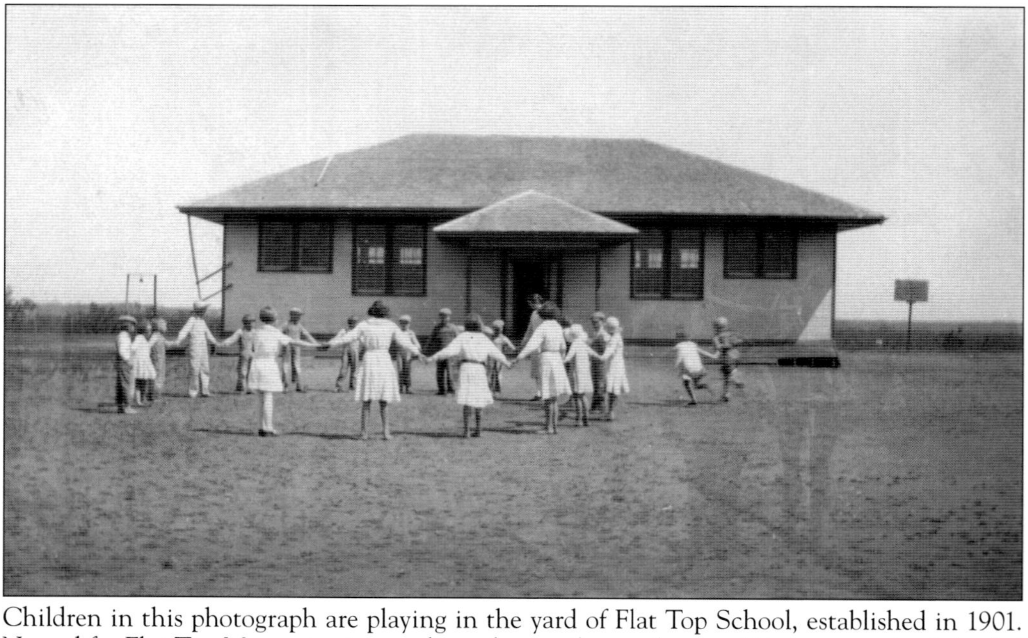

Children in this photograph are playing in the yard of Flat Top School, established in 1901. Named for Flat Top Mountain, it was about three miles southwest of Sagerton on land deeded by L. W. and R. A. Simpson. The school was called Leavitt, after the Leavitt Post Office, but the legal name was Flat Top. The schoolyard has a basketball goal and well. The school consolidated with Sagerton in 1946. (Courtesy of Bonnie Adkins Fouts.)

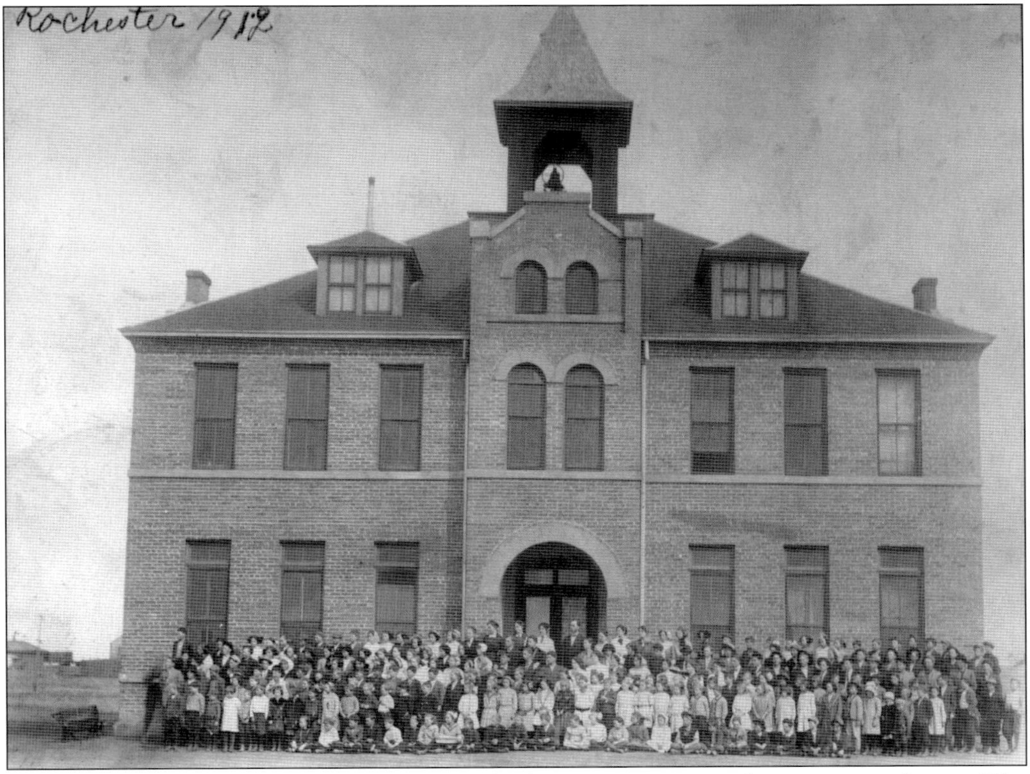

Rochester School was established in 1906. The first campus was in the west part of town. The building was heavily damaged by wind, and the remaining 1906 term and the 1907 term were in the Rochester First Methodist Church building. A four-room school was erected in the east part of town. This photograph of the brick building on Main Street was made in 1912. (Courtesy of Rochester Heritage Museum.)

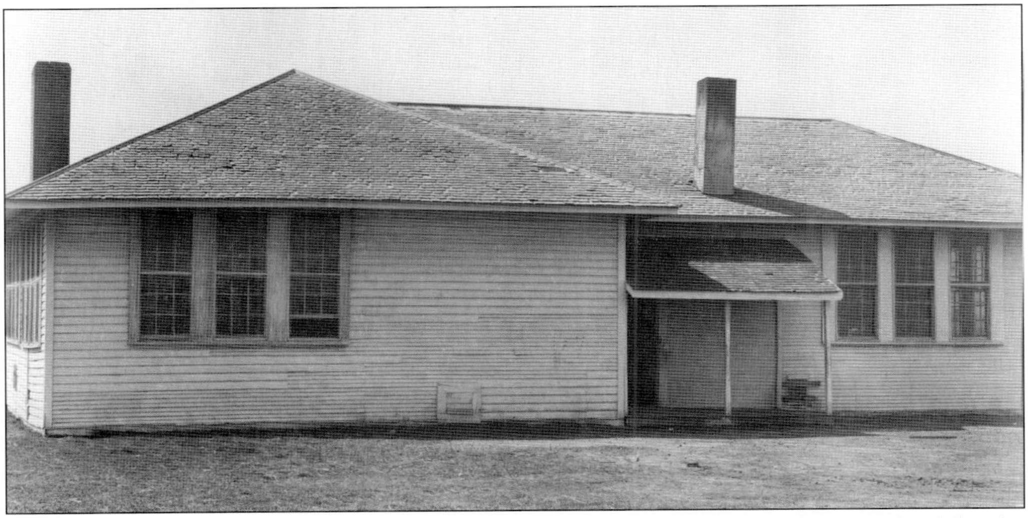

Dennis Chapel was named for the family of J. R. and Massie Dennis, who gave land for the school in 1906. A new building, costing $1,200, was built in 1912. Dennis Chapel was located southeast of O'Brien. Students there consolidated with Weinert in 1937. (Courtesy of Bonnie Adkins Fouts.)

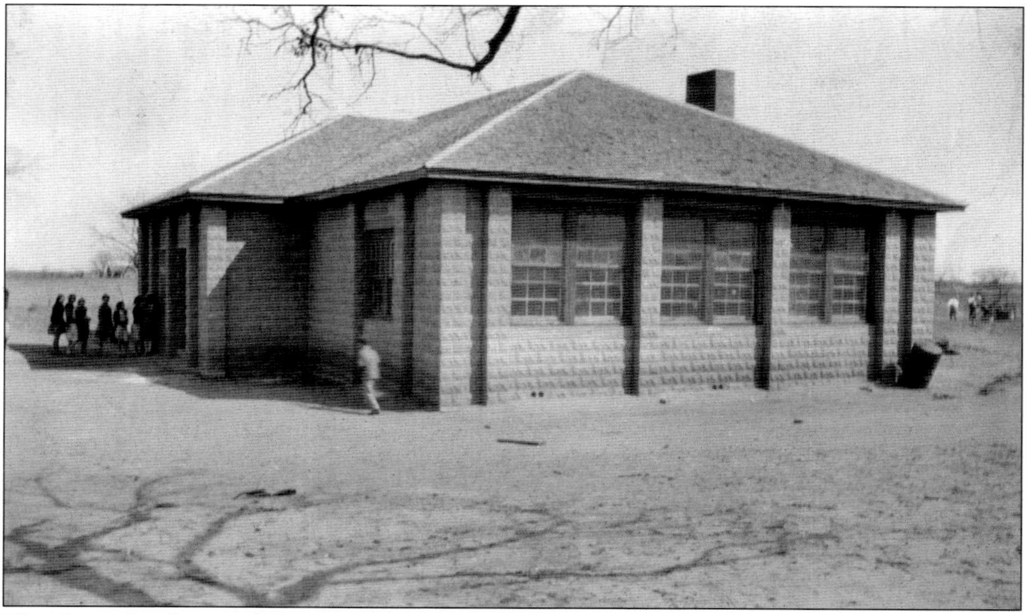

The first school named Hutto was established about 1901 on land given by Joe McReynolds. In 1902, another building 2.5 miles south of the original school was constructed on land given by H. C. Dozier. This school burned in 1917. A new school, above, was constructed of concrete blocks. Hutto consolidated with Carney Rural School in O'Brien in 1944. (Courtesy of Bonnie Adkins Fouts.)

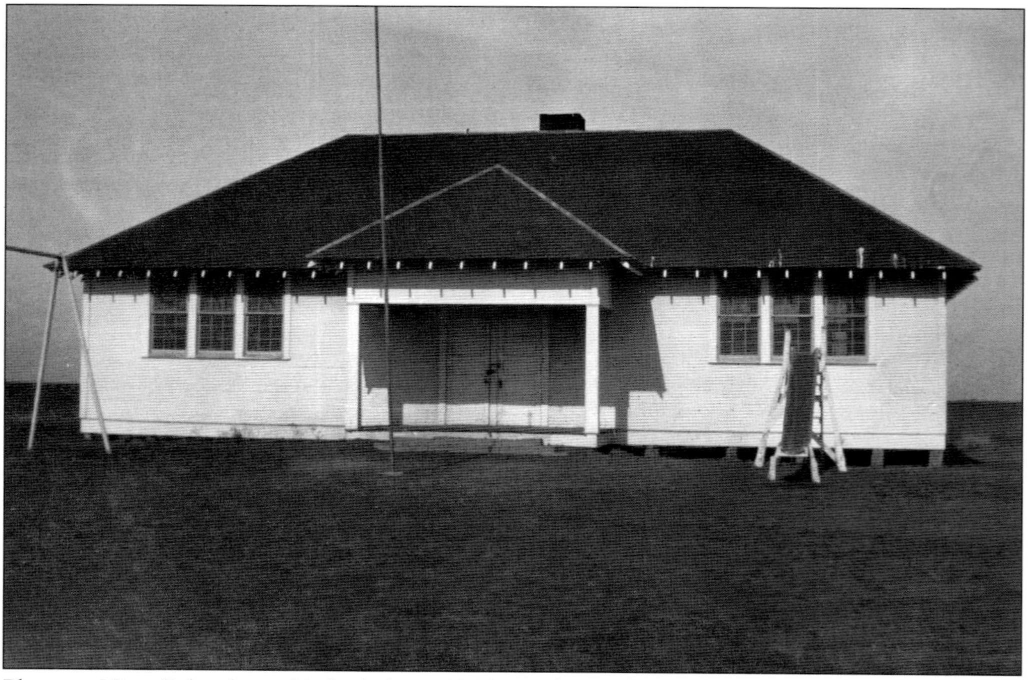

Pleasant View School, established about 1906, was located in northeastern Haskell County on land once owned by J. R. Griffith. In 1917, a bond election was held to build a $2,500 building. In 1936, all students at Pleasant View School, pictured here, contracted to attend school in Weinert. (Courtesy of Bonnie Adkins Fouts.)

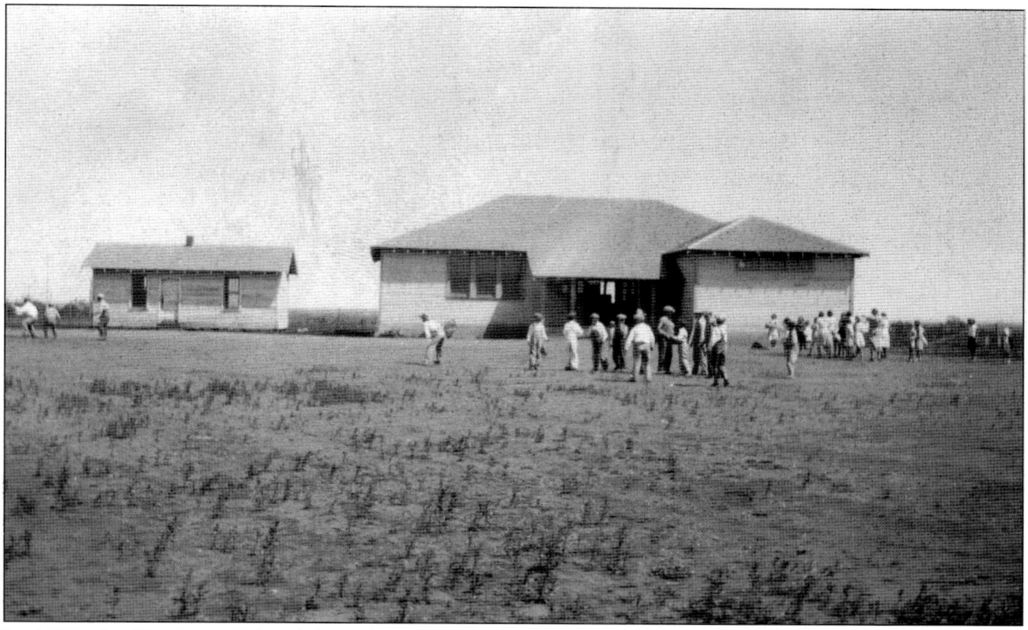

In 1907, the Grisham School, later known as Capron, was established in southern Haskell County. In 1925, the building was moved by mule teams 1.5 miles from the original site and renamed Bunker Hill, pictured here. In 1942, Bunker Hill students began contracting to Stamford. (Courtesy of Bonnie Adkins Fouts.)

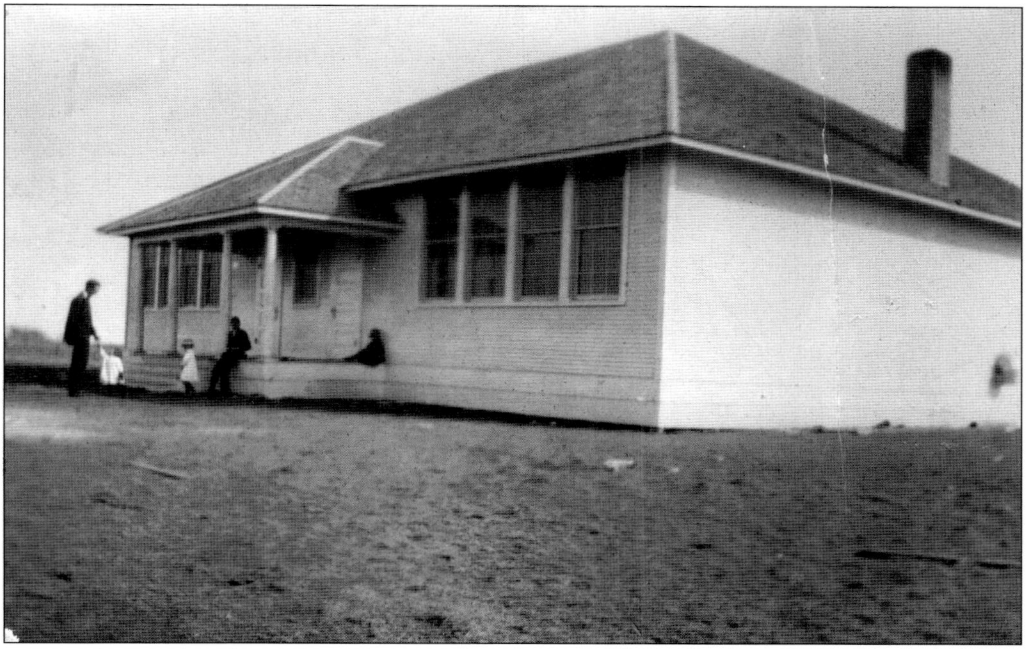

R. A. and Betty Cox donated land to build the Cook Springs School in 1905. In 1907, the building burned, and a second school was built. Cook Springs joined with Twiner and New Hope at a central location in 1915. G. W. May donated land for a Cook Springs School building, above, 3 miles north of Rule. (Courtesy of Bonnie Adkins Fouts.)

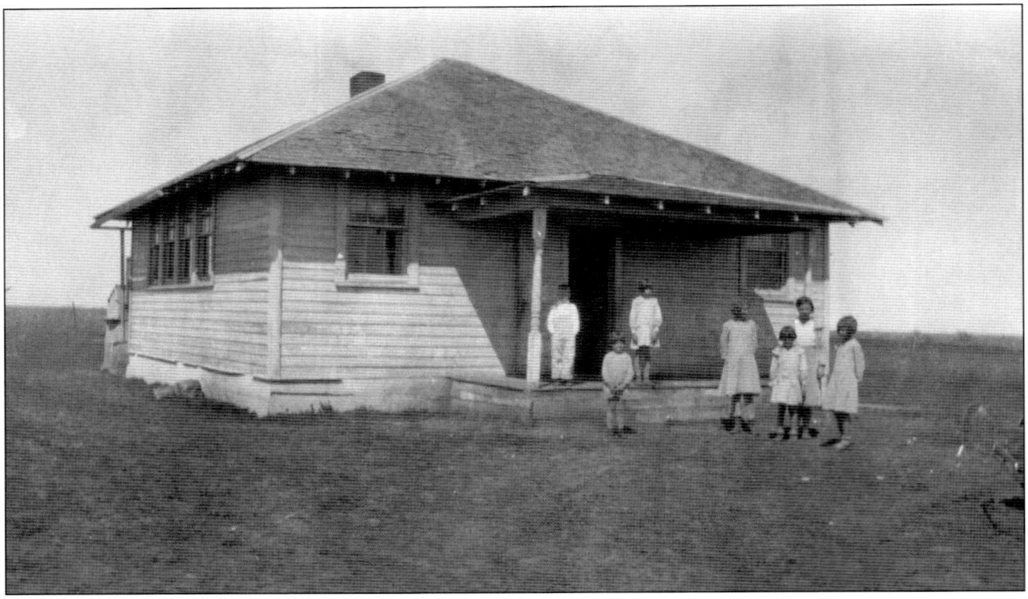

Hardy Grissom gave land to build a school in the Douglas community of southeastern Haskell County in 1909. Named Douglas, the school, pictured here, was established north of Scott's Crossing near what is now Lake Stamford. In 1921, Douglas and Baldwin (Kirkdale) consolidated, and the Douglas schoolhouse was moved north to the Haskell-Throckmorton highway. In the 1940s, students began attending Mattson or Paint Creek. (Courtesy of Bonnie Adkins Fouts.)

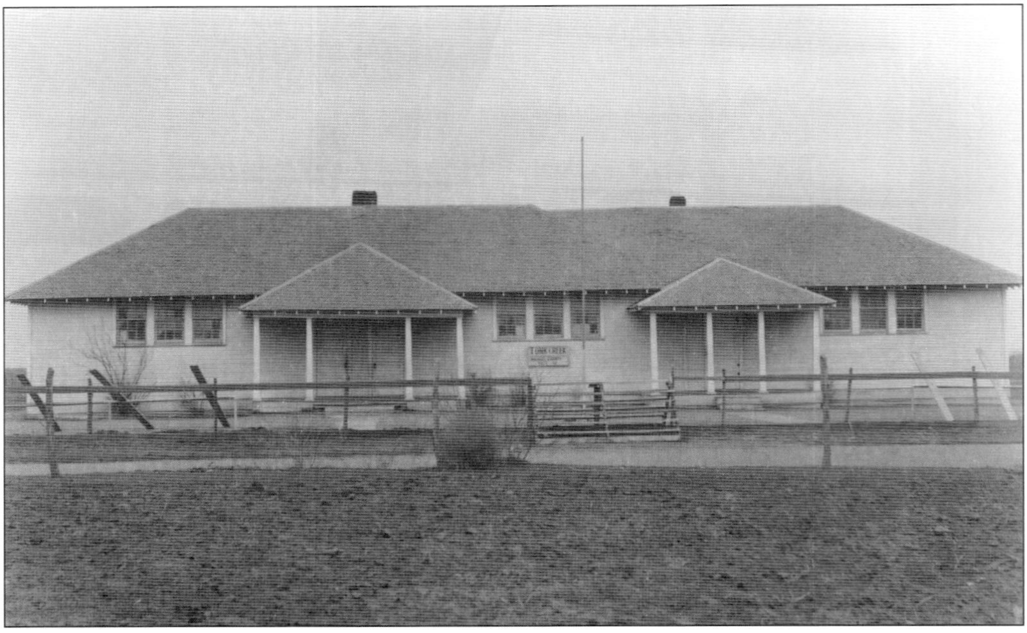

Tonk Creek School was built northwest of Rule in 1908 near the Stonewall County line. It was the only school in Haskell County west of the Brazos River. In the fall of 1940, Tonk Creek contracted students to Rule, then consolidated with Old Glory, in Stonewall County, in 1948. The wooden fence in this photograph of Tonk Creek kept livestock away from the building. (Courtesy of Bonnie Adkins Fouts.)

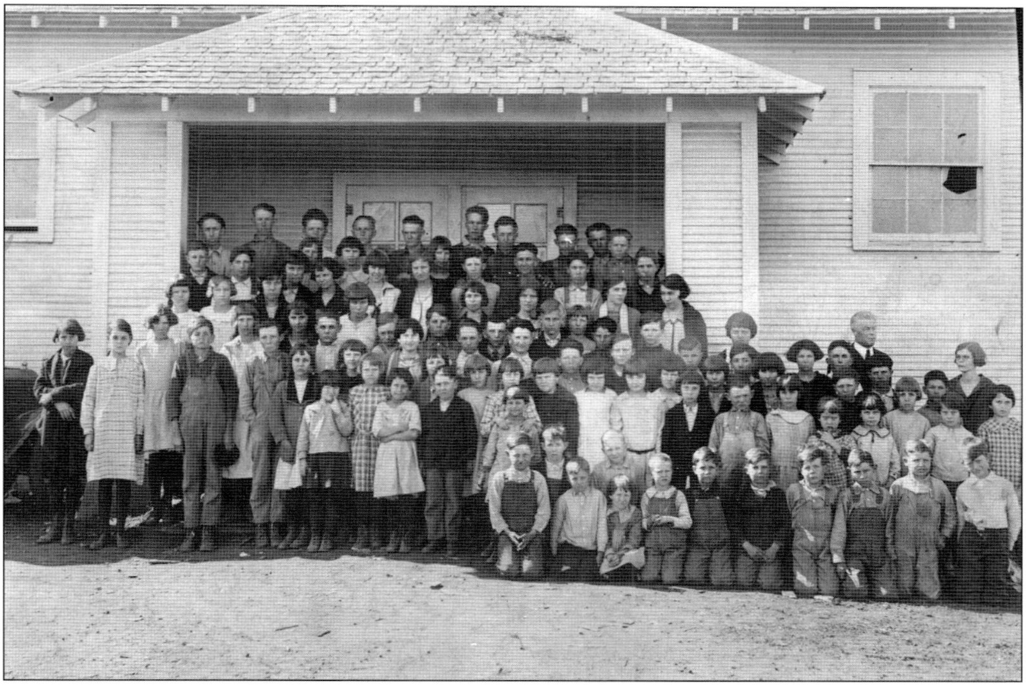

J. R. Jeter donated land for a school in the Center Point community in 1906. The one-room building, located southeast of Rule, was heated by a potbellied stove and had a barrel outside for drinking water. A teacherage was on the school grounds. Center Point, shown here with its students, consolidated with Haskell and Rule in 1944. (Courtesy of Haskell County Historical and Genealogical Society.)

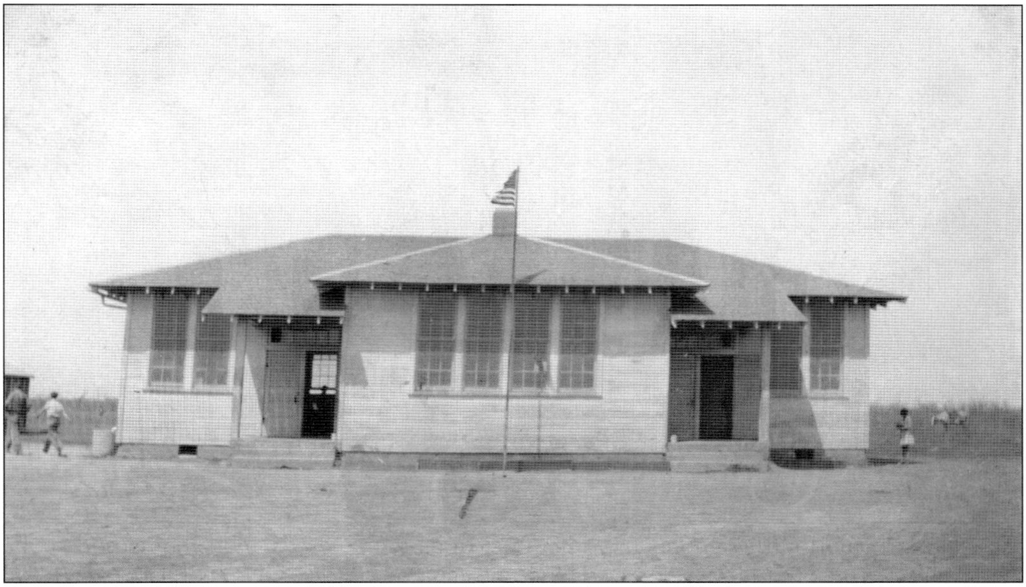

In 1907, the first Gilliam School was established. Mrs. B. J. Abbot sold land for a new school building in 1925. It was erected east and south of Rochester. One teacher taught four grades in one room, and another teacher taught three grades in a second room. Gilliam, pictured above, began contracting students to Haskell in 1938. (Courtesy of Bonnie Adkins Fouts.)

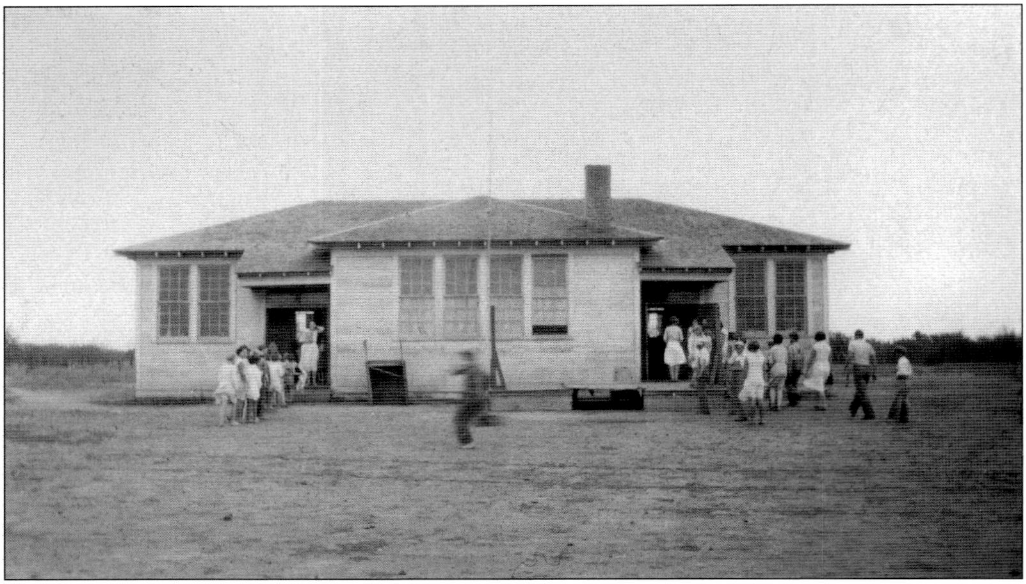

Lake Creek community, located in northeastern Haskell County, had a school in 1889. School enrollment gradually increased, and in 1927, a new three-room schoolhouse, pictured here with students lining up to go inside, was constructed. In 1938, Lake Creek consolidated with Weinert. (Courtesy of Bonnie Adkins Fouts.)

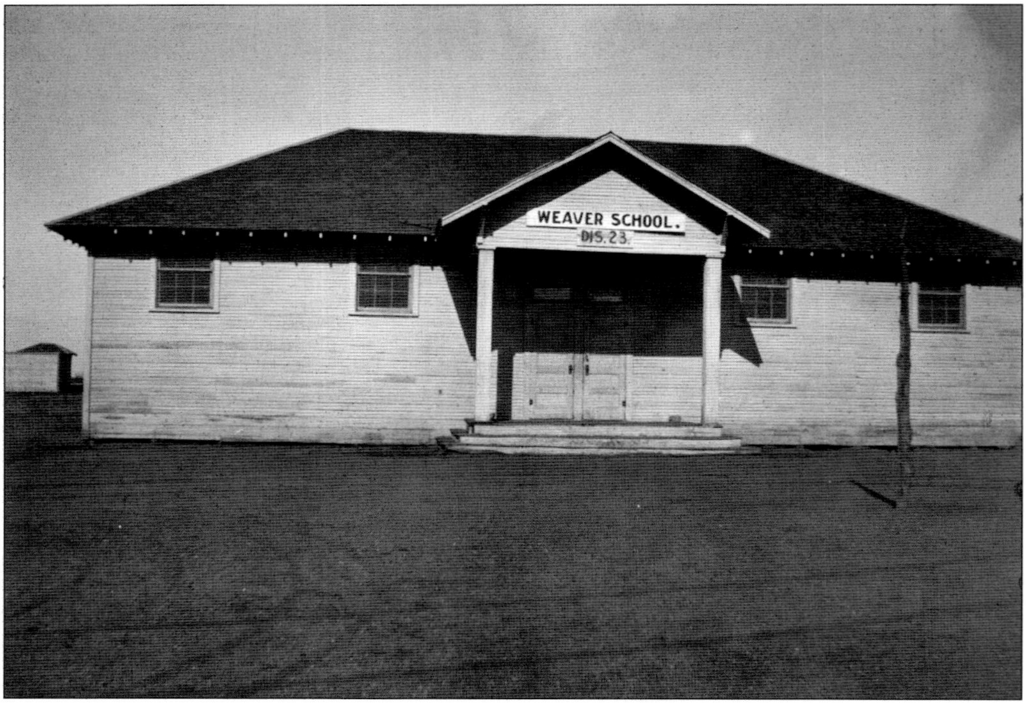

Weaver School was begun in 1909 with the donation of land by Mr. and Mrs. J. F. Weaver of the Weaver community. A second school was built in 1923 on land given by William and Fannie Pleasants. Weaver joined with other Haskell County schools to form Paint Creek Rural School in 1937. (Courtesy of Bonnie Adkins Fouts.)

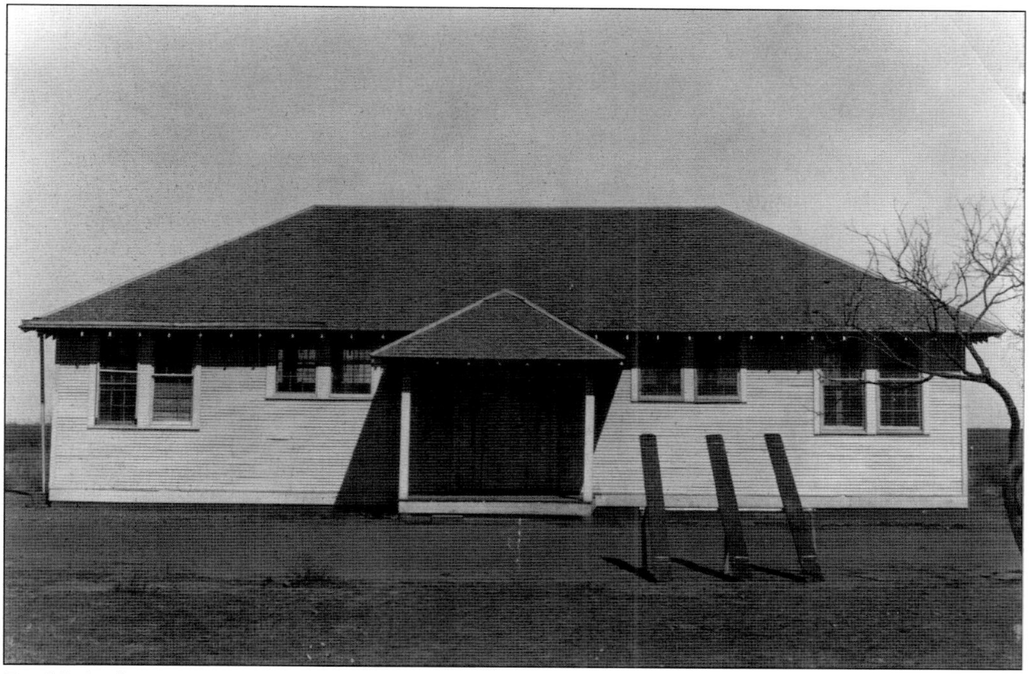

Established in 1887, Vernon School, originally known as Rawhide Bend, was built near a spring on Willow Creek. Following a fire, a second building was constructed on the opposite bank. The land was given by S. W. Vernon, so the school was named in his honor. One of the first schools in Haskell County, Vernon began contracting students to Stamford in 1946. (Courtesy of Bonnie Adkins Fouts.)

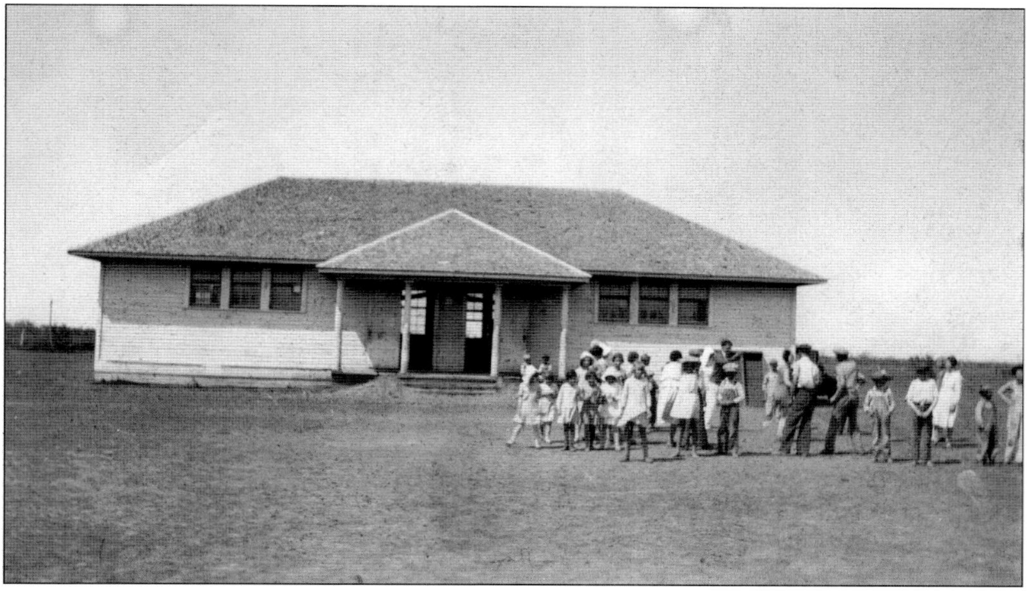

Roberts School was established northeast of Haskell in the early 1900s on land once owned by J. D. and Fannie Roberts. This photograph shows the range in age of the students typical of country schools. Roberts consolidated with Vontress, Pleasant Valley, and Cottonwood in 1936 to form Mattson Rural School. (Courtesy of Bonnie Adkins Fouts.)

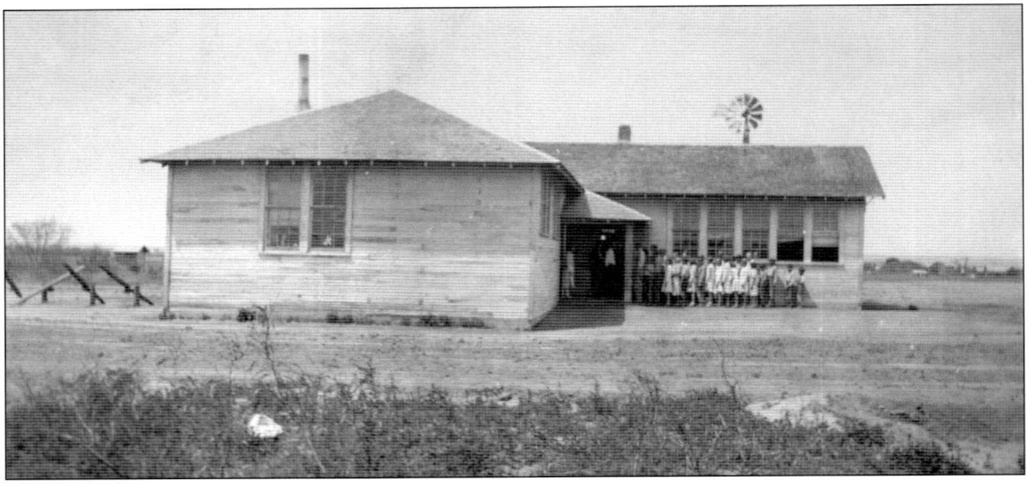

In 1907, residents of Jud, Texas, built a school building on land owned by Mr. and Mrs. A. M. Reed 6 miles southwest of Rochester. A new two-room school was erected in 1922, pictured here. Jud School had 65 students in 1938, but by 1948, only 21 were enrolled. Students consolidated with Rochester and Rule in 1949. (Courtesy of Bonnie Adkins Fouts.)

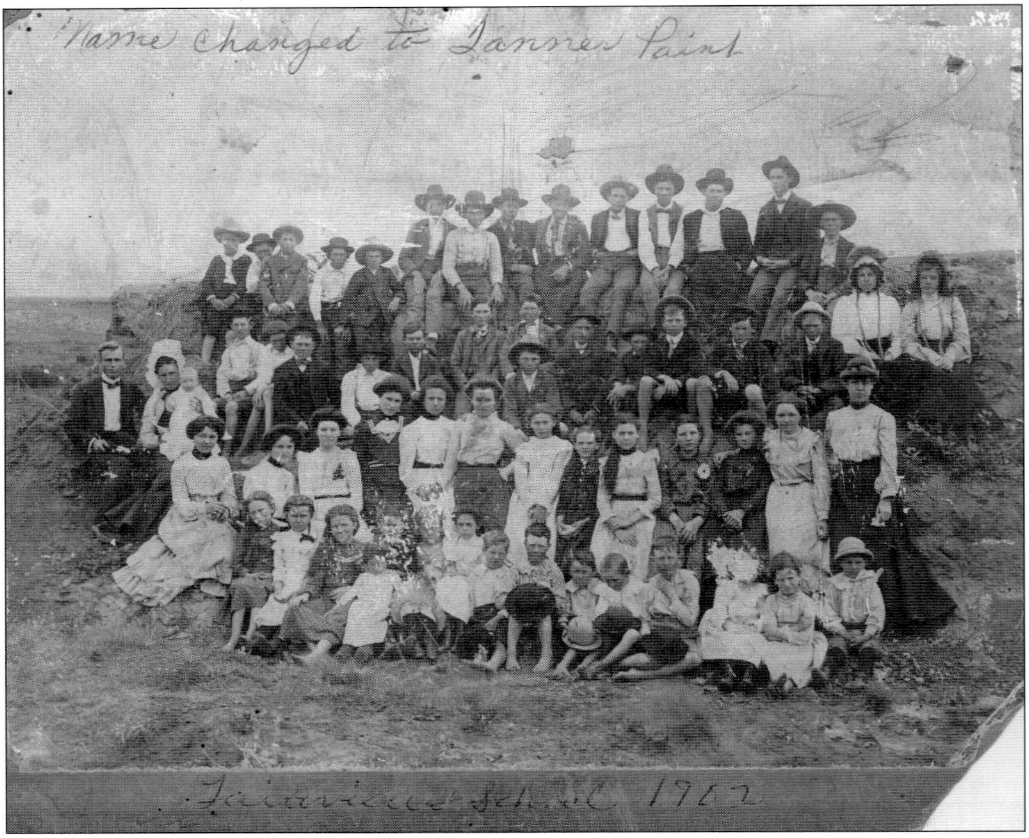

The teacher and students of Fairview School pose for a school photograph. Land was given for a church and school by Mr. and Mrs. J. E. Maxwell in 1889. Known as Fairview School, the school had 19 pupils enrolled in 1896. In 1901, a new schoolhouse, known as Tanner, was built. Fairview and Willow Paint School later became Tanner Paint, pictured here. (Courtesy of Joyce LeFevre.)

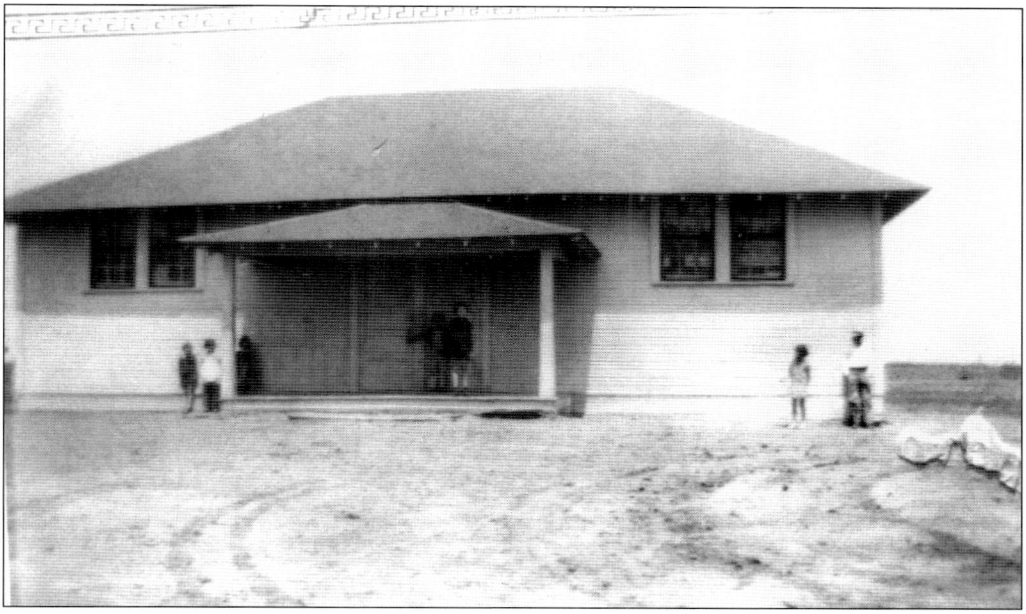

The Myers School was established in 1908 on land once owned by Kate Green. It was named for William Myers, who helped settle the Myers community in northern Haskell County. Thirty-five pupils enrolled the first year. In 1916, a new building was constructed. Myers, above, consolidated with Weinert in 1937. (Courtesy of Haskell County Historical and Genealogical Society.)

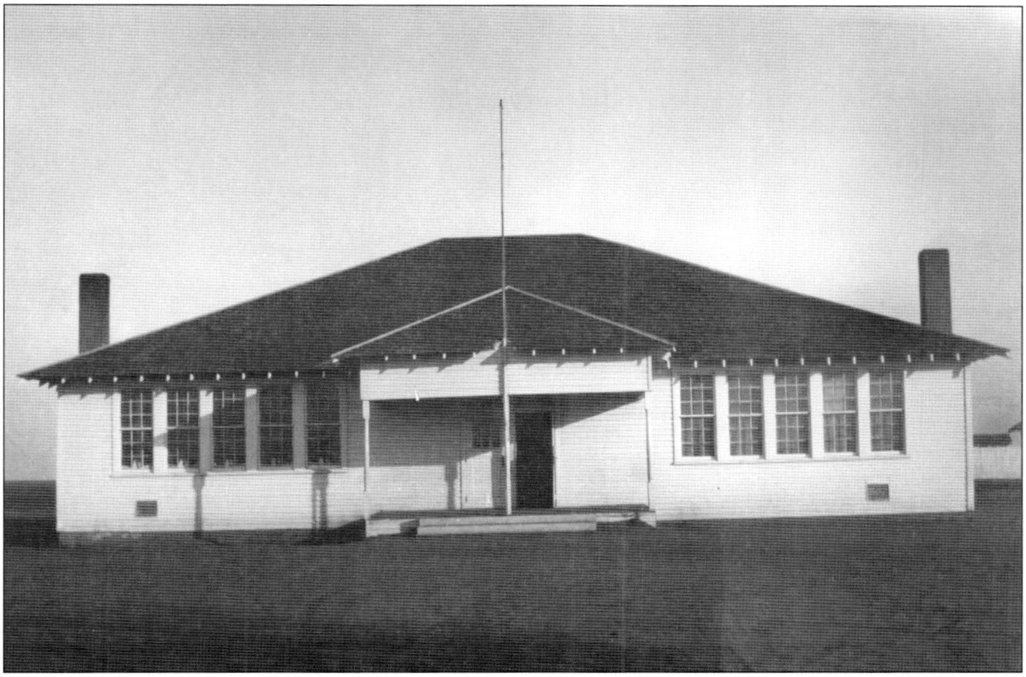

Midway School was established in 1922 when Whitman and Pinkerton merged. Midway was located 4 miles northwest of Haskell. Midway was the only school in the county at the time to have a gymnasium. In 1938, students consolidated with Rule and Haskell. (Courtesy of Bonnie Adkins Fouts.)

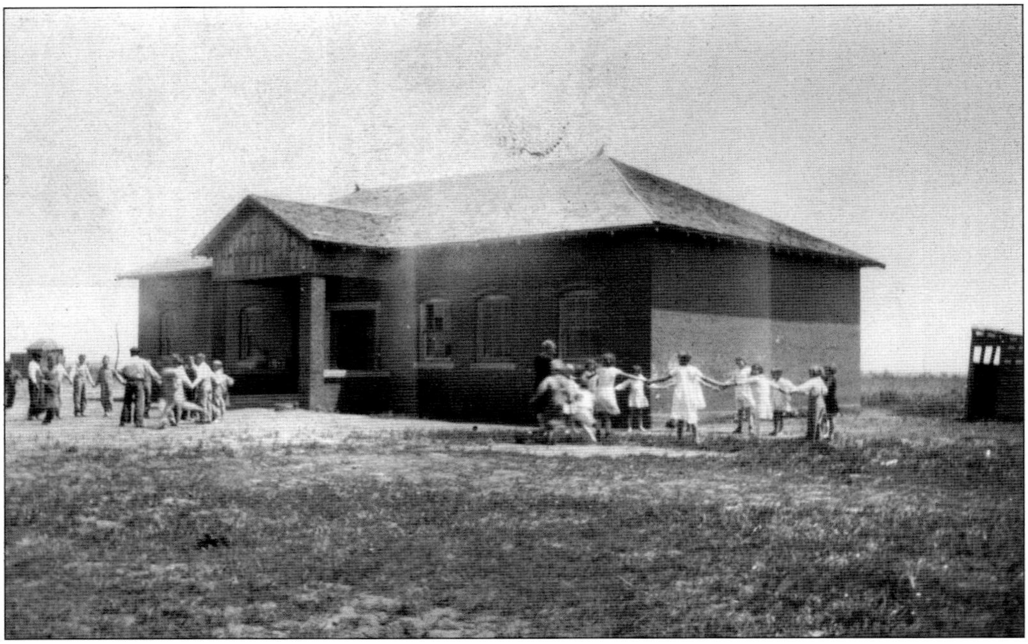

In 1903, land was taken from the Joe Bailey School District to form Plainview. When Joe Bailey closed in 1917, its students transferred to Plainview. Here students play ring games in the Plainview schoolyard. While most rural schools were made of wood, this building is of brick construction. Students began attending Paint Creek in 1940. (Courtesy of Bonnie Adkins Fouts.)

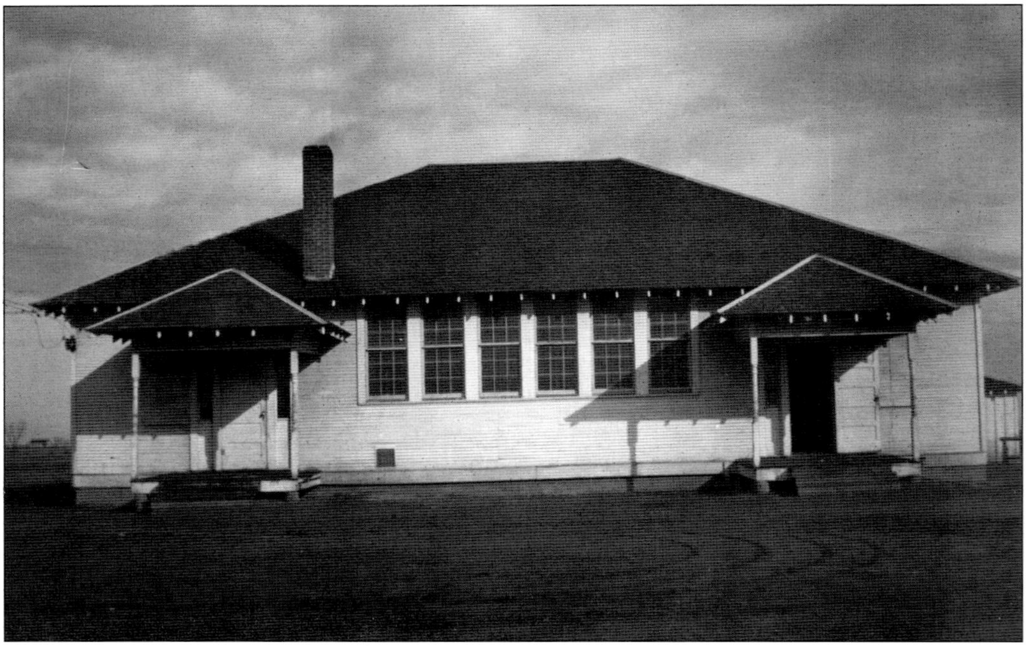

Howard School was established as early as 1903. In 1909, a new building was constructed on land deeded by Lewis and Mary Ann Howard. In 1918, some 70 to 80 students were enrolled. Howard and Whit Chapel consolidated in 1921, and a new three-room, three-teacher school was constructed in 1922. Howard combined with neighboring schools to form Paint Creek in 1937. (Courtesy of Bonnie Adkins Fouts.)

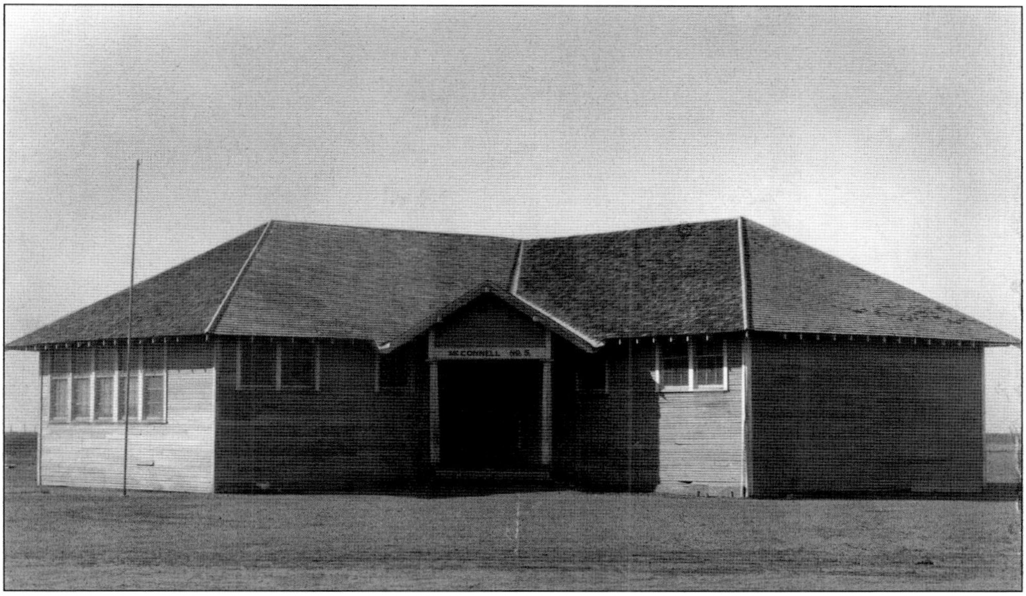

McConnell School was constructed in the north half of the Ward School District. It was a one-room building. A new two-room building (shown here) was constructed later. The two rooms could be made into one with folding middle doors. In 1937, McConnell became a part of Paint Creek Rural School. (Courtesy of Bonnie Adkins Fouts.)

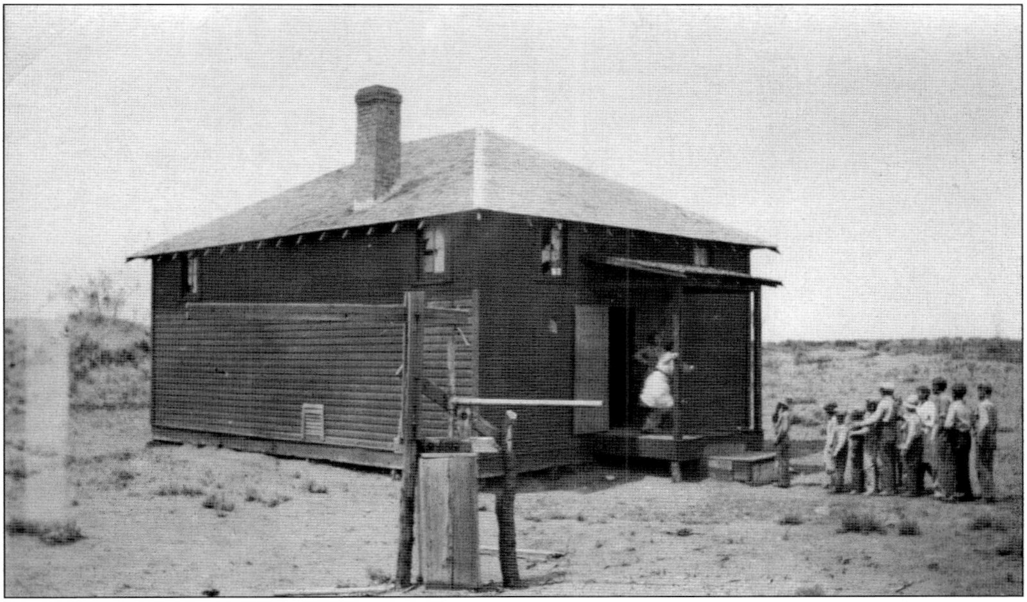

About 1887, the town of Marcy, originally given the name Mesquite by settlers, was established in western Haskell County. In 1891, land for a school building was given by Alice and W. H. McClatchy. As with most country schools, the term was scheduled to allow children to help with the cotton harvest. When the Marcy community moved east to the railroad at Rochester, most students enrolled at Rochester. Some attended Four Corners west of Marcy. (Courtesy of Bonnie Adkins Fouts.)

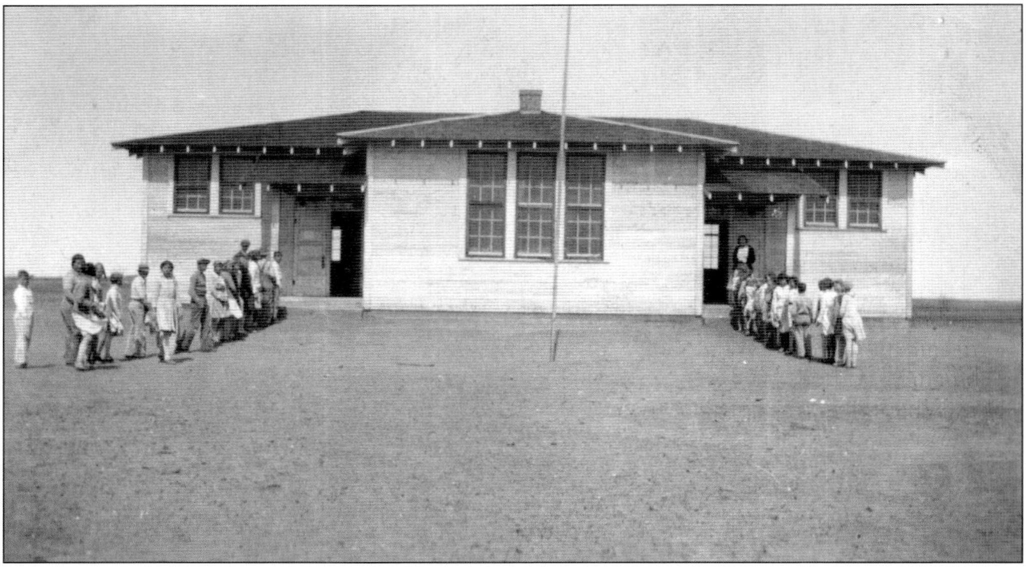

J. W. Mitchell and others donated land to build a schoolhouse in northwestern Haskell County about 1904. It was named Mitchell and, in 1908, had a large enrollment. In 1916, a new building was erected west of the original site. Another new school was built in 1925. Mitchell School began contracting students to O'Brien in 1938. (Courtesy of Bonnie Adkins Fouts.)

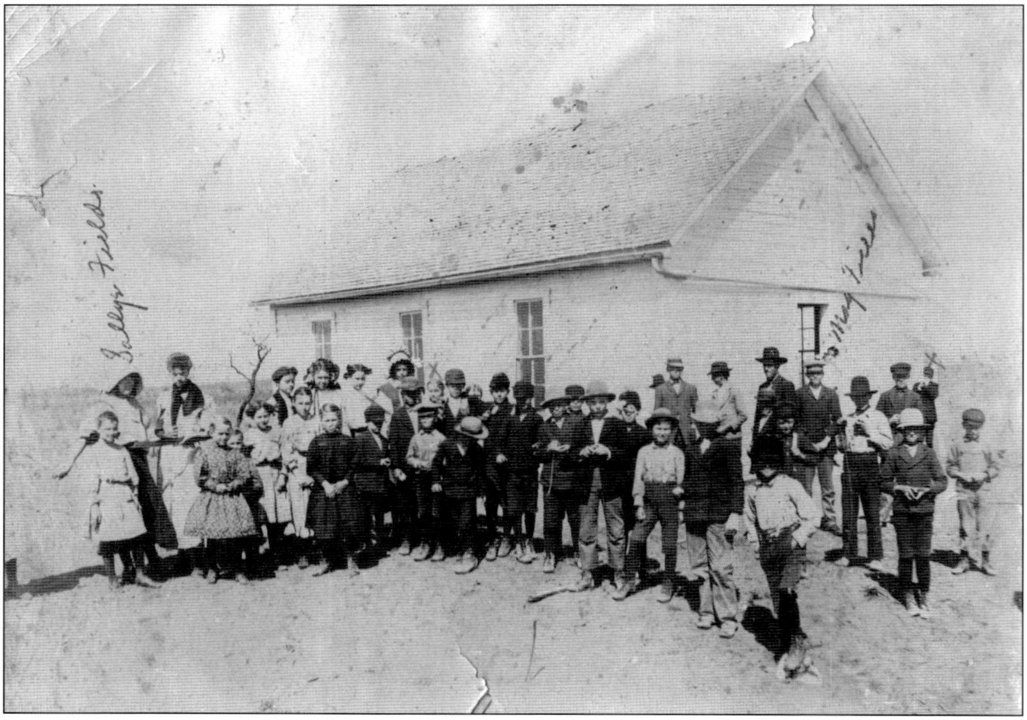

J. J. Brag, W. J. Brag, J. D. Worley, and R. W. Stanfield each gave one half acre of land for a school site west of Rochester in 1907. The school was built at the common corner of their acreages, thus the name Four Corners. Four Corners consolidated with Rochester in 1948. (Courtesy of Sharon Mullino.)

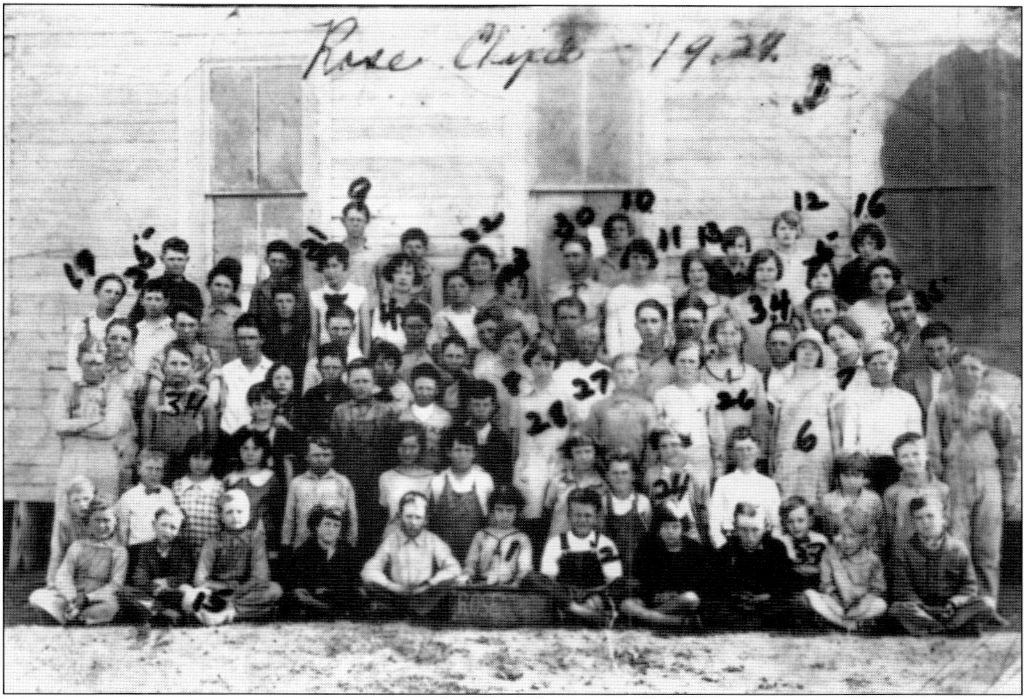

In 1905, J. A. and Willie Rose donated land for a two-room school. Known as Rose or Rose Chapel, it was located east of Haskell. Salome Anthone sold land for a teacherage. In the absence of a house provided by their schools, teachers boarded with families or rented rooms. Teachers usually walked, rode on horseback, or drove a buggy to school. Rose became a part of Paint Creek in 1937. (Courtesy of Haskell County Historical and Genealogical Society.)

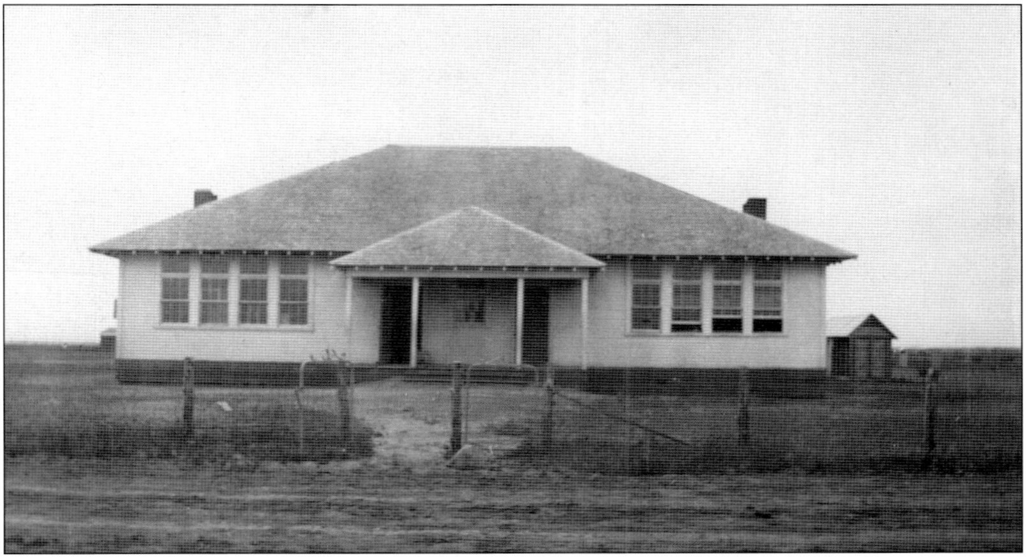

In 1888, Haskell County commissioners established the Brushy School District in northeastern Haskell County. J. S. Boone donated land on which the Brushy Creek School was built. The Brushy School was moved in 1907 to land once owned by J. A. Bowman. The school was destroyed by fire in 1933, and a new building was erected. Students began attending school at Weinert and Goree, in Knox County, in the 1930s. (Courtesy of Bonnie Adkins Fouts.)

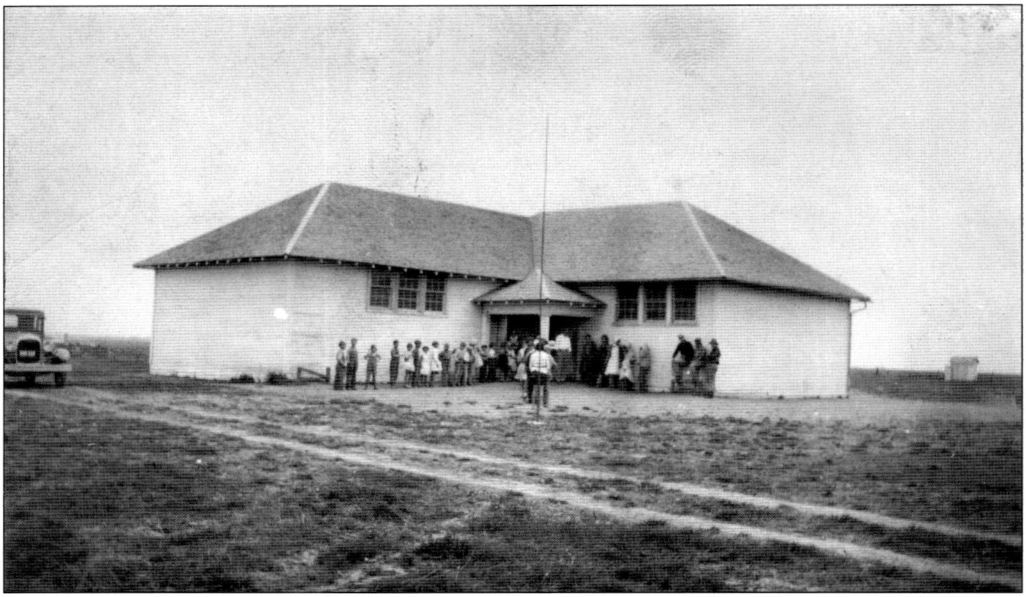

Willow Paint and Fairview combined to become Tanner Paint School. In 1918, the schoolhouse burned, and classes were held in two rooms of the five-room teacherage. Edward J. Cloud, future State Representative from Haskell County, was a principal of this school for a time. In 1937, Tanner Paint began contracting students to Rule. (Courtesy of Bonnie Adkins Fouts.)

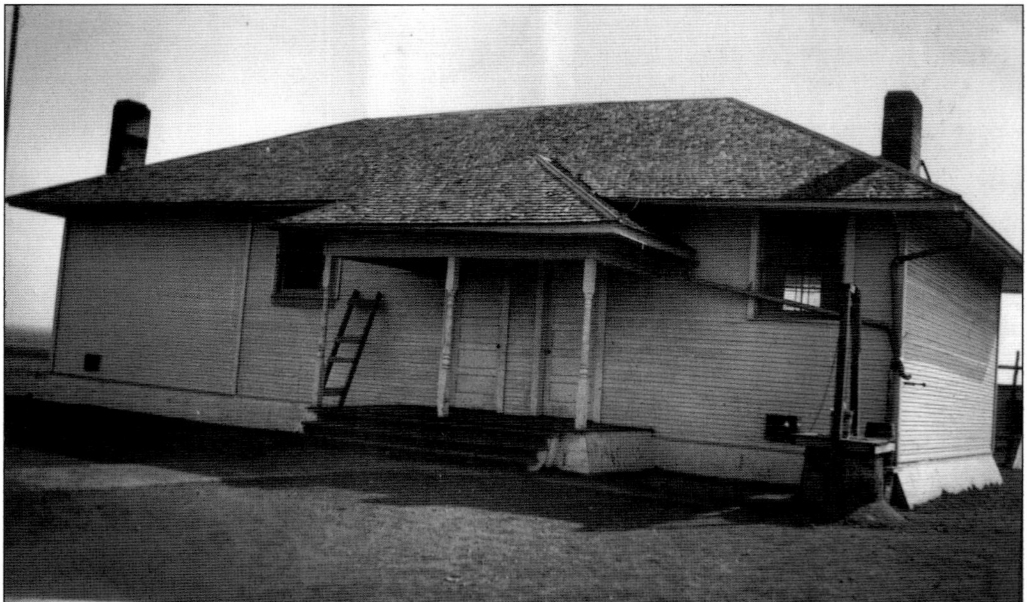

August and Frances Guesendorf gave land for a school in 1904 to the German settlement of Irby, 13 miles east of Haskell. Ten grades were taught at Irby, which had an enrollment of 70 students in the early 1920s. The building was heated by coal, which the boys brought in each afternoon. Irby became part of Mattson School District in 1949, though students has begun attending Haskell Schools by 1948. (Courtesy of Bonnie Adkins Fouts.)

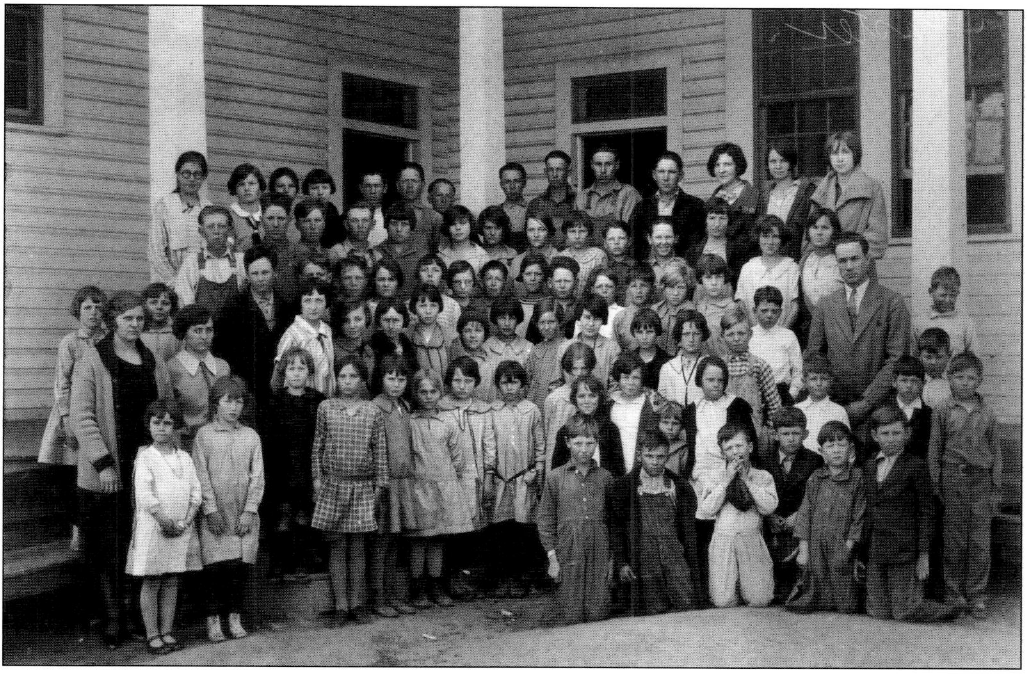

Foster Rural School was established about 5 miles southeast of Rochester in 1901. In 1912, a new two-room building was constructed. During the 1938–1939 school year, students began attending school at Rochester. Foster schoolhouse was moved to Rochester for a school lunchroom. (Courtesy of Frances Harrell Bowen.)

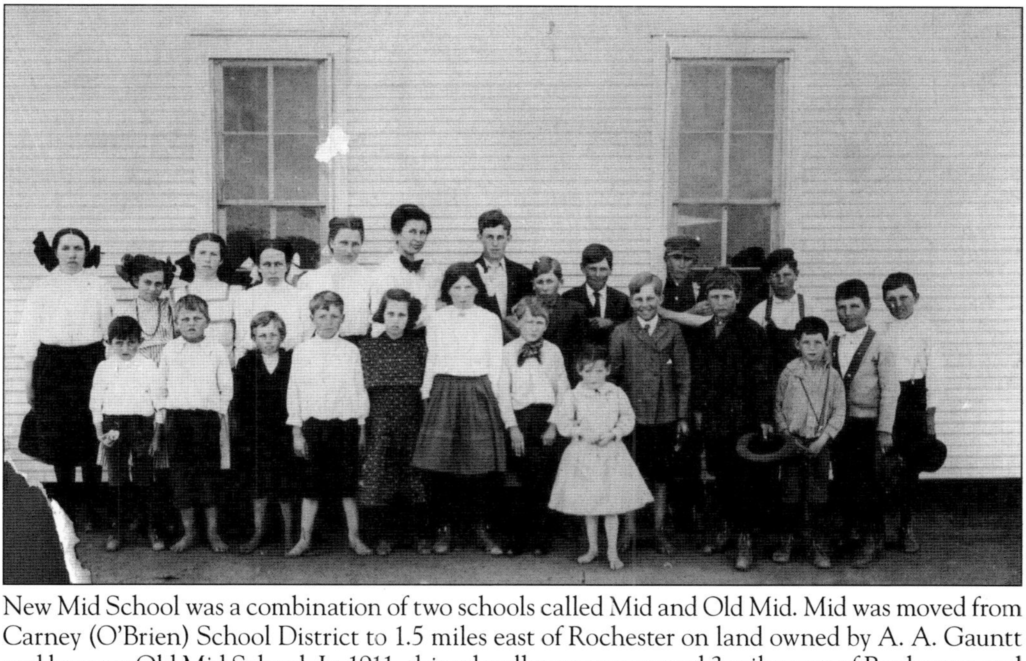

New Mid School was a combination of two schools called Mid and Old Mid. Mid was moved from Carney (O'Brien) School District to 1.5 miles east of Rochester on land owned by A. A. Gauntt and became Old Mid School. In 1911, this schoolhouse was moved 3 miles east of Rochester, and the name was changed to New Mid. Eunice Gauntt Michaels (second row, sixth from the left) was a teacher at New Mid. (Courtesy of Rochester Heritage Museum.)

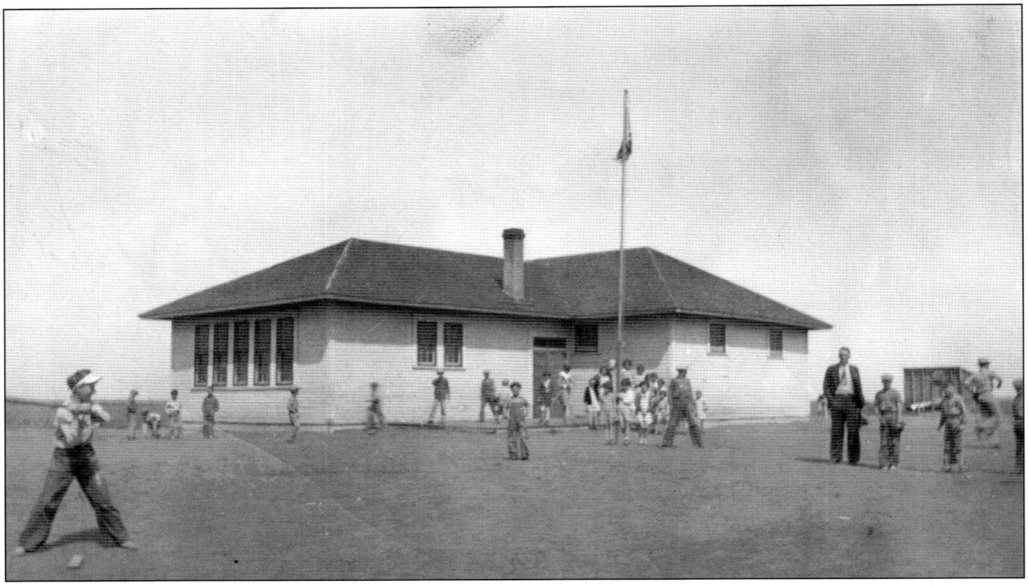

Cliff School was located in the northwestern part of Haskell County. It was named for M. A. Clifton, who gave land for the school. In 1913, a new two-room school was built on land donated by R. A. Tankersley. In this photograph, students play baseball in the Cliff schoolyard. Cliff students contracted to O'Brien and Weinert beginning in 1938. (Courtesy of Bonnie Adkins Fouts.)

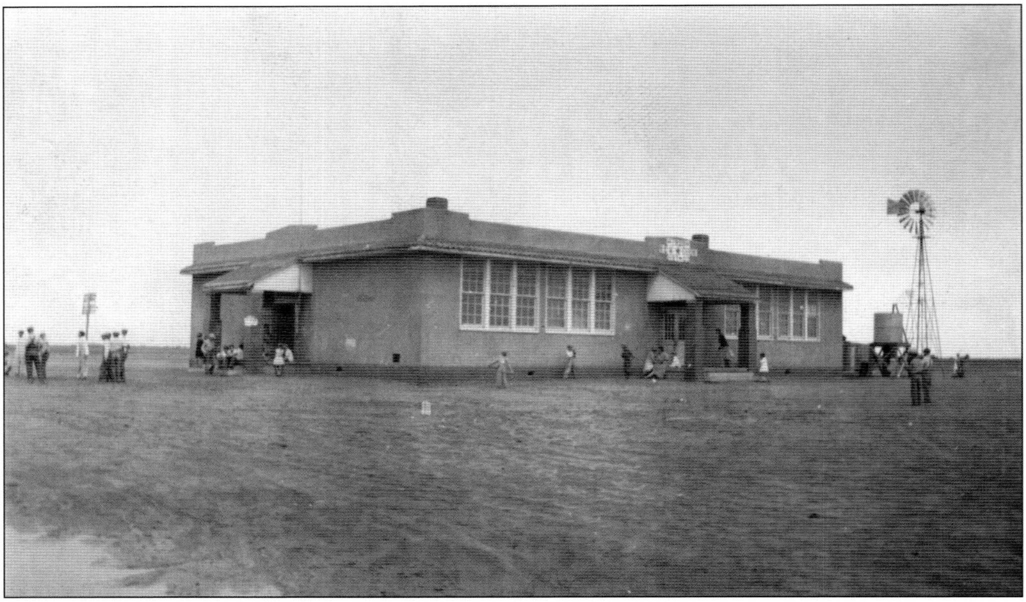

New Cook was a consolidation of Cook Springs and Corinth. The four-room schoolhouse, complete with book room and stage, was built in 1929. A windmill and basketball goal are in the schoolyard. There was also a four-room teacherage. New Cook consolidated with Rule and Rochester in 1945. (Courtesy of Bonnie Adkins Fouts.)

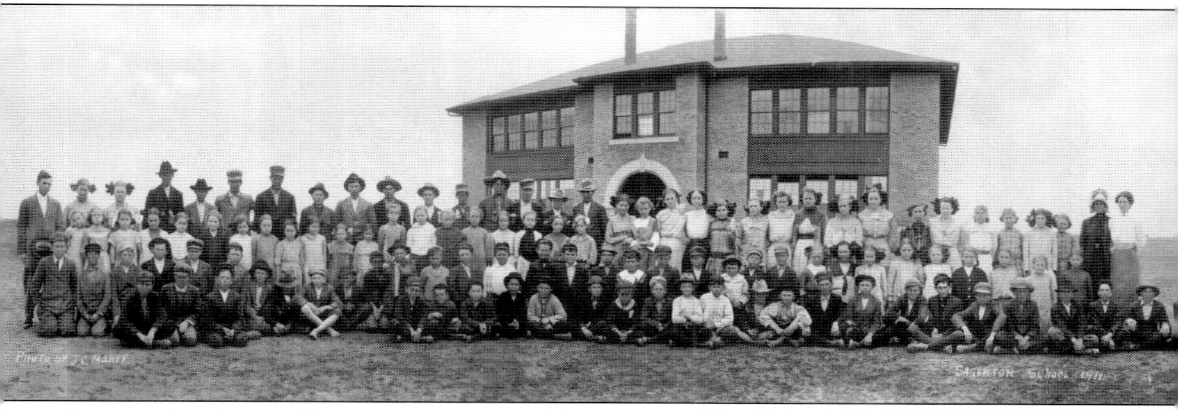

From its founding in 1902, the population of Sagerton grew rapidly. In 1907, residents voted to establish a public school system for Sagerton and the surrounding area. Students soon outgrew the classroom set aside for them east of the Sagerton First Methodist Church. A $10,000 bond was passed in 1909 to secure a new building. On the northeast corner of the Sagerton townsite, a two-story red-brick building was constructed. It was designed with four classrooms downstairs and classrooms, offices, and an auditorium on the second floor. In the 1910–1911 school year, it employed three teachers and enrolled about 150 students. Early settlers of Haskell County had many hardships, and survival was often a serious struggle, but the first priority, after establishing basic shelter and provisions, was getting children an education. From simple classrooms held in storerooms, homes, and one-room buildings, education was soon housed in the finest facilities its patrons could manage. Many students educated in these rural schools went on to succeed at the highest levels of education and make immeasurable contributions to society. (Courtesy of Joyce LeFevre.)

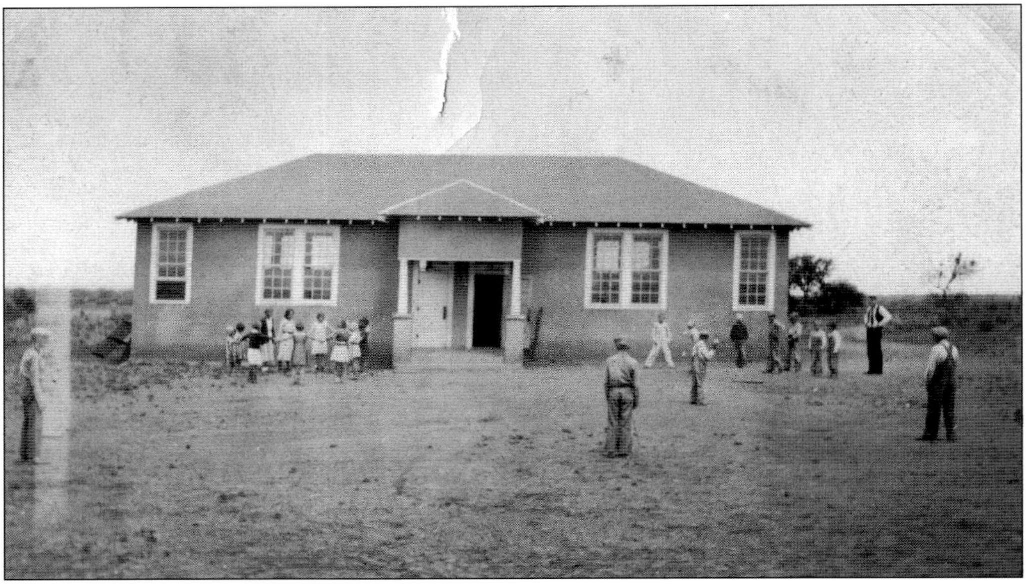

The Idella Schoolhouse was originally built on land owned by George W. Cook and his wife, Idella. Located 7 miles west of Rochester, Idella is said to be one of the earliest established schools in Haskell County. J. C. Helton gave land to build a new school in 1908. A two-room schoolhouse was built in 1927. Twenty-seven students consolidated with Rochester in 1937. (Courtesy of Bonnie Adkins Fouts.)

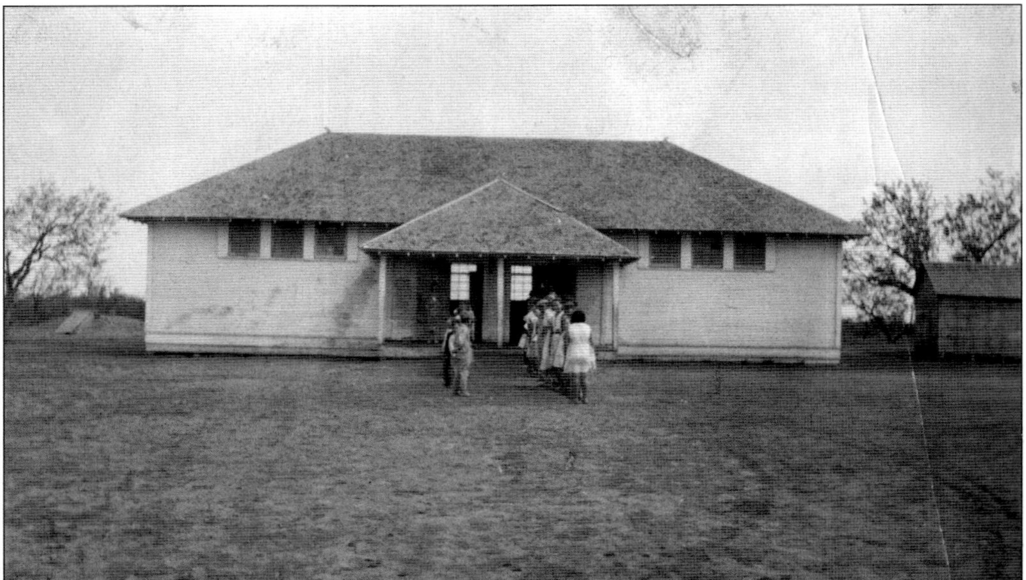

Commodore Nicholson, ? Berry, and George Taylor built a small schoolhouse on land in northeastern Haskell County in 1903. Known as Cottonwood School, it employed two teachers in 1910. In 1936, Cottonwood consolidated with other districts to form Mattson Rural School. (Courtesy of Bonnie Adkins Fouts.)

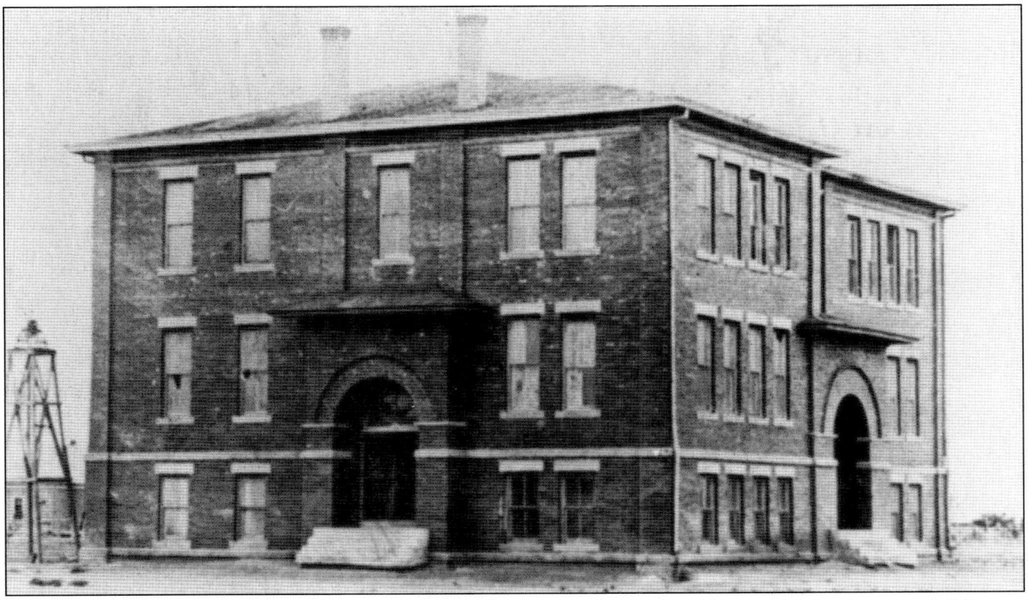

Land for the first school in Rule was donated by Mr. and Mrs. Jim Davis. According to *A History of Rule* by Mr. and Mrs. Jack E. Westbrook, the school, known as Ivanhoe, began its first term in 1899. Nicknamed Bug Scuffle, it came to be known as Rule Public School. Sagerton, New Cook, Tanner Paint, Midway, and Center Point all eventually consolidated with Rule. (Courtesy of Rule Independent School District.)

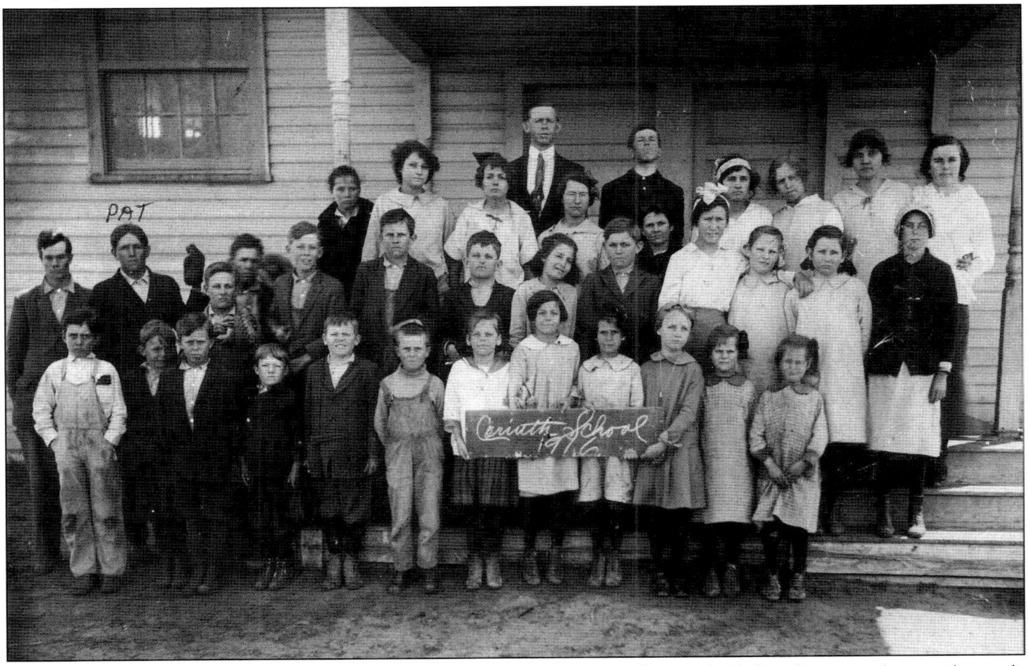

G. W. Hutto gave land to build a school in 1904. Known as Corinth School, it was located north of Rule. Corinth served as a social meeting place and as a church. The school building was moved in 1923, and a new building was constructed on the original site. Corinth consolidated with Cook Springs to form New Cook in 1929. Students eventually consolidated with Rule in the 1940s. (Courtesy of Teresa Scoggins.)

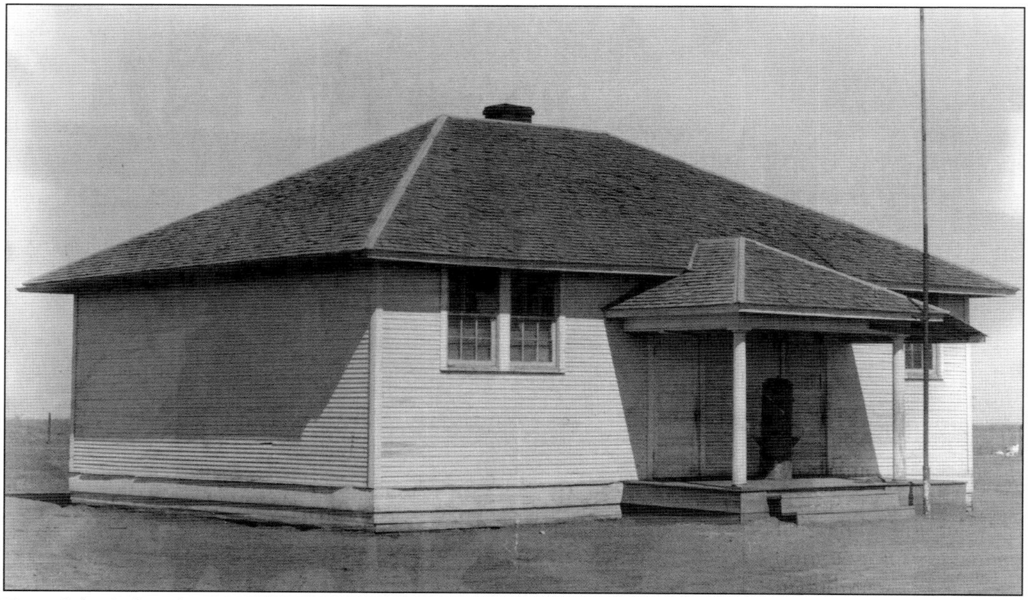

Ericsdale School was constructed in 1906 in southeastern Haskell County. It was destroyed in 1913, and a new building was erected in 1914. Desks for this school were ordered from Sears, Roebuck, and Company. Ericsdale began contracting students to Paint Creek in 1938. (Courtesy of Bonnie Adkins Fouts.)

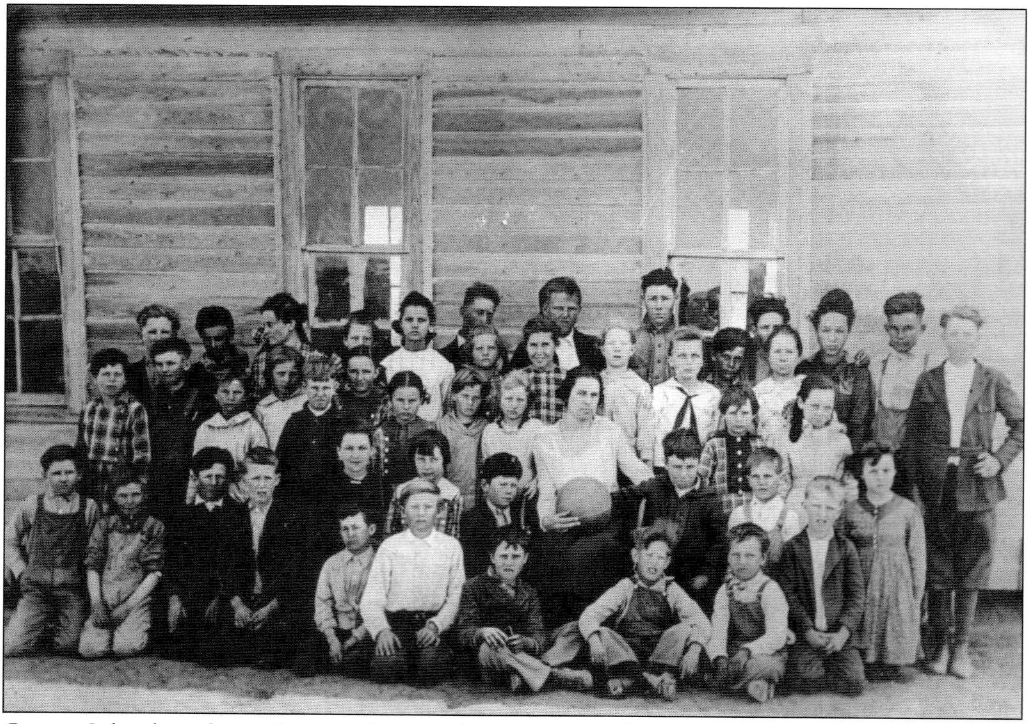

Gauntt School was located east and south of the town of Rule and 6 miles west of Haskell. In 1920, approximately 45 students were enrolled. A. A. Gauntt secured the bonds to build the school, which was built on land belonging to Tom Sims. Gauntt School began contracting students to Haskell in 1940. (Courtesy of Haskell County Library.)

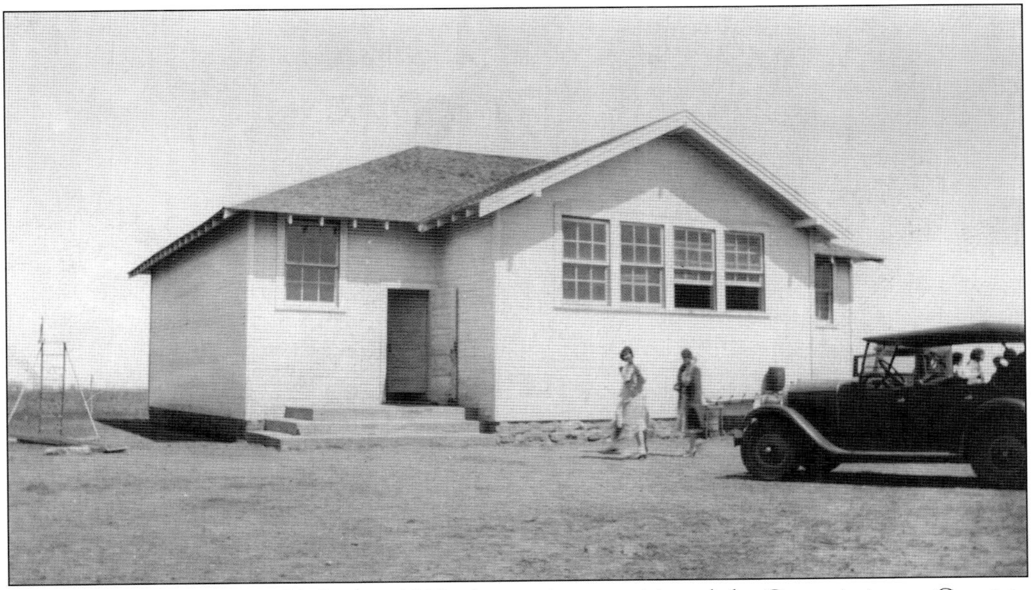

Rockdale School was established in 1903 when citizens petitioned the Commissioners Court to create a district in the far southeastern corner of the county. In 1923, a new two-room schoolhouse was built. Fire destroyed this building in February 1928. In May, patrons voted to replace the building. Rockdale, shown above, later consolidated with Paint Creek School. (Courtesy of Bonnie Adkins Fouts.)

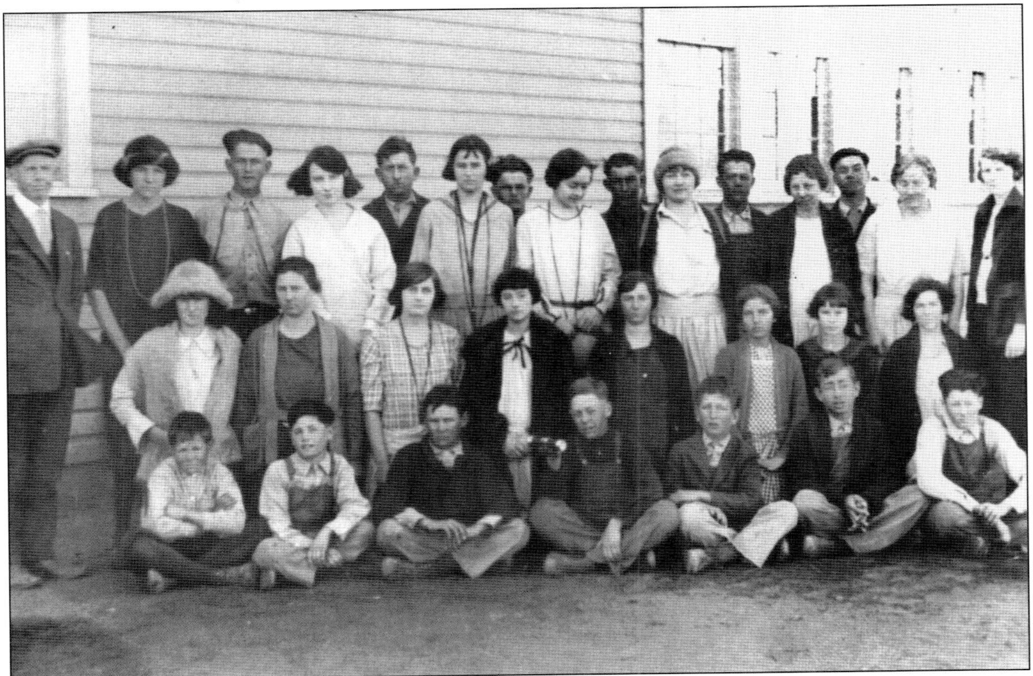

Land for a school was given to Haskell County by W. P. Whitman in 1909. Known as Whitman, the school was located 5 miles northeast of Haskell. Classes met six months of the year. Whitman students are pictured here beside their school. Whitman and Pinkerton consolidated to form Midway School in 1921, eventually joining students in Haskell and Rule. (Courtesy of Haskell County Historical and Genealogical Society.)

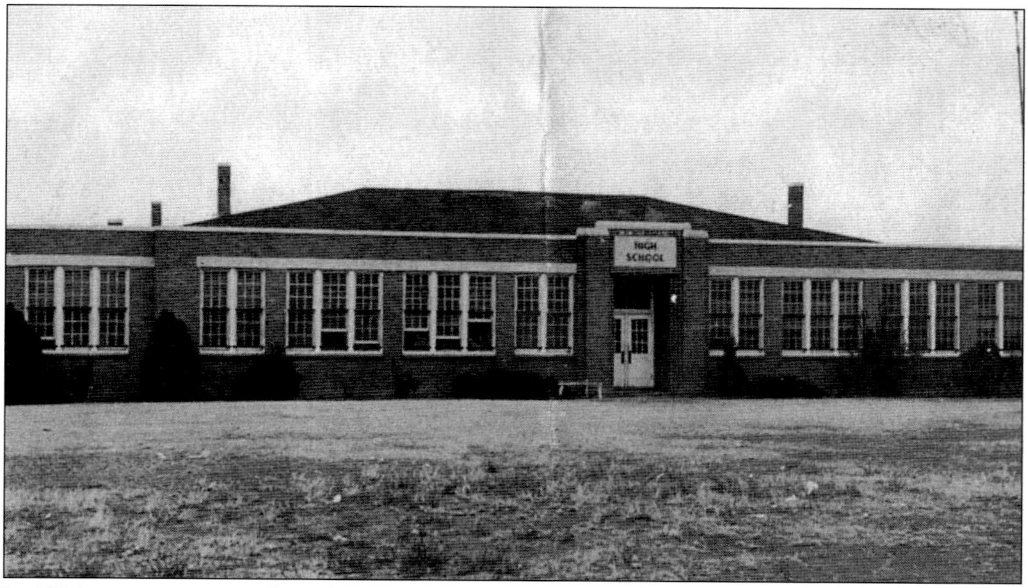

In 1906, a two-story wooden school building was constructed in the town of Carney (O'Brien). A brick building was erected in 1916. Though the name of the town changed, the school continued to use the name Carney. In 1928, Carney School had its first bus, a Model T Ford truck. In 1943, Mitchell, Hutto, and Cliff consolidated with Carney Rural High School in O'Brien, pictured here. (Courtesy of Thelma Cox Burt.)

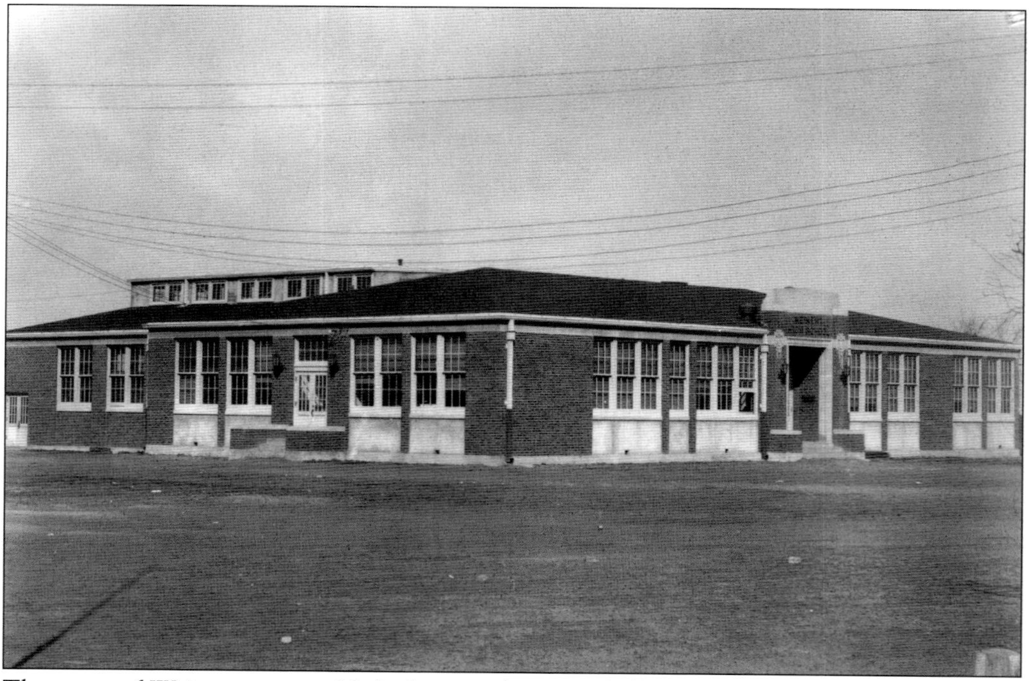

The town of Weinert was established in northern Haskell County in 1906. The first school in Weinert was the land office building located on Main Street. Later, a one-room school was constructed. Enrollment had reached 116 in 1909, and a larger building was built in the southwest part of town. Ballew, Cliff, Myers, Lone Star, Lake Creek, Pleasant View, and part of Brushy School District consolidated with Weinert. (Courtesy of Bonnie Adkins Fouts.)

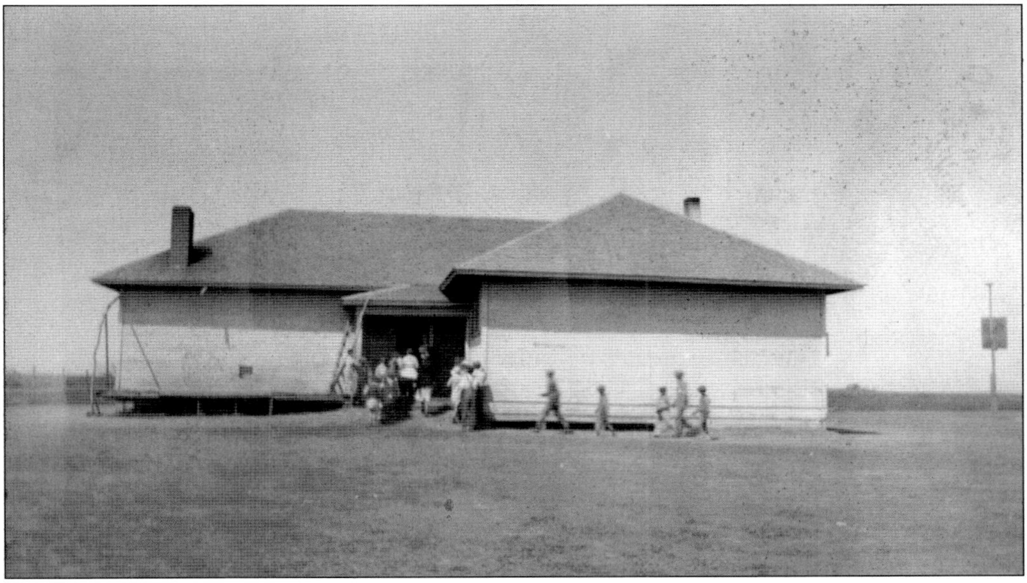

The Post School was located about 8 miles south of Haskell on land once owned by Sid Post. In 1913, residents passed a bond to fund a larger school building. The school served the Post community until 1938, when it joined other area schools to form Paint Creek Rural School. (Courtesy of Bonnie Adkins Fouts.)

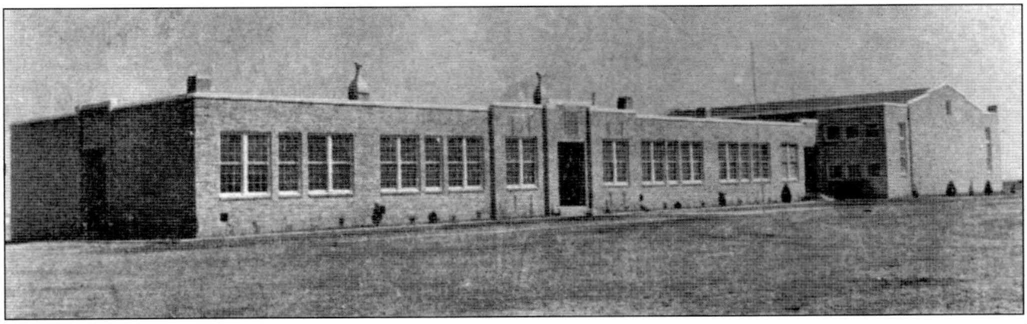

Land purchased from Mr. and Mrs. E. A. Schaake and from the Thane estate became the site of Paint Creek Rural School. Its name was chosen from the name of a creek running through the district. Howard, Weaver, Post, Rose, McConnell, Ericsdale, Ward, and Plainview consolidated to form the new school district. The first term began in 1938. Pictured here is Paint Creek High School, home of the Pirates. (Courtesy of Haskell County Historical and Genealogical Society.)

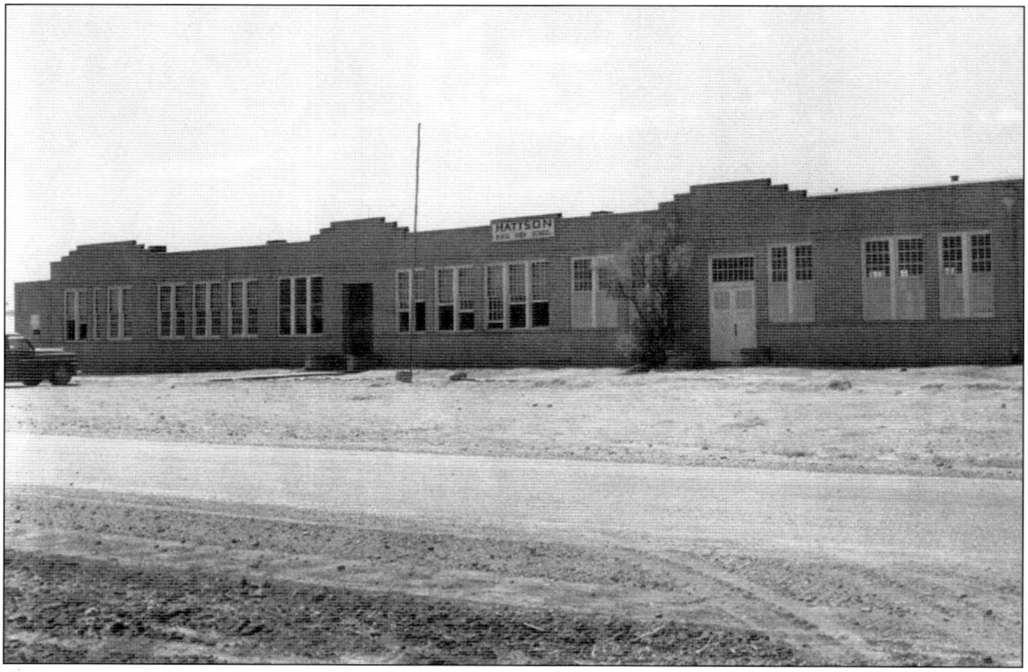

Mattson Rural School was established in northeastern Haskell County when surrounding schools consolidated beginning in the 1930s. Schools that joined with Mattson were Powell, Vontress, Pleasant Valley, Ferris Ranch, Irby, Cottonwood, Roberts, Baldwin (Kirkdale), and a portion of the Douglas School District. (Courtesy of Haskell County Historical and Genealogical Society.)

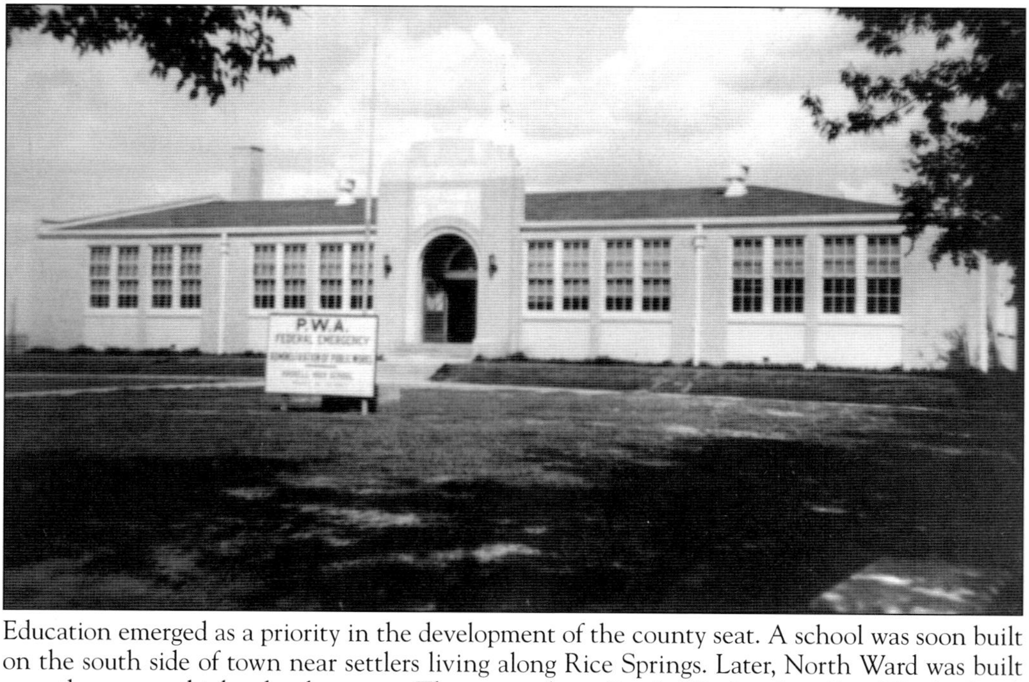

Education emerged as a priority in the development of the county seat. A school was soon built on the south side of town near settlers living along Rice Springs. Later, North Ward was built near the present high school campus. There was also a South Ward and an East Ward school. The Haskell High School Building shown here was built in the 1930s through the Public Works Administration. (Courtesy of Haskell Consolidated Independent School District.)

Eight

Preserving the Past

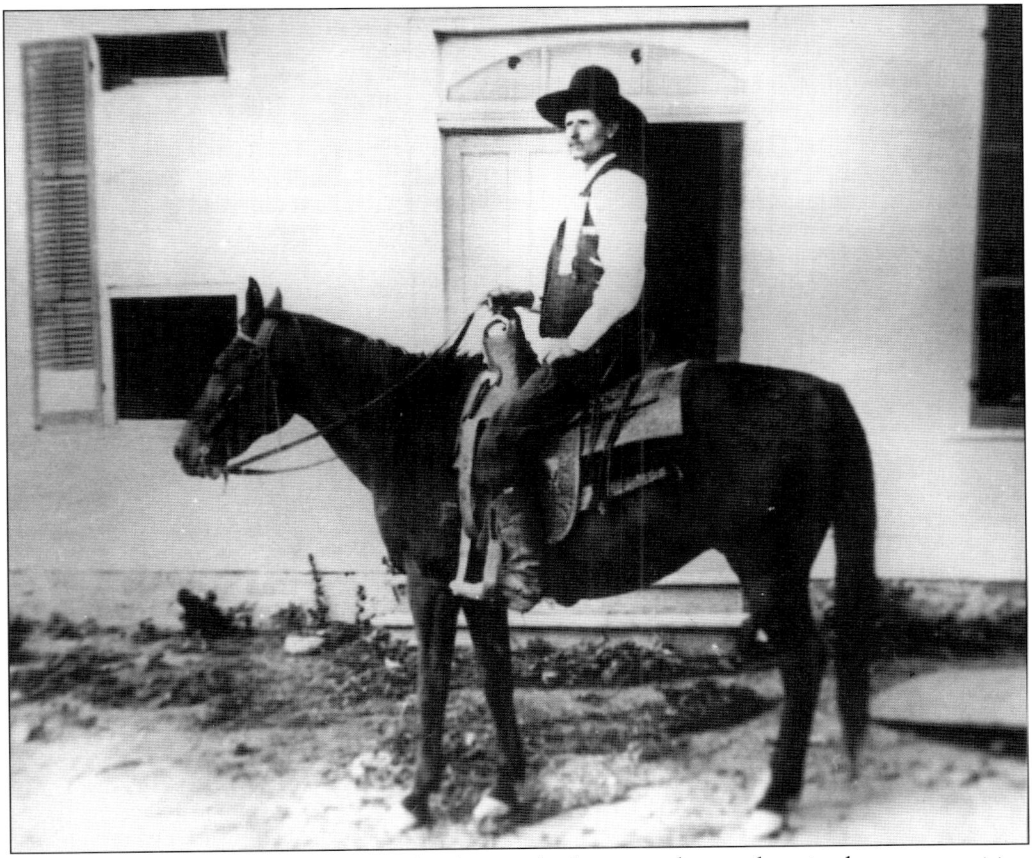

Sam Graves, above on a horse called Old Hub, won the first ever advertised cutting horse competition at a July 1898 Cowboy Reunion in Haskell, Texas. Eleven riders competed for the $150 purse. The 22-year-old horse bested the field. Estimates say 10,000 people attended the reunion. The annual Sam Graves Memorial Cutting held during Wild Horse Prairie Days Ranch Rodeo commemorates this historic event. (Courtesy of the National Cutting Horse Association.)

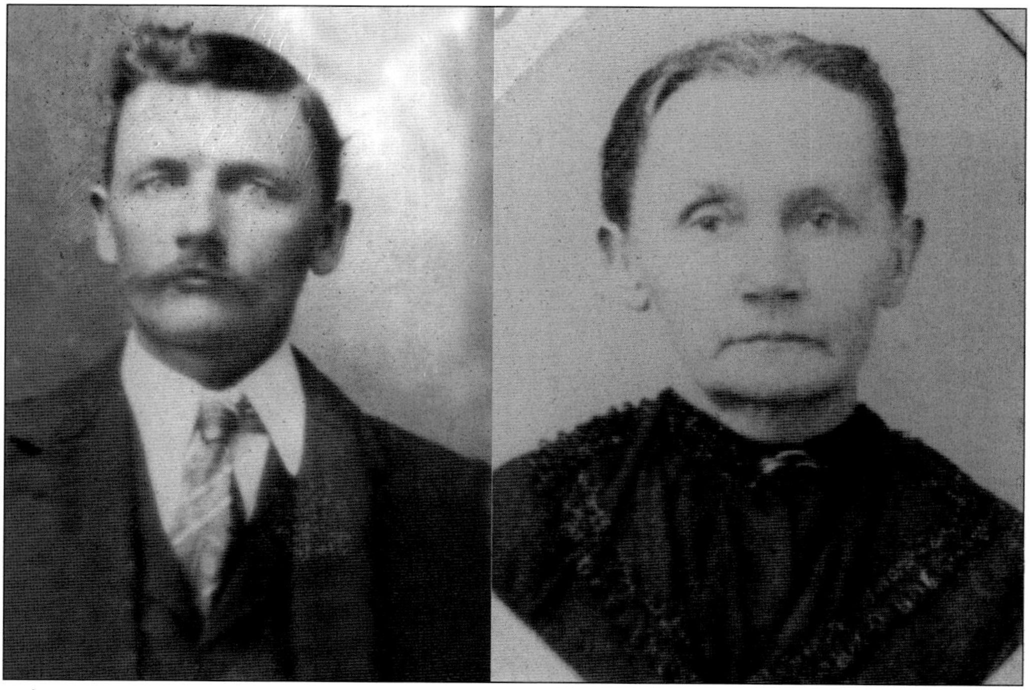

When pioneers settled the treeless prairie of Haskell County, their first homes were often made in the prairie itself. These homes were a hole dug in the ground or into the side of a hill or rise. Half-dugouts were partially underground, with the front portion built of other materials. Martha Temperence Woods Dunnam and her son, Andrew (left), lived in a dugout when they first came to Haskell County by wagon in 1917. (Courtesy of Wanda Dunnam Ham.)

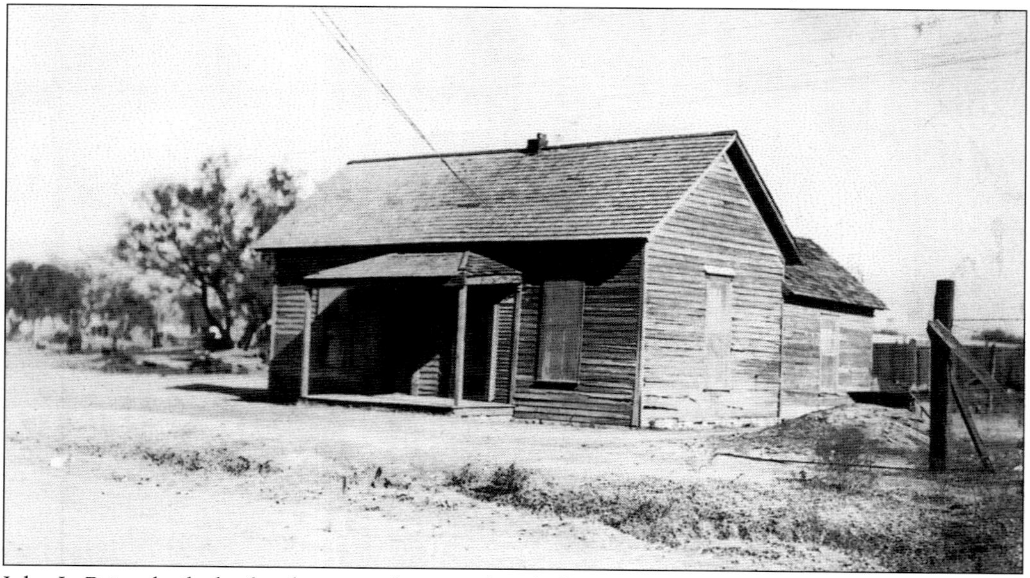

John LaBriere built the first house in the city of Haskell in 1883. Lumber for the two-room structure was hauled by wagon from Albany. LaBriere was a cattleman and county hide and animal inspector. In 1884, he drove 3,000 head of steer from Haskell County to Caldwell, Kansas. The LaBriere house stands today in the Haskell City Park and is maintained by the Haskell Progressive Study Club. (Courtesy of Haskell County Historical and Genealogical Society.)

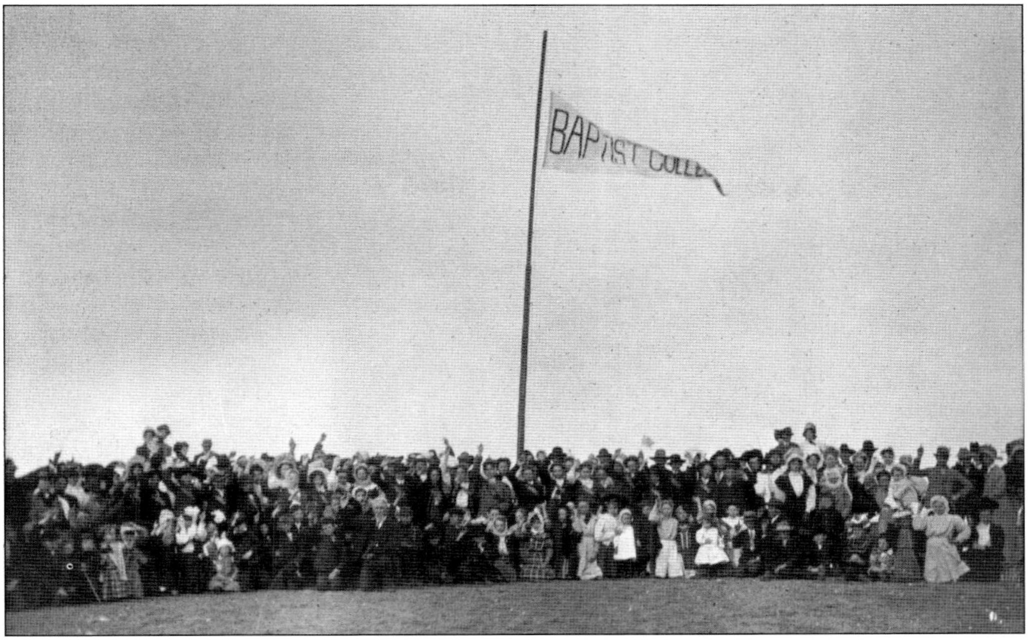

With a growing population in 1906, attempts were made to form a Baptist college in O'Brien. A Reverend James initiated the project. A meeting was held to raise money, and a load of bricks was brought to the building site at Park Avenue and Seventh Street. Brother James died shortly after this, and the project went no further. The O'Brien First Baptist Church later constructed a building near the site. (Courtesy of C. H. Underwood.)

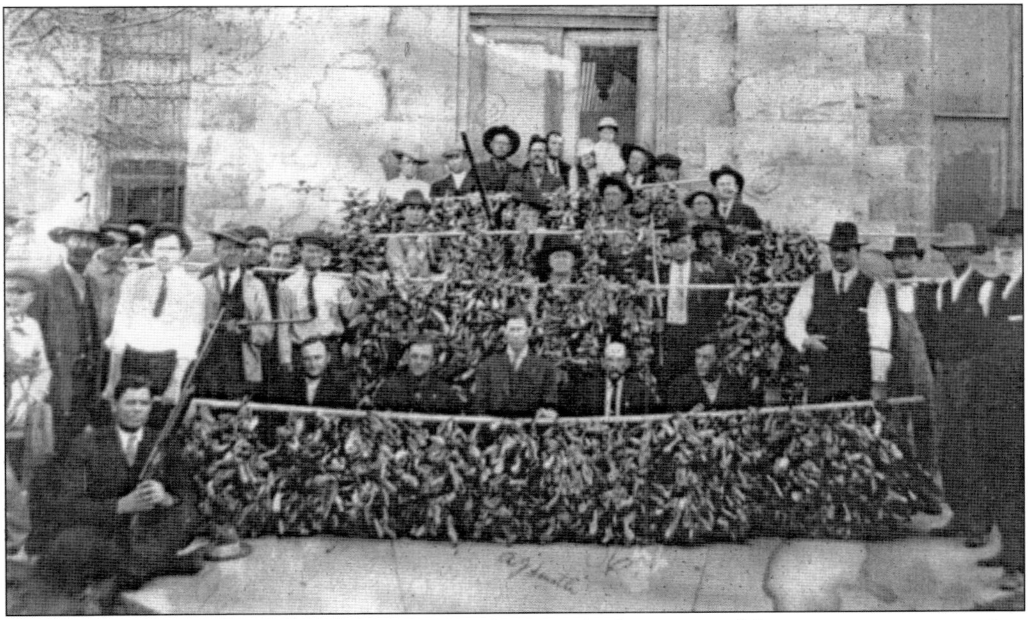

A state scalp law was passed in 1891 to supplement the bounty paid by counties on a number of animals destructive to crops and livestock. County records list jackrabbit ears at 8¢, prairie dogs 4¢, coyotes $2, wildcats $1, and panthers $5 each. In this undated photograph, county residents display rabbit ears on the courthouse steps. (Courtesy of Haskell County Historical and Genealogical Society.)

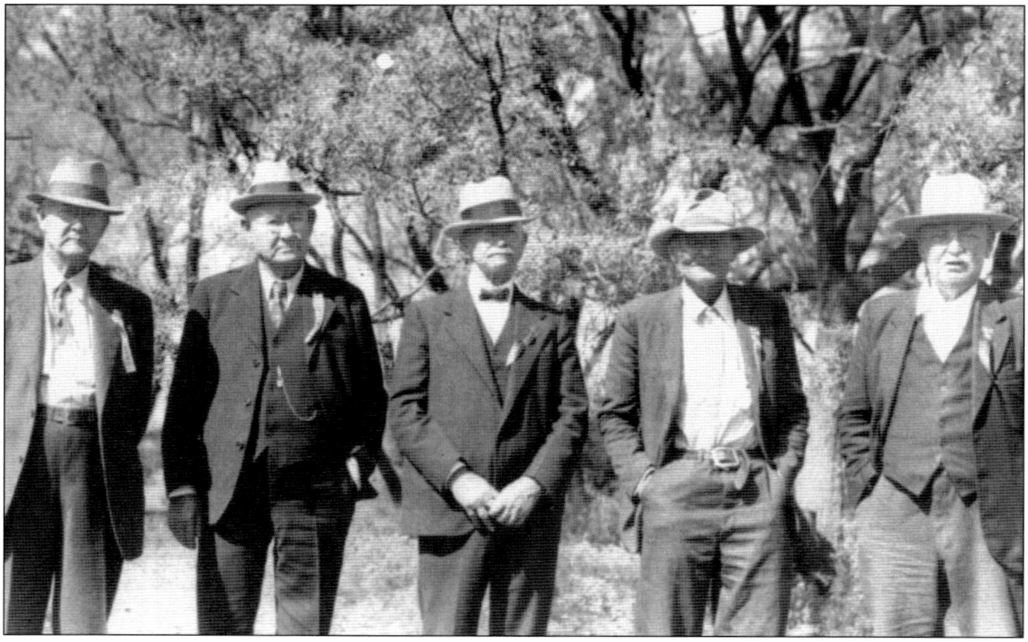

These pioneer cattlemen came to Haskell County when there were no fences. In this photograph, taken about 1886, are, from left to right, R. D. C. Stephens, Will Springer, F. G. Alexander, John Humphress, and M. S. Shook. According to R. E. Sherrill in *Haskell County History*, they and other Haskell pioneers found the land "fresh from the hand of the creator." Their names are long remembered in the rolls of county history. (Courtesy of Haskell County Historical and Genealogical Society.)

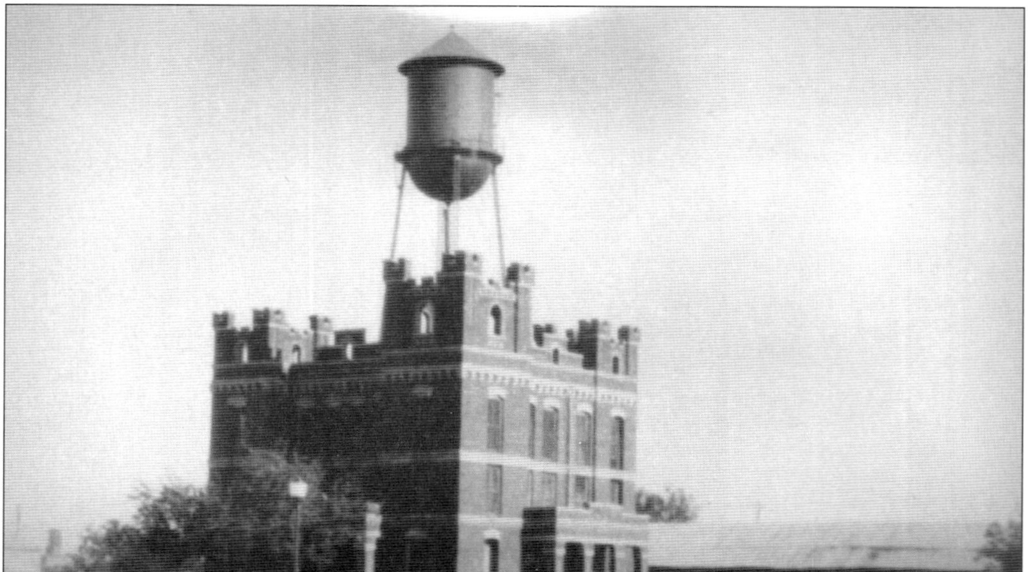

The first Haskell County jail was located three blocks west of the square. Travelers and immigrants often stayed here as they were passing through. The second jail, pictured here, was built in 1909 by Southern Structural Steel Company of San Antonio, Texas. Joe Irby was county judge. The three-story jail, complete with gallows, was located on the corner of what is now South First Street and Avenue D. (Courtesy of Haskell County Historical and Genealogical Society.)

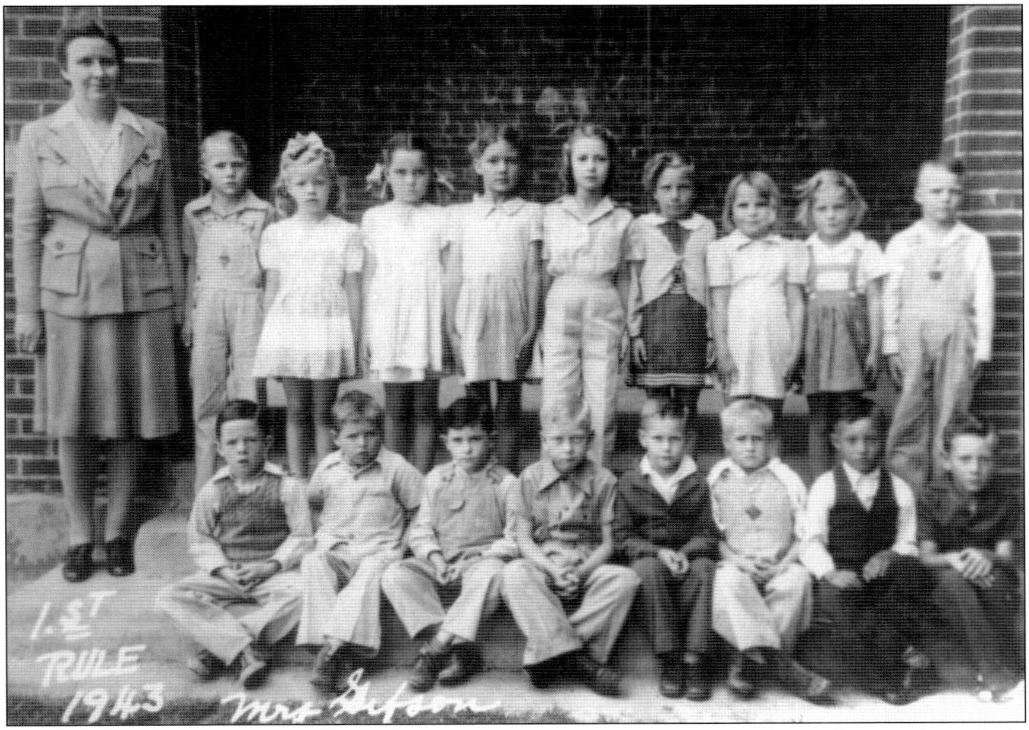

Haskell County native David Counts is shown here (second row, far right) as a first-grader at Rule Elementary School. Counts served as a state representative from Knox County. He retired as a colonel after 32 years in the Texas National Guard, attaining the rank of brevet brigadier general, and was named grand master of Masons for 2008–2009. (Courtesy of Alma Counts.)

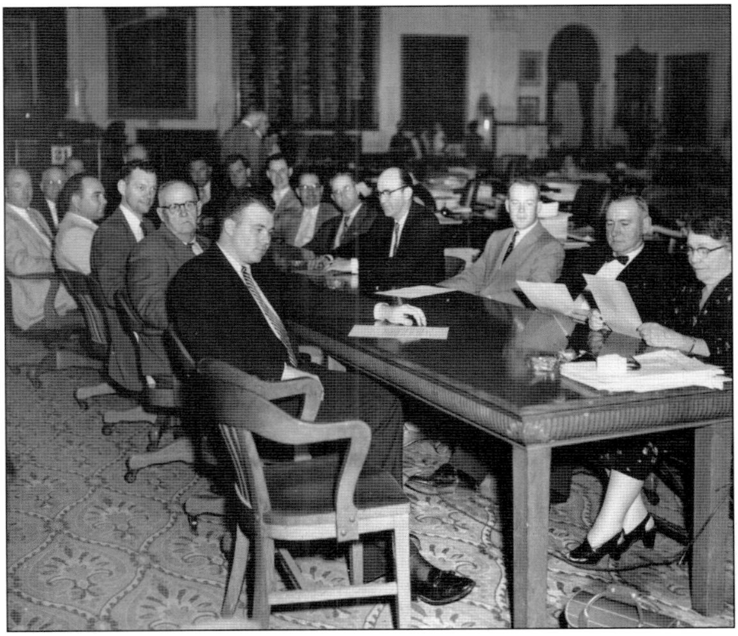

Edward Jacob Cloud came to Rule on horseback in 1900. He attended school at Ivanhoe in Rule and was a teacher in several Haskell County schools. From 1955 to 1961, he served three terms in the Texas House of Representatives, representing Baylor, Knox, Haskell, and Throckmorton Counties. He is pictured here (beside the vacant chair) on the floor of the Texas House in Austin. (Courtesy of Alma Counts.)

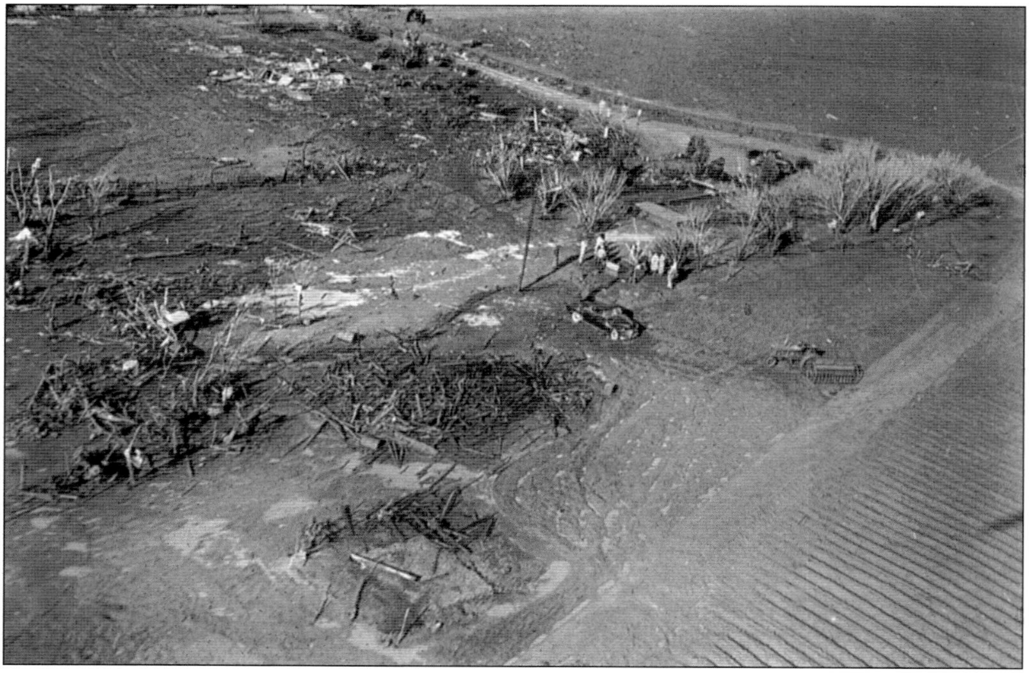

On Friday, March 13, 1953, a tornado struck the far western edge of Haskell County, continuing well into Knox County. The tornado, which would today classify as an F4, left 17 dead and 60 injured. Five people died in one family. This storm is still considered one of the top 500 most significant tornadoes in Texas. This photograph shows the extensive destruction of winds up to 260 miles per hour. (Courtesy of Haskell County Historical and Genealogical Society.)

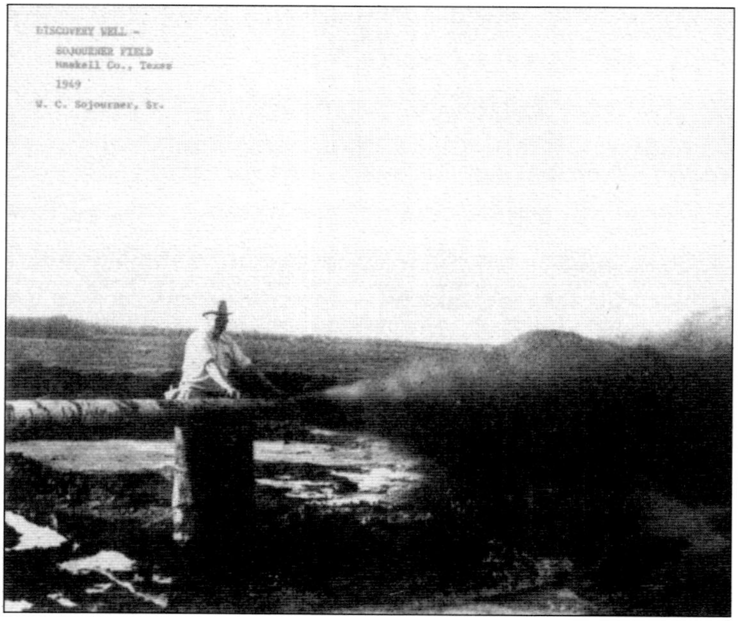

The Sojourner Field is located 2.5 miles west of Haskell. Late in 1949, the Crown Central Petroleum Corporation farmed out six 80-acre tracts to the Sojourner Drilling Company. In January 1950, Sojourner completed the No. 1 W. P. Crouch as a discovery well for a potential of 250 barrels of oil per day. Oil was first discovered in Haskell County in 1929. (Courtesy of Sojourner Drilling Company.)

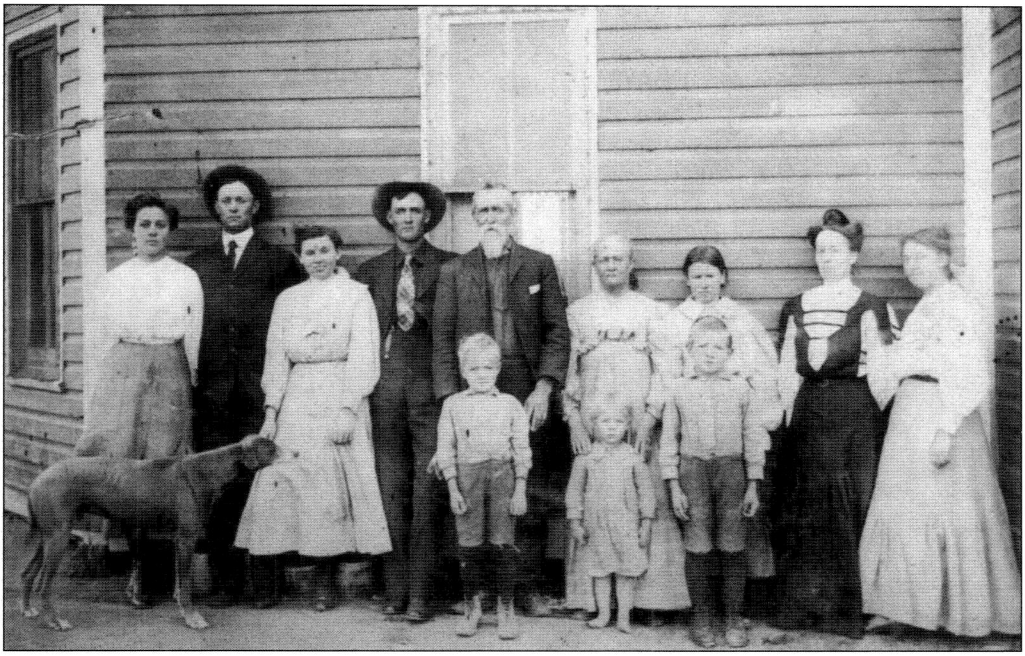

Many veterans of the American Civil War settled Haskell County. One of these was Clem Barbee, who served with Gen. Robert E. Lee. Barbee was released from prison and took the Oath of Allegiance to the United States of America on June 23, 1865. He walked 160 miles of his journey home to North Carolina. In 1903, he moved to Haskell County. He is fifth from left in this photograph. (Courtesy of Teresa Scoggins.)

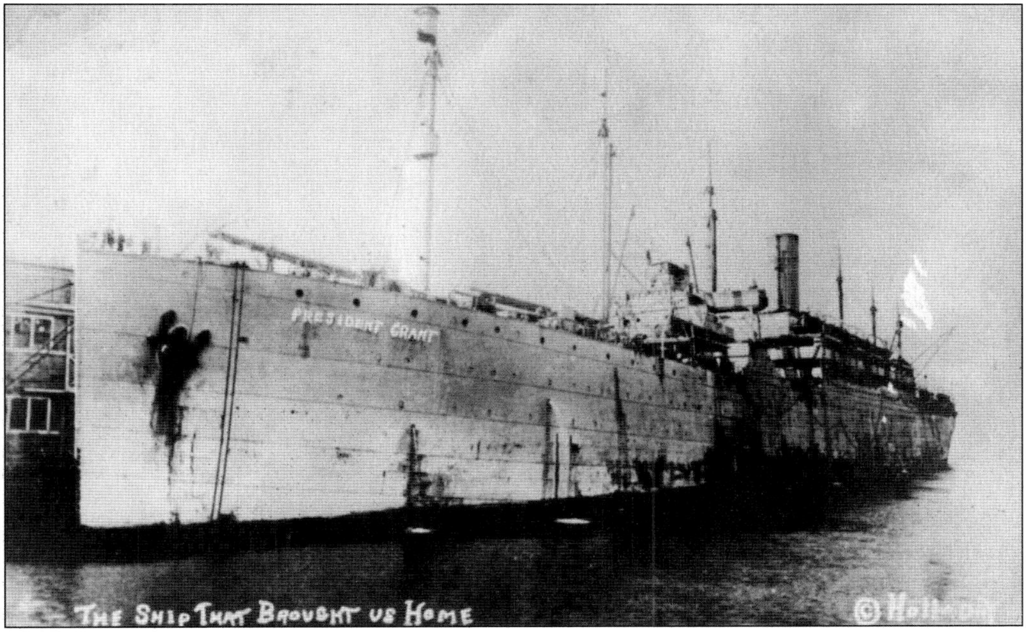

During World War I, Haskell County sent many sons from her cotton fields to the battlefields of Europe. Sailing from Le Havre, France, in 1919, the USS *President Grant* returned PFC John W. Scoggins to his West Texas home, landing first at Newport News, Virginia. (Courtesy of Johnny Scoggins.)

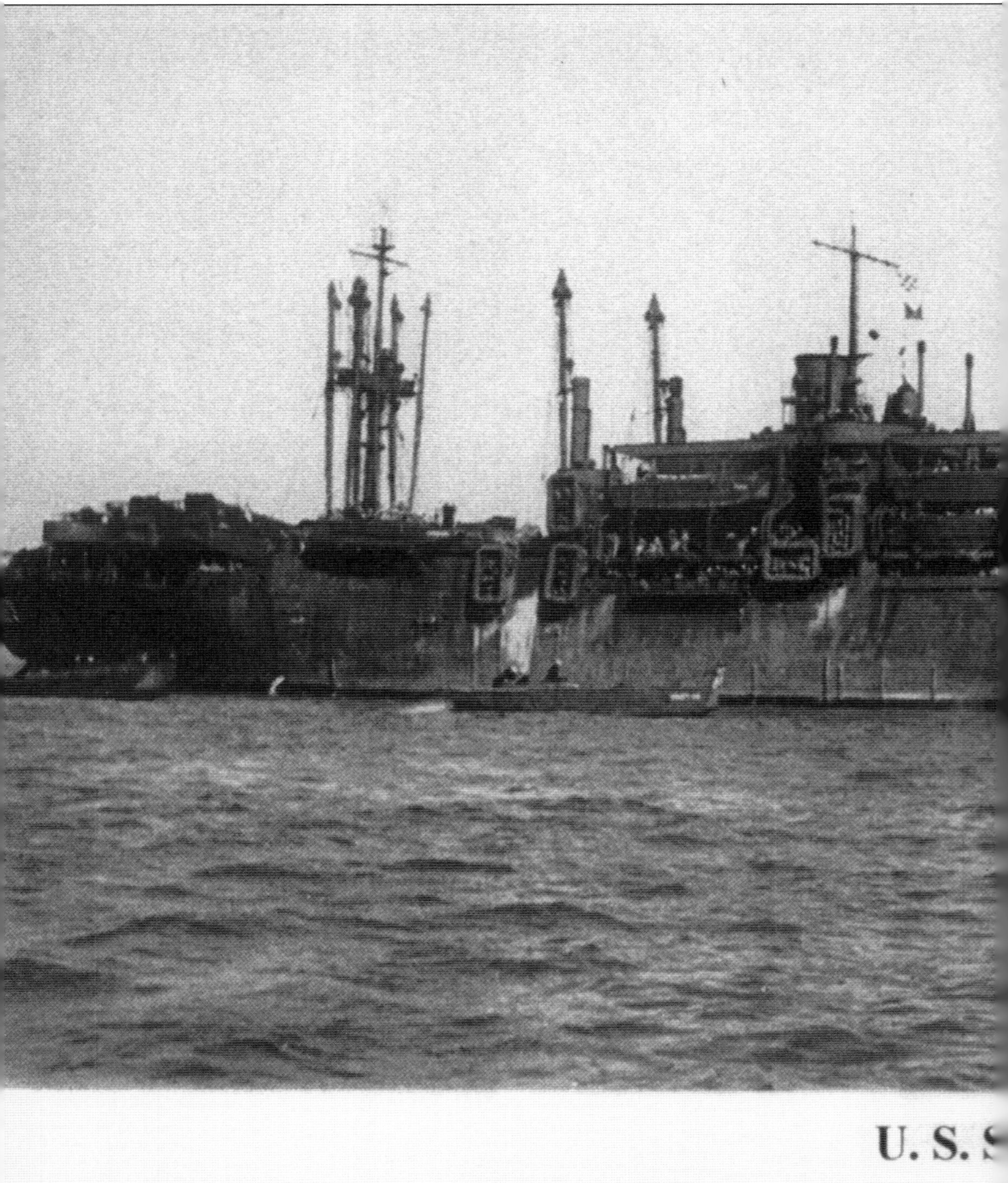

The USS *Haskell*, named for Haskell County, Texas, Oklahoma, and Kansas, was a victory ship transport launched June 13, 1944. Commissioned September 11, 1944, in San Pedro, California, the ship was designed both to attack and to land troops and equipment on enemy beaches. Decommissioned May 22, 1946, it was placed in the National Defense Reserve Fleet until 1965, then transferred to the James River in Virginia, where it remains. Haskell County native Leroy

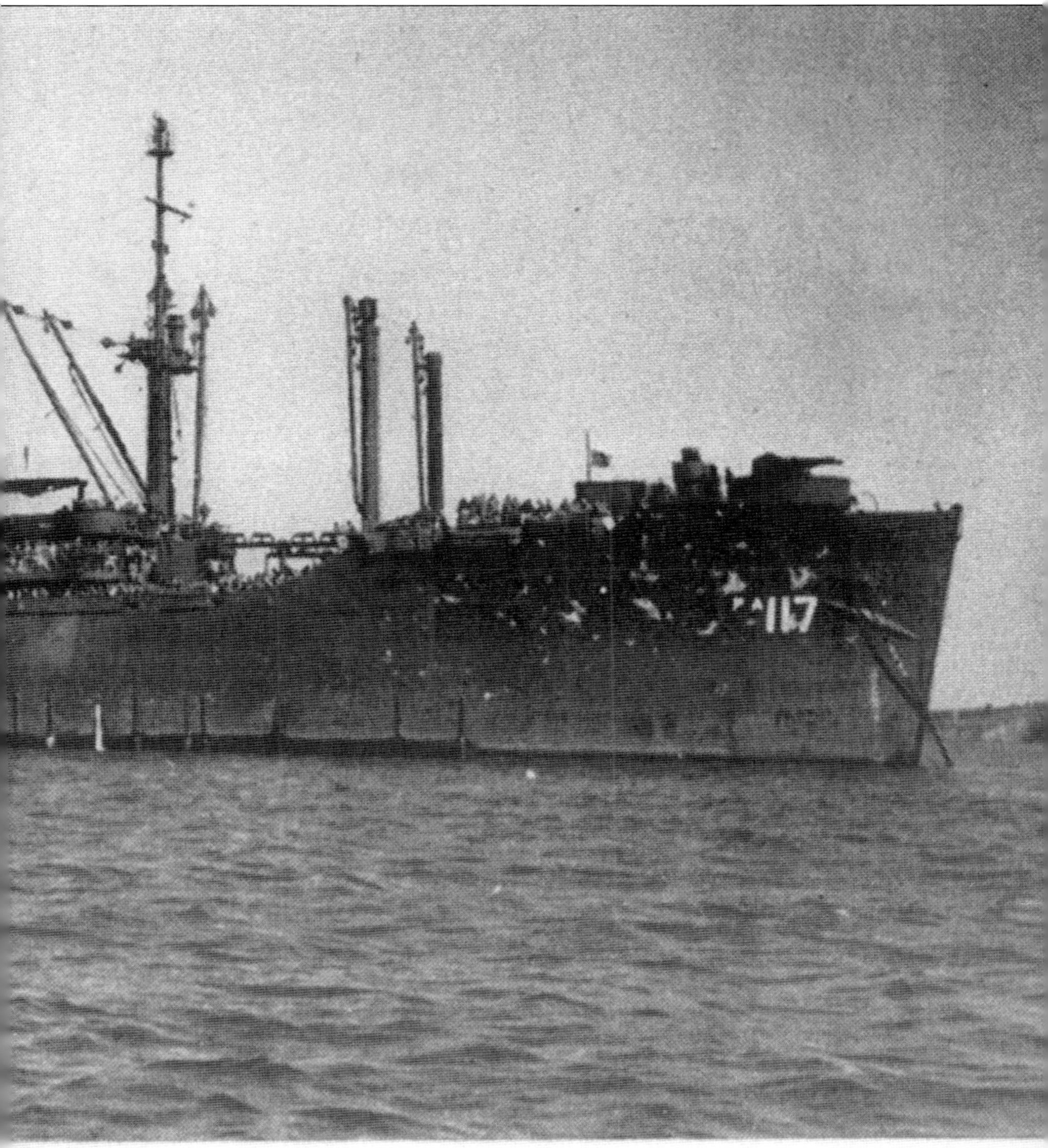

SKELL

Wreyford of Rochester served on this ship throughout its tour of duty. The *Haskell* crossed the International Date Line 10 times, the equator four times, visited 15 foreign lands, and survived three submarine attacks and dozens of air attacks. The ship also endured a typhoon with winds of 185 miles per hour. During its short tour of duty, it recorded only one killed and 28 wounded. (Courtesy of Johnny Scoggins.)